# LOSING MOGADISHU

# LOSING MOGADISHU

## TESTING U.S. POLICY IN SOMALIA

JONATHAN STEVENSON

NAVAL INSTITUTE PRESS

Annapolis, Maryland

Library of Congress Cataloging-in-Publication Data
Stevenson, Jonathan, 1956–
Losing Mogadishu: testing U.S. policy in Somalia / Jonathan Stevenson.
p. cm.
Includes bibliographical references and index.
ISBN 1-55750-788-0
1. United States—Foreign relations—Somalia. 2. Somalia—Foreign relations—United States. 3. Operation Restore Hope, 1992–1993.
I. Title.
E183.8.S58S74 1995
327.7306773—dc20 94-23853
CIP

Printed in the United States of America on acid-free paper ♾

02 01 00 99 98 97 96 95 9 8 7 6 5 4 3 2

First printing

For my parents,
Eric and Judith Stevenson
*and*
To the memory of my grandmother,
Laura Muzio Herrick
1903–1994

*The people of Somalia need a friend—not just another oppressor in desert camouflage utilities.*

MAJOR GENERAL CHARLES C. WILHELM, USMC
Memorandum re: 30-day Attitude Adjustment
UNITAF Headquarters, Mogadishu, January 12, 1993

*Force, blind themselves to its sanction as the right-thinking may, provides the ultimate constraint by which all settled societies protect themselves against the enemies of order, within and without; those with the knowledge and will to use it must necessarily stand close to or at the very center of any society's power structure; contrarily, power-holders who lack such will or knowledge will find themselves driven from it.*

JOHN KEEGAN, *THE MASK OF COMMAND*

*A coherent plan which involves the political, humanitarian, and security needs for the country has yet to emerge. Control of Mogadishu has been lost.*

GENERAL JOSEPH P. HOAR, USA
September 1993

# CONTENTS

# Acknowledgments

On the ground: Willy Huber often provided me with the best lodgings and bodyguards in Mogadishu and through culinary artiste Ibrahim Abdi Mahamoud, the best lemon-meringue pie anywhere; both have my thanks. I'm grateful to Matthew Bryden for emigrating from Canada to Somalia and for teaching me about one-tenth of what he knows about the Somali people and thereby making me at least a probationary expert. Dr. Hussein Mursal likewise has embraced two worlds, and I appreciate his generously sharing his cultural wealth with me. I owe Todd Shields and Didi Schanche for making East Africa homey enough to be comfortable, and Tom Rhodes for bringing his own "circus act" to Nairobi for my amusement, edification, and sanity.

Elsewhere: I'll record here that Clay Burkhalter provided me with the girding of unconditional friendship at critical phases, even though he knows it already. My father, on his own initiative, systematically kept me abreast of stateside coverage of Somalia and made my task far easier; thanks, Dad. Finally, thank you, Lionel Shriver, for reading the book's early incarnations and taming it with your power, and for making daily life so gobsmackingly grand.

# Introduction

On December 1, 1992, eight days before the American landing in Somalia on December 9, Smith Hempstone, the U.S. ambassador to neighboring Kenya, sent an urgent cable to the State Department. He warned Washington that once under the United States's foster care Somalia would become a "tar baby" that nobody else would want to adopt.[1] The language was typically florid and neocolonial—in his 1961 book on Africa, Hempstone referred to Liberia as Uncle Sam's "black nephew"[2]—but the point was an informed one. He had recently seen Somalia's anarchy firsthand and apprehended a people that after the populist ouster of a ruthless dictator had imploded on its capital, flashed into the postapocalypse, and mushroomed refugees over its borders into Kenya and Ethiopia. What remained was a scabrous layer of scavenging combatants. Thirty years earlier, Hempstone had railed presciently against the politically motivated intervention of the United Nations in the Congo, now a post–Cold War basket case known as Zaire.[3] Moreover, Hempstone was a Republican ideologue, a former East Africa correspondent for two major newspapers and a Bush political appointee. Though resented at Foggy Bottom for his ungilded style, he was championed by the Bush administration against his critics.[4] Still the president didn't listen.

Somalia was, of course, the world's leading candidate for humanitarian intervention. Its famine had been planted by drought and fertilized by war. At the peak of the hunger crisis in August 1992, the International Committee of the Red Cross estimated that 75 percent of Somalia's population, or 4.5 million, were in danger of starving. Aid organizations gave up huge proportions of their budgets to Somali protection rackets that stole the food they were paid to guard. In October, the United Nations effectively scuttled its own campaign to coordinate relief operations and induce Somali cooperation by firing special envoy Mohamed Sahnoun, the one man the warlords would heed. When General Mohamed Farah Aidid declared Sahnoun's second, David Bassiouni, persona non grata, the United Nations went from hobbled to paralyzed. If Somalia was to be saved from mass starvation, it seemed that someone else was obliged to step in.[5]

Horrific pictures of starving babies catered to the American public's taste for melodrama and its sense of noblesse oblige and provided George Bush with a popular stage for his grand finale. As if the Somalis' salvation were a fait accompli, American troops landed to a media brass band, with glaring television lights and excited journalists. The administration line was that the U.S. troops—which would eventually number over twenty-five thousand in-country—would simply open up food channels with an overwhelming show of force and be gone by January 21, Clinton's inauguration. Nervous marines embarrassed themselves by roughly bracing friendly Somalis with their M-16s. Even so, the world saw this stern muster of U.S. force as an acknowledgment, perhaps an exaltation, of the Third World itself as a locus of Western concern, even while Yugoslavia roiled with what U.N. Secretary-General Boutros Boutros-Ghali had petulantly called "the rich man's war." American troops, after all, had graced Somalia before Bosnia.

But January 21 came and went without the Unified Task Force (UNITAF), as the U.S.-led force was called, having established any security for relief operations outside their "areas of positive control." The soldiers had to stay. Their brooding presence broke the famine, but neither the United States nor the United Nations could leverage that success into civil and political rehabilitation. In early January, pitched battles between the two dominant Mogadishu clans occurred only a few kilometers from

UNITAF headquarters. A well-orchestrated ambush on January 14 produced the first dead G.I., Domingo Arroyo, of Operation Restore Hope. Though the Somalis had initially beheld the Americans as saviors, their failed attempts to make Somalia a kinder, gentler place through invigorated disarmament operations had perversely made them seem both feckless and furtive, like the United Nations before them. Mogadishu started to conjure images of 1963 Saigon: the ungrateful beneficiary.

All the while, Ismat Kittani, Boutros-Ghali's marginalized special representative, had grinned through press conferences like a Pollyanna. Operation Restore Hope, he said, was still a U.N. operation, authorized as it was by a Security Council resolution. He talked about "eliminating the daylight between the U.S. and the U.N."[6] In what seemed a literal attempt to realize the objective, the secretary-general replaced Kittani with an American, retired Admiral Jonathan Howe, in March. The appointment coincided with the end of a peace conference in Addis Ababa. The conference was essentially a sham. Fractured by fighting in Kismayu between Aidid's forces and Siad Barre loyalists, the meeting produced the concept of a "transitional national council" but no means of composing it. The incompleteness of the program doomed political reconciliation to remain a rheumy vision from a lost weekend. Six weeks later, on May 4, Marine Lieutenant General Robert Johnston handed over formal command of the U.N. forces in Somalia to General Cevik Bir, a Muslim Turk thought to be palatable to Muslim Somalis. The United States had failed to sanitize the United Nations. In fact, by then Somalis reviled Americans almost as much as they did the United Nations. To them all foreign troops were disempowering occupiers—an accurate perception.

Continued attempts at disarming General Aidid's forces did not jibe with his angling for hegemony over the southern port of Kismayu. From his radio station he began broadcasting propaganda encouraging his minions not to give up their weapons. They complied. On June 5, Aidid's militia killed and mutilated twenty-four Pakistani soldiers as they finished a weapons inspection next to his radio station. A month later, members of his clan killed four foreign journalists; three were stoned to death, the fourth shorn of his flak jacket and shot in the chest.

The summer did not witness the sprouting of even a primitive indigenous government. Because of the June 5 massacre, Howe had put a bounty on Aidid's head. U.N. persecution turned Aidid into an outlaw folk hero. By August, Howe was not even bothering with the U.N. command structure, directly cabling Washington for the preferred support of American soldiers, his fellow alumni. What he got was airborne Rangers, the Army's elite grunts, as well as commandos from Delta-force, the antiterrorist unit whose existence the Pentagon at that time still did not officially acknowledge.

On October 3 the ringers flanked and then hit Aidid's suspected hideout; eighteen Americans were killed and seventy-seven wounded. It was the bloodiest single combat episode involving U.S. casualties since Vietnam—worse than anything in the Gulf War. A dead GI was dragged unclothed through the streets, a captured helicopter pilot videotaped pleading for American restraint. As the Americans prepared to pull out of Somalia altogether in early 1994, Mogadishu clans were re-arming in preparation for regaining occupied territory and scrounging ordnance left behind by departing troops. Banditry and strong-arm tactics were on the rise. Aid organizations had hired more guns. Although nineteen thousand U.N. troops remained, the most able, experienced and feared soldiers—the Americans, their Western partners, and the Turks—had all withdrawn by March 31, 1994. The U.N.'s deterrent was gutted.

A year later the United Nations gave up and pulled out all foreign troops. By all indications, Somalia's capital descended back into the anarchy from which Restore Hope had given it tenuous relief. Ambassador Hempstone did "not think Somalia [was] amenable to the quick fix so beloved of Americans."[7] He was right.

The experience of October 3 confirmed one of the key lessons of Vietnam, namely, that fighting guerrillas on their home turf is far more dangerous than massing troops to set-piece battles. That realization, however, is by now a banality. On any level but this superficial one, it is wrong to compare Somalia baldly to Vietnam. In Somalia, with the Cold War decisively over, the United States had no ostensible geopolitical or economic ambitions, faced no hidden political enemies backing direct combatants, and confronted neither a unified nor a collectively manipulable population. Washington no longer needed the Horn of Africa as a forward base for the Middle East. Somalia's oil reserves, though extant and largely untapped, are mere drops compared to the vat that the United States fought for in 1991. Colonial handlers (Britain and Italy) are basically aligned with the United Nations on Somalia, and former Cold War antagonists like China and North Korea aren't interested. As a people, Somalis are atomized, their allegiances veering toward clan and away from country or grand theory, so that no one figure can charismatically command all of them. Aidid is no Ho Chi Minh.

Most saliently, the United States did not find even a corrupt, unprincipled government, like the Republic of Vietnam, as its ally on the ground. Instead it found itself stranded in a power void, in the maw between erstwhile rebel groups closing on territory neither had ever ruled. It found itself, in short, having to build a nation from anarchy by hesitantly killing people, to cull an unruled and unruly population of its rogues. So revealed, Operation Restore Hope even at the outset was a heady and formidable task. Rogues, humans or elephants, are disruptive, but they are also part of the natural order. Eliminating them is not easy. Thus, at first it seemed fitting that the American initiative was an unprecedented deployment of the U.S. military—qualitatively, quantitatively, politically. Never before had U.S. troops been used for humanitarian purposes, dispatched in such large numbers (some one hundred thousand) on a noncombat mission, or deployed under eventual U.N. command. But American policy makers had only a glancing understanding of the Somalis' unique culture. The mission was far more difficult to execute than either President Bush or General Colin Powell had imagined. That they conceived of Restore Hope as the poignant closing of Bush's "foreign policy presidency" was testament to the persistence of American military confidence and sanguineness. Operation Restore Hope was the United States's first test in the "new world order." The United States did not score highly.

There were, of course, substantial reasons for committing American troops, logistical wherewithal, and firepower to Somalia. The thick residue of weapons left over from Washington's support of Somalia in its war with a Soviet-subsidized Ethiopia in the eighties, along with Soviet hardware from the earlier Cold War chapter, stoked and fueled Somalia's anarchy. But does the United States owe Somalia its succor, just because it was Somalia's final Cold War sponsor? Before Restore Hope opened up food routes from Mogadishu port to starving Somalis in the bush, 350,000 had died from starvation while the ineffectual United Nations fiddled. But as the world's richest nation, and at times ventriloquist to the Security Council's dummy, is the United States obliged to help walk Somalia to political self-sufficiency? Southern Sudan and Mozambique, and now Rwanda, have lost perhaps even more people than Somalia to war and starvation. What makes Somalia the more worthy recipient of help?

These are questions about the moral duties of a nation. By the cessation of the Cold War, their answers are rendered ideologically unencumbered but, without the evil empire as lurid foil, harder to formulate. The U.S. operation in Somalia, as the first protracted American military engagement after the Cold War, constitutes a veritable laboratory for American military policy, U.S. foreign policy in the Third World and Washington's proper relationship with the United Nations.

From the American experience in Somalia, I extract lessons that though provisional I believe are demonstrably correct as far as they go. In scope, duration, and tragedy, the American involvement in Vietnam obviously dwarfs its involvement in Somalia. But the Vietnam experience still so dominates American policy and strategy that comparisons do help explain the psychology of American decision making, though not always its soundness. For this reason, I have not been timid about drawing such comparisons. At the very least, Operation Restore Hope has shown that U. S. policy makers and soldiers have learned the lesson of Vietnam mainly by rote and have yet to turn it into an integrated intervention policy.

# LOSING MOGADISHU

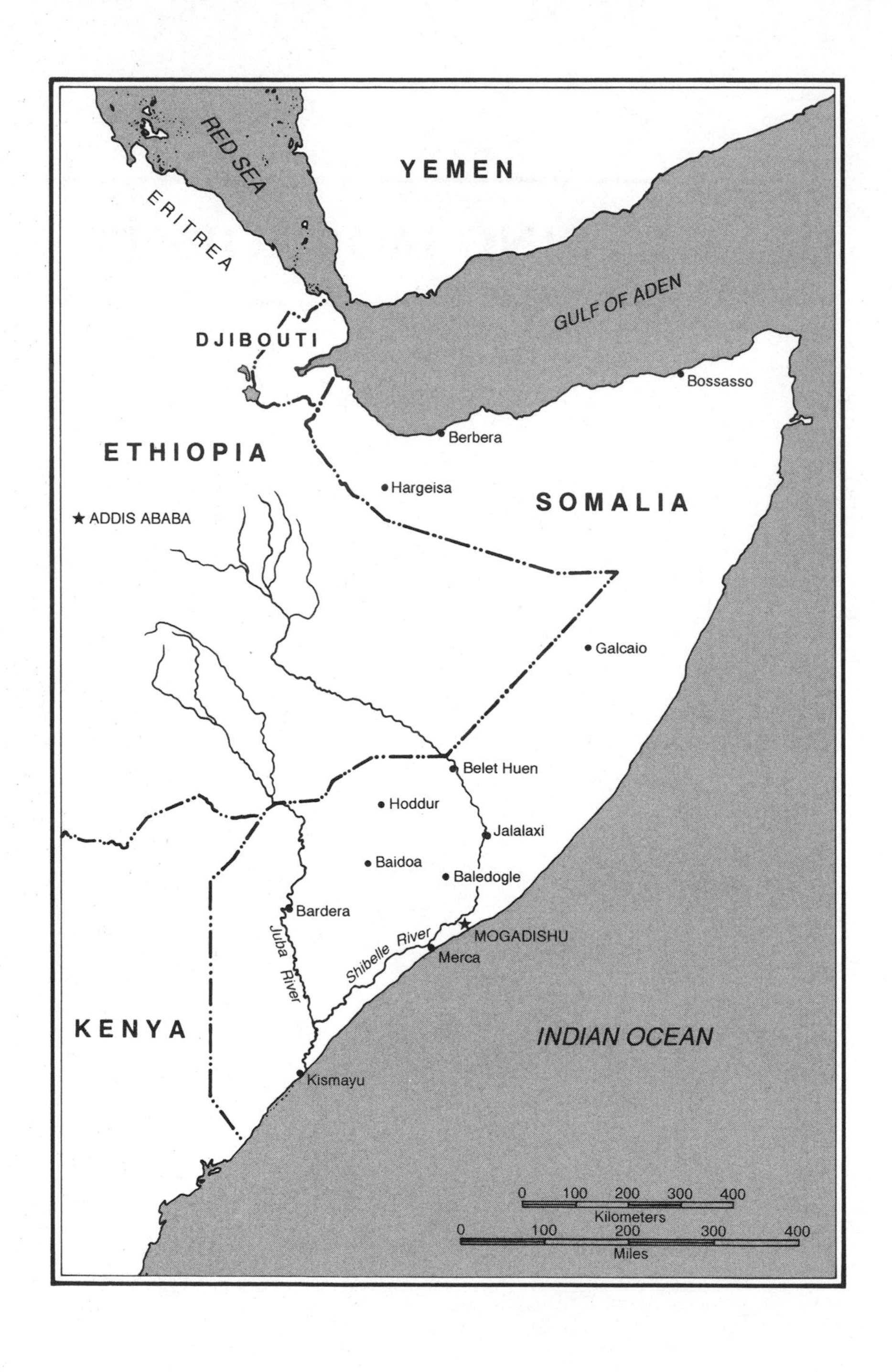
RED SEA
YEMEN
ERITREA
GULF OF ADEN
DJIBOUTI
Bossasso
Berbera
ETHIOPIA
Hargeisa
SOMALIA
ADDIS ABABA
Galcaio
Belet Huen
Hoddur
Jalalaxi
Baidoa
Baledogle
Bardera
MOGADISHU
Shibelle River
Merca
Juba River
KENYA
INDIAN OCEAN
Kismayu
0 100 200 300 400
Kilometers
0 100 200 300 400
Miles

# 1 Dissemblance as Ethos

Somali culture is what makes Somalis so singularly unmalleable, so reluctant to take guidance. The lone but typical exception to the rule is war against a common foe. Somalis are possessed of a racist psychology—with inferiority complexes. Rendered ethnically homogeneous by generations of blending among Arab maritime traders from the north and east, and pastoral Cushite tribes from the west and south, most Somalis trace their lineage to a single mythical patriarch, the Samaale. They regard Arabs as gifted brothers and black Africans as handicapped cousins. The upshot is resentment toward both. After Pakistani troops befriended Somalis, they ambushed and mutilated those troops. Somali street kids called the Nigerian U.N. contingent "niggers." It is fair to say that their Arab-African schizophrenia makes Somalis tend to disdain everyone but themselves. Although their evolved homogeneity has imbued the Somalis abstractly with a sense of a common heritage and destiny, it now manifests itself merely as exclusion and not as unity.

With one another, Somalis are distinctly callous. Somali women are the most heavily circumcised in the world—over 90 percent have their clitorises "clipped," sometimes at three different stages of preadolescence. In the final stage, the lips of the labia are scarred and joined together (sometimes by suturing), only to be reopened forcibly by the husband's penis on the couple's wedding night. (The initial procedure is called *clitoridectomy,* the final procedure *labial infibulation.*) For young women, this cultural practice makes for an adolescence of pain and infection and a lifetime of sexual numbness. Young men are let off relatively lightly with the dread and potential stigma of failure on the wedding night. If a Somali groom doesn't achieve penetration, the marriage can be annulled and the man and woman are placed back in circulation to repeat the same ordeal. Originally imposed by male Muslim elders to ensure chastity among Somali women, these practices are slowly falling out of favor. Ironically, the holdouts are mainly obdurate mothers with nubile daughters, reinforced by traditional superstitions.[1]

All Somalis are complicit in clan contentiousness. Although the women are less beholden to clan than the men, at the Addis Ababa peace conference in March 1993 even among the Somali women's groups talks broke down according to clan. Despite Islam's stern exhortations of female demureness, Somali women traditionally assumed the role of haranguers during wartime.

The United States took on Somalia as a client in the late seventies, after Siad Barre had engaged his people in a battle for "greater Somalia" against Ethiopia. The vast Ogaden region of eastern Ethiopia was populated by ethnic Somalis whom Siad Barre and other Somalis considered their brethren and properly under Somali dominion. Northeast Kenya also borders Somalia and is populated largely by ethnic Somalis. While that region as well as the Ogaden is technically considered part of "greater Somalia," Siad Barre agreed not to contest northeast Kenya in exchange for President Daniel arap Moi's pledge not to attempt or help to destabilize Siad Barre's government.

Although the Soviet Union had supported Somalia and built up its military infrastructure, the socialist tilt of Mengistu Haile Mariam and geographical proximity of Ethiopia to the Middle East proved too tempting for Moscow to pass up. The Soviet Union abruptly shifted its support from Somalia to Ethiopia. The United States, which itself had earlier backed Haile Selassie, stepped to Mogadishu with like opportunism. This sort of shifting of subject and object was the idiom of the

Cold War, and it was often iterated in times of uncharacteristic national unity in the host country. The United States initially spied a tough, cohesive people, fighting fiercely against a Soviet client. It did not know what it was getting into.[2]

There is practically no such thing as a Somali patriot or a Somali nationalist. By tradition Somali nomads are self-sufficient. From this heritage they developed a transcendental sense of individual superiority and the conviction that they are accountable only to God. Somali diaspora pepper East Africa and the Horn, where they are known as canny and aggressive traders and cunning smugglers. To the extent that they are politically motivated at all, these willing expatriates move abroad and angle for profit in the interest not of their country but of their clan. Likewise, those who stay at home do so for their clans and subclans. The clan is the only palpable political entity the Somali knows. It is the essential unit of Somali culture.[3]

Clans are extended patrilineal networks that go back several hundred years—not terribly different from the Hatfields and the McCoys of Appalachian legend. The clan system—which stresses segmentation over community—developed not out of any affirmative desire for interdependence or religious solidarity but rather out of a reluctant need to bolster the individual. A Somali proverb nicely captures the uneasy nature of clan bonds: "Me and my clan against the world; me and my brother against the clan; me against my brother." Clans still function only to protect outnumbered members. Customarily they competed for some central stake—generally, grazing land or livestock—but banded together to protect that stake against encroachment from stronger subclans or clans. Property was defined not by legal ownership but simply by occupation, and no particular moral stigma attached to theft or even murder.[4] In Somali poetry, participation in a successful camel raid is a badge of honor. The modern Somali counterpart is a car hijacking. Traditionally, one family could make amends for a homicide with one hundred head of camel. Now exoneration costs six hundred thousand Somali shillings—about six hundred dollars. Because a wound calls for expensive convalescence, it costs two million shillings. Somalis prefer killing to maiming. Calculation sums up character.

In nomadic tradition, it was as much through skirmishes as negotiation that subclans reached material and territorial equilibrium. Nomadic treachery is still considered macho and debonair. Osman

Hassan Ali, known as "Osman Ato," Aidid's second in command and chief financier, boasted that he sold guns to a subclan allied with his nemesis Ali Mahdi because he could easily steal them back before the collaborators would have a chance to use them. In fall 1992, Ato landed a contract to supply fuel to the European Community for its reconstruction of Mogadishu's water system. It was common knowledge that he had stolen the petrol from EC cargos.

Somalis are ethnically homogeneous (99 percent Muslim), which means clans are not "tribes" in the ordinary sense. In fact, until the civil war in 1991, Western experts considered this feature of the society an especial source of hope that Somalia would not succumb to the brand of vicious tribalism that has riven much of sub-Saharan Africa.[5] But the divisive clan ethic dilutes even Islamic dogma—the Somali political contract, known as Heer, subordinates Muslim sharia penal justice to traditional forms of retribution whereby personal guilt is vicariously transmitted to the culprit's kinsmen. As nomads, Somalis historically maintained their distinctness by virtue of the land they occupied at a given moment. Government was not centralized. To enforce boundaries, preserving clan identity meant fighting for turf.

Before Siad Barre, most families were self-sufficient and rarely needed to rely on their subclans for sustenance. It was rarer still that one subclan needed to turn to another for help, and assistance was rendered parsimoniously—even then only when the besieged subclan was unequivocally overmatched. Once the family or subclan in need of help was back on its feet, the hierarchically superior group would withdraw and friction between clans or subclans would recede. Coexistence, albeit tense, did tend to prevail over conflict.[6] The experts may not have been all wrong: Clans may yet stand a chance of coexisting when politicians aren't around to tweak old rivalries. Members of different clans often are not categorically chauvinistic and often profess that they are "all Somalis."

A proud and haughty bearing is characteristic of most pastoral nomadic peoples; it does not perforce make them virtual criminals. The Masai and Turkana of Kenya and Tanzania, and the Dinka and Nuer of Sudan, for example, share this countenance and carry it nobly. So did the Somalis before Mohammed Siad Barre's regime. Indeed, they remain singularly prepossessing. A remarkably handsome people, Somalis are typically tall and slender, with long triangular faces, finely chiseled features, piercing eyes, and ready smiles. They are by inclination gregarious—a trait that adds to their seductiveness and therefore their cunning. In untarnished nomadic societies—like pre-Siad Somalia—it was perfectly normal for a person to use these native qualities casually to steal livestock and expropriate land for grazing, for wealth was "on the hoof." Because the people came to understand that everyone behaved that way, they did not descend into outright war and merely dealt with depredations ad hoc through the clan ethic. The accepted fact that they were "all Somalis" kept conflict at the level of mere skirmishing.

But Siad Barre, the military dictator who ruled the country from 1969 until forced into exile in April 1991, transmogrified Somali culture. He did not treat his people as if they were "all Somalis." Instead, at the expense of other groups, he favored his own Marehan subclan, and secondarily the Darod clan comprising it, with selective political appointments and government largess. To other clans he offered only violent persecution. His discriminatory brutality forced members of other clans to remain artificially insular for the sake of self-preservation.

In 1982, the Ogaden war ended in defeat, Somalia having gained little territory. Now without the prospect of aggrandizement to temper Siad's ruthless grabbiness, disfavored clans clung all the tighter to historically controlled territories and ostracized any interlopers. Although the clan ethos in its pure genealogical form tied status to kin rather than place, Siad's nepotistic policies forced others to take refuge in land as the sole source of social security. He had thoroughly corrupted the clans' perspective. They were able to unite briefly to get rid of Siad Barre. Nomadic tradition dictated a return to equilibrium, but Siad Barre had poisoned that tradition by making the other clans mistrustful of the customs of coordination and restraint that had once preserved parity by breaching them for so long. So each clan sought the monolithic and exclusionary power that Siad Barre had enjoyed. "Siad Barre dominates the psychology of this country," commented a prominent Mogadishu businessman. "All clans want what his clan had."[7]

Some clans want more. General Aidid's aggression in the southern port of Kismayu—an area not historically held by his Hawiye clan—is a bald attempt by the Hawiye to erase traditional encirclement by Siad Barre's Darod brethren, who populate areas both north and south of Mogadishu. This Darwinian behavior has persisted throughout the recent American occupation and U.N. military stewardship.

Traditional boundaries, though frayed by Siad's provocations, tenuously endured through most of the 1980s. Somalia remains divided among six clans of substantial political influence (although there are many more). Each territory is in turn divided among subclans, of which about twenty-five are politically significant. On its face this structure is anathema to any centralized politic: the very dynamic of Somali culture is, oxymoronically, that of shifting loyalties and fluid allegiances. Loyalty extends only as far as the subclan; farther than that, it is both proper and expected that the subclan's collective alignment will roll with the moment. When Siad Barre victimized the Majerteens after taking power, although they too were Darods, they readily accepted the hospitality of Coptic Ethiopians over the border—historically their sworn enemies.[8]

Deeper considerations made prospects for the modern state look even bleaker. As residual survival mechanisms, clan networks worked well when Somali society was truly nomadic and parity was just a matter of expropriating a few camels, a little land, or a bit of food. But under Siad Barre, central government, urbanization, modern weapons, and artificial disparity were superimposed onto Somalia's crude, schismatic pastoralism. It was a tragically bad fit, but the change was secular and structural. Somalia cannot go back to what it once was. Yet the cultural and ethical traditions that the twenty-one-year trauma of corrupt modern government rendered obsolescent will not die. Hence the jangled Somalia of today.

Though now afflicted with a vengeful and paranoid acquisitiveness, once-disadvantaged clans and subclans made it their first order of business after ousting Siad Barre to regain the historical strongholds Siad had brutally confiscated over two decades. The large and nomadically dispersed Isaaq clan isolated northwest Somalia and proclaimed it independent Somaliland, with the same boundaries as the British Somaliland of the colonial era. One Darod subclan started fighting another northeast of Mogadishu, and a third near the southern port of Kismayu. But by far the most destructive conflict was the battle between two Hawiye subclans for Mogadishu itself, Somalia's capital city and largest port. The Hawiye were the historical denizens of Mogadishu, but Siad Barre had crowded them out economically and politically. In four months of nihilistic mayhem the two subclans reduced Mogadishu to rubble. When they finally proclaimed a truce in March 1992, Ali Mahdi Mohamed of the Abgal had secured the northern part of Mogadishu and General Aidid of the Habar-Gedir the southern part.

Even in peacetime, the Somali economy had no margin. Three-quarters of the population remained vagrant nomads and lived at the subsistence level on camels, sheep, goats, and cattle. Cyclical drought produced mass starvation on a regular basis. Somalia had long depended on the permanent presence of foreign relief organizations to feed those its economy could not. In the early nineties, Somalia was still reeling from the historic drought of 1984 and 1985, having lost perhaps 30 percent of its livestock. Nearly a million refugees from the Ogaden war and Ethiopia's war for Eritrea strained the already diaphanous fabric of Somalia's economy. Inflation was running at 100 percent in 1990. In the same year, because of a $100 million arrearage, the International Monetary Fund refused to extend new loans. In 1991 another major drought hit, coinciding with civil war and the subsequent anarchy. Many of Siad Barre's troops fled to Somalia's most arable land, west of Mogadishu, and disrupted farming with terror and rapine. Others moved south and plundered livestock. Lack of security scotched important agricultural projects like the Bardera Dam and forced expatriate development workers to evacuate. There was no longer any central government, therefore no longer any central economic planning. Virtually all of the nomads in southern Somalia became destitute and helpless. The inevitable result was famine.[9]

The indigenous population of Mogadishu still looked to the subclans for food, even though its ultimate sources by 1992 were almost exclusively expatriate donors and emergency aid groups. Food came into the port, where CARE and Red Cross workers off-loaded it. But, perversely true to form, the Somalis demanded that anyone wishing to provide them with charity pay them first. Because the subclans had the firepower—Land Cruisers quaintly known as "technicals" mounted with heavy machine guns and grenade launchers, the odd tank or rocket launcher, AK-47s, M-16s, leftover Berettas, all the spoils of rebel victory—subclan elders could and did insist that food be distributed through them. Where the measure of a man had once been the size of his herd—"Somali" means both white camel and camel milk—the new gauge was the number of weapons he owned.

Some elders earnestly tried to channel food to the people who needed it most. The allocation of food among Mogadishu's districts was nominally determined through a Joint Committee for Relief Assistance, which consisted of three representatives each from the Abgal, the Habar-Gedir, and the United Nations. But if one subclan decided that the allocation arrived at by the committee were unfair, its members would simply steal food at gun point. During one week in June 1992 alone, CARE personnel in Mogadishu were involved in twenty-one incidents of looting or gunplay.[10]

To amplify the problem, a large proportion of the displaced population consisted of members of the Rahanweyn clan and unaffiliated Bantus. The Rahanweyn were traditionally farmers rather than nomads and consequently were dispersed and vulnerable to aggression from other clans. The Bantus are not ethnic Somalis but farmers who originally emigrated from Tanzania. Many of them had once been virtually enslaved. Siad Barre had ostracized and systematically starved both groups in their habitat in central Somalia.[11] Enlightened Somalis in Mogadishu weren't inclined to treat them any better. In summer 1992, dozens of them could be seen draped over the sea wall, a stone's throw from Red Cross feeding centers, dying from malnutrition. In July 1992, some 3,400 of those who couldn't find nourishment tried to make it to Yemen in an old freighter, but at least 150 perished short of the coast when an armed gang killed 70 and the rest drowned fleeing ashore.[12] Todd Shields, recently *U.S. News and World Report*'s Middle East correspondent and then based in Nairobi, called the voyage "a belch from hell." The remark didn't see print, but it reflected the consensus.

The feeding system was a farce but still consistent with the Gestalt of clan predation as an expression of self-reliance. Unfortunately, that idiom didn't translate to a commodity that had to be universally rationed. But the Somalis' culture had perpetually skewed their eye inward toward their clan, so that the only morality they knew beyond survival was blood obligation. Altruism is simply not an attitude Somalis come by easily, if at all.

Again, in a nomadic subsistence economy this social deficit was of little consequence. In fact, pastoralist anarchy actually worked until the advent of Siad Barre's military dictatorship. But after his soldiers raped land and herd, leaving a wealthless people utterly destitute, Somalis' inexperience with mass deprivation became momentous. Displaced persons flocked to Mogadishu for the dole they knew would arrive at the port, doubling its population to one million in six months. These people were separated from their subclans and had nowhere to go except Red Cross kitchens for food. They gravitated toward other displaced members of their own subclans for emotional comfort, but the reconstituted groups had no territorial roots in Mogadishu. They could offer little material support and could solicit none from local clans.

The world understandably saw the Somalis' abrasive lack of community as barbaric lawlessness—a form of cultural retrogression. From the Somalis' point of view, though, there was never any political structure to lose; all that ever mattered were clan and subclan. However perverse that conviction was in a society forced by war into urban welfare, clans and subclans were the only sources of identity Somalis could appreciate. In August 1992, U.N. special envoy Mohamed Sahnoun offered the pregnant but incongruous observation that clans were "politically interesting and important because they check power."[13] That is true, but how could that militate to the benefit of all? Over one hundred thousand Soviet and American weapons left from the Cold War were in random circulation, and they gave contentious clans very big teeth. A touchy American political officer cracked, "Guns don't kill people; Somalis kill people." Another caustic diplomat offered the observation, "Telling a Somali to kill is like telling a dog to lick his balls—the problem is getting him to stop." Behind all the warped humor lay the persistent view that however different they were, to whatever extent the superpowers had egged on their bellicosity, the Somalis had brought their plight on themselves with helterskelter skirmishing and the venal neglect of starving innocents, debasing their vaunted ethic, religious uniformity, and proud edict to protect their brothers.

By default, Sahnoun's was the best prescription at the time: ideally the clan structure would remain intact while the grasping, exclusionary ethic that traditionally drove it was moderated. In August 1992 there were no signs of that happening. Although clan elders were able to stave off an outright breach of the cease-fire, random, individual acts of violence were commonplace. They increased exponentially with the arrival of food cargo. Two U.N. observers were shot shortly after they arrived. On the same day there was a massive looting at the port spearheaded by three tanks—a show of force that could not have occurred without Aidid's backing, or at least his acquiescence.[14]

Even then it was clear that the first step toward civil stability was safe and orderly food distribution. But over a thousand teenage gunmen, wired on khat (an herbal amphetamine) and galvanized by infamy they'd never dared dream of, ruled the port. They were organized into six clan-based security groups, each of which insisted on protection money from CARE and the Red Cross for safe off-loading and convoy passage to remote food distribution points. CARE paid them five thousand dollars a day, plus a kilogram of dry food per man. Even so, they would often loot the very convoys they were escorting. Less than half of the food unloaded at the port made it into the mouths of the people most in need in the famine vortices—Baidoa, Bardera, Merca—that radiated from Mogadishu.[15] In August and September, the weekly body count in Baidoa alone approached two thousand.[16] War and scarcity had turned a tough and individualistic people into a callous and venal mob. Journalists leveraged their sense of irony with jokes. After enduring an afternoon of bullying swagger from the urban hooligans of Mogadishu, they would wearily pose to newcomers the three biggest lies in Somalia: There is petrol in the car, the safety is on, and I didn't know he was my brother.

In their hearts of hearts, though, the United Nations and the non-government aid organizations knew that any attempt to tame Somalis with condescension and disgust would have proven futile. Somalis were simply doing what was inbred and used to work for them and lacked the moral frame of reference necessary for wholesale reform. In other words, they didn't know any better—a conclusion that smacks of patronizing disdain in spite of itself. It took only a logical half-step to decide that if they didn't know better, perhaps they couldn't be taught. They were not used to rationalist learning, much less to taking instruction from benevolent masters, having only had a written language since 1973.

Yet the aid community's mission was to help people in need. Philosophically, yielding to the Somalis' stingy clamor for food and profit over anyone else's dead body would have frustrated the very purpose of humanitarian aid. The view donors adopted—with the broad and alacritous support of the media on both sides of the Atlantic—was simply to flood Somalia with food. The idea was that even though cynical local merchants controlled the looters through their subclans and hoarded food either to feed militia or to jack up the eventual price of survival, sooner or later the food would reach the people. The key was to keep the food pipeline full enough to portend lower prices and liberate hoarded stockpiles, wherever they were. This approach, according to a CARE worker, would lead to a "monetization of the market"—and, eventually, to civil stability.[17]

In August 1992, though, fifty thousand metric tons of food per month were needed to feed Somalia, and only thirty-two thousand tons were in the pipeline.[18] One-third of the people in southern Somalia—1.5 million—were in immediate danger of dying from starvation, and malnutrition was approaching 80 percent in some areas.[19] In terms of the proportion of the population affected, Somalia's famine was worse than Ethiopia's benchmark famine of 1984 and 1985.[20] The Red Cross's commitment to Somalia increased to absorb a record 35 percent of its world budget. Later it climbed to almost 50 percent. With Operation Provide Relief, the U.S. Air Force began to airlift food into remote regions in Somalia's interior not serviceable by cheaper and more efficient truck convoys because of looting.[21]

The realities of food logistics in Somalia's anarchy doused any prospects of creating a stable and legitimate food market there: the aid agencies themselves funneled most of their money to the men with the guns, and as long as those men had the guns they weren't about to use their money for food. Instead, they would use it for more guns, more khat, which Somali men chew habitually, more cigarettes, more T-shirts stenciled unabashedly with "I am the Boss." Money only fueled an invidious shadow economy.

The best example was the khat trade. Abstinence would have freed up at least six dollars per day per user. That was enough to buy twenty kilos of maize or rice and feed six people for a week, and in the aggregate maybe even enough to transfuse an economy bled of currency by the khat traders themselves. Yet none of the political players dared even suggest that the khat trade should be curtailed. Some of them—like Aidid—benefited directly from sales. Others simply knew that the result of a ban would have been more unrest. In September a Somali employee of a French relief agency who was paid half in food instead of all in cash detained several expatriate doctors and nurses in an operating theater with an unpinned hand grenade until he got his way. Food couldn't buy khat.

Beyond the simple economics of khat versus food, the remarkable survival of the khat industry through war and anarchy demonstrates both how able and how cynical the Somalis can be.[22] Khat, known in Kenya as *miraa,* is a green leaf that secretes heavy concentrations of an amphetamine (cathinone) similar to the speed found in trace amounts in antihistamines. Muslim religious leaders and devotees traditionally used it to zing through marathon sessions of Koran recitation, but during this century it has become widely used by Somalis as a recreational stimulant. Chewing khat for a few hours, the way a good old boy would munch a plug of tobacco, is chemically about like taking a liberal dose of dexedrine. The drug is considered a hip distraction among the teenage boys who wield the guns in Somalia, for whom it punctuates an otherwise humdrum day of glowering intimidation.

Khat also generates a strong and insidious psychological addiction. The natural temptation is to compare it to cocaine. But khat does not provide that stark sense of omnipotence, nor does it lubricate the fleeting minutes with the steady, salty metronome of postnasal drip. Instead, it turns the saliva into a brackish froth, necessitates rabid spitting (though experts swallow), and tastes bitter and putrid. For the first two hours the chewer feels happily animated. During the third hour depression, fatigue, and distrust kick in, yet sleep is impossible. The bladder may fill, but urinating is akin to straining honey through cheesecloth. These wire-crossing features make the high one of gnawing agitation, not crystallized power. The impetus to action seems to come from a need to escape the drug's languid foulness. When a colloquy of Somali intellectuals are sitting around in London or Rome talking about a "political solution," the khat buzz manifests itself benignly as a string of urgent tirades. When a provincial young Somali in need can actually see product and feel a new jolt coming, though, he loses any sense of decorum.

Before Operation Restore Hope, gunshot wounds in Mogadishu—the so-called cease-fire produced thirty to fifty per day—peaked out in the early evening hours, when the gunmen were at the apex of the khat spree. As the day wore on, restless adolescents got more and more cranked up and less and less rational. By late afternoon, the jangled nerves and raw tempers started to show up as reckless driving, senseless arguments, and what a Somali doctor called "just joking around"—that is, the playful exchange of gunfire. A drug-conjured insistence on personal supremacy turned the power of the gun and pubescent energy into casual, cheap violence. "You find easy solutions to all your problems on khat," said Mohamed Abshir, a prominent member of the one viable Somali political faction that frowns on khat, in September 1992. "The problem is that Somalis' problems now are other Somalis."[23]

Somali merchants stoked this creeping malevolence by keeping the flow of khat unimpeded amid anarchy and famine—an undertaking so logistically complex that only the lure of the easy money that drug dependence guarantees could explain it. Khat requires loose, volcanic soil and kilometer-high altitudes not found in Somalia. Some of Somalia's khat comes from Ethiopia. But the strongest stuff, and the bulk of Somalia's import crop, is grown legally in central Kenya, trucked to Nairobi, and flown into Mogadishu at a rate of about six metric tons per day. This process must occur 365 days a year, as khat loses its potency one day after it is picked. The Kenya-Somalia import trade alone yields over $100 million annually to wholesalers, transporters, and street dealers, and the import value of khat dwarfs that of any other imported commodity, particularly food. Now the thirty-five thousand Somalis who fled to Britain, where khat is legal, anchor a global khat trade estimated at $75 million annually, and growing.[24]

The real beneficiaries of khat are the warlords. Osman Ato is widely reputed to be the industry kingpin—though Ato himself vehemently denied any involvement in the trade when asked about it as he flew back to Nairobi from Somalia after a khat delivery.[25] He is said to have built the airstrip (known as K-50 after its distance in kilometers from Mogadishu) that receives most of the khat for that specific purpose. As many as six of the ten planes that fly khat from Kenya into Somalia on a given day reportedly carry his product, much of which is allocated to Aidid's forces. Ato's official title is Coordinator General of Somalia Relief and Rehabilitation for the Somali National Alliance, Aidid's fractious coalition.

Ato and his fellow wholesalers enjoy a 200 percent profit thanks to their ethnic Somali brethren in Kenya, who drive unconscionably hard bargains with unworldly Kenyan farmers across the border. The money, of course, ends up in Rome bank accounts and does Somalia's economy no good whatsoever. Worse still, there is broad speculation that the merchants export looted food and fuel to fund further khat purchases, rather than cutting into their retained earnings.

On top of the offshore war chest, khat gives the warlords genuinely lean-and-mean young fighters. The warlords mete it out to their soldiers along with daily food rations—which can be that much smaller since khat suppresses the appetite—and nudge clan resentment toward outright hatred. As a bonus, they save on saltpeter, as khat makes most men sexually disinclined or incapable. There are rumors that Aidid's men are also allotted synthetic amphetamines and barbiturates, which combined with enough khat could produce an army of Manchurian rogues.

But the khat habit is sociopathic enough all by itself. At K-50, a spontaneous duel is a constant possibility when one hundred or so eager addicts start unloading khat, under armed scrutiny, from seven or eight planes. Disputes over which khat belongs to what dealer occur every day, and if less than the expected number of planes arrive, the frayed civility of the couriers on the ground can degenerate into claim jumping. The intellectual community concedes that khat's widespread use is a culprit in Somalia's violent anarchy, as do the United Nations and the nongovernmental relief agencies. Osman Ato himself coyly admitted that "khat is a luxury item" on which Somalis should not squander any wages they are lucky enough to earn. But they do. A 1980 U.N. report condemned khat as physically and psychologically debilitating. But, fearing rebellion by an addicted male population, neither the United Nations nor UNITAF before it could do anything to inhibit the khat trade in favor of a less corrupt economy or, far less ambitiously, food sufficiency. It took Ato's involvement in the June 1993 massacre of the Pakistanis to get him arrested.[26]

The food-dumping strategy, then, was the Western notion of trickle-down stubbornly applied to an arcane and unaccommodating foreign culture in the Horn of Africa. It failed to finesse the looting problem or the khat problem. And in its basic contours—blithely throwing money at privation in lieu of a more probing and fastidious solution—it was a common enough Cold War mistake, first committed more than a decade earlier when Washington inherited Somalia from Moscow.

# 2 America's Patronage during the Cold War

The Soviet Union and later the United States needed a strong dictator, not dispersed clans, to rally Somalis to geopolitical vigilance—and in the Americans' case, war against a Soviet-backed Ethiopia. By taking turns rewarding Siad Barre financially and militarily for his shifting allegiance during the Cold War, the two superpowers gave the Somalis a good reason to favor dictatorship over pluralism and to try to manipulate the strategic players and later the United Nations. The Cold War superpowers, and then the United Nations and George Bush's kinder, gentler America, were to the Somalis simply other clans whose allegiances were for bartering.

Siad Barre came to power by coup in 1969, probably with covert Soviet help. His spiel was Marxist-Leninist socialism, and he cast the Somali people as an opportunistically eclectic blend of socialists, pastoralists, and pious Muslims. In 1974, Somalia became the first sub-Saharan African nation to sign a treaty of friendship and cooperation with the Soviet Union. Although the Americans had poured money into Somalia immediately after independence, their alliance with Ethiopia, Somalia's ancient territorial foe, had tainted the relationship. By 1977, after years of abuse, the U.S. aid mission pulled out. Siad Barre's government tapped the American embassy's phones and opened its mail. Western journalists were banned. Siad's show of partisanship was aimed solely at garnering Soviet support for Somalia's battle for the Ogaden, which the Ethiopians had inherited from the British, who in turn had taken it from the Italians in World War II.[1]

In a way, the con catered to the Somalis' defiantly treacherous nature, their countenance always situational, depending on what face would accrue to their advantage, except for the residuary resort to violence should ruses and connivance fail. Among outsiders, the Soviets bought the first ticket. In the early seventies, the Soviet Union gave Siad surface-to-air missiles in exchange for facilities for their Indian Ocean fleet—in particular, a cruise-missile retooling plant in the northwest port of Berbera. This was the era of Soviet adventurism, after the United States had faltered badly in Vietnam and Angola. Self-doubt and hesitancy in Washington had fueled Moscow's strategic ambitions inside the "arc of crisis," in Zbigniew Brzezinski's phrase, encompassing the Middle East, from Afghanistan to Somalia.[2] By 1974, Soviet-Somali cooperation had cemented the Soviet Union's deepest foray into Africa and yielded a long-coveted outpost in the Indian Ocean, from which Moscow flanked the Middle East and lorded an implied threat over the oil shipping lanes that served Western Europe.

Although the war in the Ogaden nominally began when Haile Selassie was still the emperor of Ethiopia and a staunch American ally, Mengistu took over in a coup in December 1974 and adopted state socialism. By December 1976, he had signed an arms agreement with the Soviet Union. Somali troops were now facing fresh T-54 tanks, supplied by the very regime that was supposed to be backstopping them. The Soviets tried to convince Siad Barre that Mengistu was a tractable good guy, a comrade in the world socialist movement, but Siad wasn't having it. Mengistu, he said, was "the Abyssinian wolf in sheep's clothing." Siad would have known. But the obligatory reconciliation meeting was front-loaded to ensure Siad's nominal acquiescence, chaired as it was by Fidel Castro. Siad sulked away from the meeting in Aden on March 17, 1977, having reluctantly agreed in principle to solidarity between Somalia and Ethiopia.[3]

Surreptitious overtures to the United States, Britain, and France were unavailing. Officially, Somalia remained a Soviet client. In fact, the simultaneous tilt of both Somalia and Ethiopia toward the Soviet Union was a source of both embarrassment and concern for the United States in the Horn of Africa. Siad Barre's next gambit was to infiltrate the Ogaden covertly with twenty thousand troops masquerading as a renegade Ethiopian separatist group, styled the Western Somali Liberation Front. (He could get away with at least the pretense because ethnic Somalis from the Ogaden and Somalia proper are indistinguishable.) Between July and September, these troops had taken 97 percent of the Ogaden but were stopped cold by crack Cuban units.[4] Siad persistently refused to admit that the advancing soldiers were his, though winking offhandedly that Somali troops on leave were allowed to "volunteer" for duty with the local guerrilla force, and on August 28 he flew to Moscow to plea for help. The Soviets may well have privately marveled at this shameless display of disingenuousness, but they would not humor the man. Publicly embarrassed by Siad's impulsiveness and their apparent inability to control a putative satellite—Moscow had promised Mengistu that Siad would behave—the Soviets insisted that he remove his men from Ethiopia.[5]

Siad Barre folded his hands, ignored the Soviets' exhortations, and shifted to Plan B. In a veritable parody of Cold War volubility—David Lamb has called the machinations over the Ogaden war during 1977 "the most extraordinary flip-flop of superpower partnerships independent Africa had ever seen"[6]—the Soviets promptly transferred 1,200 military advisers, along with accompanying hardware, from Mogadishu to Addis Ababa. Having secured in July a modest U.S. commitment for defensive arms, on November 13, 1977, Siad Barre repudiated the Soviet-Somali Friendship Treaty, expelled the Russian military and all but a few diplomats from Somalia, and severed relations with Cuba. On that cue, the Soviets airlifted and sealifted massive numbers of arms and advisers into Ethiopia to subdue the Somali troops. Over the course of six weeks, the Soviet Union sent a billion dollars' worth of weaponry to Ethiopia—four times what the United States had supplied to Haile Selassie over the previous twenty-five years—and dispatched 12,000 Cuban soldiers and another 1,500 Soviet military advisers to Ethiopia. The reversal of alliances was obvious and draconian. Soviet trade with Somalia dropped from twenty-three million rubles in 1977 to zero in 1978.[7]

Somalia had lost the war and the Soviet Union but was now America's proxy in the Horn of Africa. The direct military aid it received was small by comparison to what the Soviets had bestowed before—about $36 million per year from 1983 through 1986, but dropping to $8.7 million in 1987. Soviet military aid in 1970 alone came to $40 million and increased through the seventies. In today's Somali gun market, AK-47s far outnumber M-16s and M-16 ammunition is especially hard to come by. The fighter carcasses that litter Mogadishu International Airport are all MiGs; there is not an F-4, an F-5, or an F-16 among them. And the military airfield at Bale Dogle that American troops made it their first order of business to secure was built by Soviet engineers. Soviet advisers and soldiers in Somalia had peaked at six thousand in the 1970s, an order of magnitude higher than U.S. in-country personnel strength in the succeeding decade.[8]

During Somalia's terrible drought of 1975, well before the decisive Soviet-American swap of Somalia and Ethiopia in 1977, Siad Barre had shopped Somalia's woes to the United States, China, and the conservative bloc of Arab States as well as its principal sponsor, the Soviet Union. Moscow was deeply offended and exhorted Siad to reduce his dependence on foreign capital. Siad essentially ignored the admonition and behaved with the hypocrisy characteristic of the nonalignment charade once in vogue in the Third World. To attract American largess, in July 1975 he invited a congressional delegation to Berbera to allay Washington's suspicions that the Soviet Union had built an offensive missile base there. Though the inspection tour was heavily sanitized because of Soviet pressure, Siad's small gesture at transparency was enough to open the U.S. Treasury to Somalia. Through the United States, Somalia garnered "soft" development and financial aid totaling an enormous $1.8 billion during the 1980s.[9]

America was a munificent benefactor but still guided by the spirit of the armchair liberal. Washington never really got acquainted with Somalia. In a speech at Cornell University in March 1993, former U.S. Agency for International Development official Michael Maren, now a journalist, recalled the willful artlessness of American economic aid to Somalia: "I was working for USAID in Somalia in 1981, when we started pumping food into that country. It was clear to many of us, even then, that the program was working to prop up a corrupt dictator and turn nomads into relief junkies. Refugees poured over the borders and into camps, where they were fed day after day, year after year, by private voluntary organizations, while little effort was made to break their growing dependence. In 1987 a World Food Program report stated that Somalia had actually produced a surplus of food that year, yet private voluntary organizations continued to distribute free food and collect U.S. government money for administering the delivery. Inevitably, indigenous food-distribution networks withered and died. The country's economy adapted to foreign aid—not to production. Meanwhile, the private voluntary organizations and corrupt government officials got fat and rich."[10]

Under a similarly nearsighted military policy, Washington reacted vaguely and sluggishly to Somalia's periodic brazenness and practiced only cosmetic damage control. Against the backdrop of the Soviet Union's early tilt toward Mengistu, the Carter administration told Siad that it was "not averse to further guerilla pressure in the Ogaden" and would "consider sympathetically appeals for assistance from states which are threatened by a build up of foreign military equipment and advisers on their borders, in the Horn and elsewhere in Africa."[11] This pronouncement led to an agreement in principle to provide defensive weapons to Somalia in July 1977. A month later, "shocked," à la Claude Rains, at the magnitude of the fighting in the Ogaden, Washington rescinded the offer and nixed the transfer of weapons via third-party intermediaries pending the restoration of Ethiopia's territorial integrity. The move, parsed and precious as it was, carried world opinion with it.

In an effort to salvage its dual position in the Horn, the Soviets officially accused the United States of "fanning nationalism and separatism to discredit African regimes and to smear their links with the Soviet Union."[12] But the Cuban troops' direct engagement of Somalis closed Moscow's window on Somalia. Siad severed all ties with the Soviet Union, and Moscow lost its base in the Indian Ocean. In keeping with the Janus-faced Somali ethic, Siad "never again uttered a favorable word about Marxism," writes Lamb.[13] But Siad also exuded the other salient Somali feature: sheer gall. Forthwith he roundly castigated the United States for failing to support Somalia against Ethiopia. His audacity toward the two superpowers revealed a jauntiness rare among Third World leaders. But what seemed like a shot from the hip was in fact carefully aimed—Siad knew that mere words and gestures would not queer his relationship with the superpowers because of Somalia's strategic resonance. Such unalloyed duplicity was vintage Somali. And in short order, Siad's mood swing conditioned the West to give Somalia its cautious backing. Although President Carter, Secretary of State Cyrus Vance, Defense Secretary Harold Brown, and the joint chiefs all opposed a theater U.S. military presence to counter the Cubans, Siad found a friend in Zbigniew Brzezinski, the national security adviser, who lobbied (unsuccessfully) for a naval show of force in the Red Sea to discourage the Soviets. The best the United States would do was stave off an invasion of Somalia by Ethiopia with presidential rhetoric, after Mengistu's counteroffensive in November 1977 had obliterated virtually all of the Somalis' gains.[14]

Washington remained aloof from the Somali people even as its involvement in-country deepened. The northwest port of Berbera in 1980 formally became the U.S. Rapid Deployment Force's Indian Ocean base, and the RDF engaged in exercises with Somali troops throughout most of the 1980s. (In 1983 the RDF became the U.S. Central Command, which, though no longer based in Berbera, had responsibility for American operations in Somalia from Operation Restore Hope forward.) But again the United States refused to commit its own manpower to Somalia's cause after Mengistu invaded Somalia, probably with Soviet backing, in July 1982 and began a six-year period of Ethiopian border incursions and complicity with Somali dissident groups against Siad Barre's government. In fact, the Somali rebel groups—the Somali Salvation Democratic Front (SSDF) in the northeast and Kismayu and the secessionist Somali National Movement (SNM) in the northwest—vaguely styled themselves socialist national liberators and drew at least rhetorical support from the Soviets themselves.

Meanwhile, the United States spent almost one hundred million dollars overhauling facilities in Berbera and Kismayu to accommodate greater naval power, which the United States planned to project from its Indian Ocean base at Diego Garcia.[15] Increasingly disenchanted Somalis identified the United States with militarism and Siad Barre. American reticence after both Siad Barre's bombing of Hargeisa in 1989 and his massacre at Jesira beach of more than two hundred members of the secessionist Isaaq clan did not help. It is telling that on the eve of Siad's flight from Mogadishu in January 1991, the CIA's Mogadishu station chief's principal source of intelligence on rebel troop strengths was still a Siad Barre crony.[16] Yet, the Reagan administration had used CIA-financed propaganda campaigns to keep alive its hopes of toppling Mengistu.[17] It was an objective that would likely have been compromised had Washington actively supported Siad's irredentism in the Ogaden yet seemed increasingly realistic as Ethiopia became dependent on American food aid during and after the horrific famine of 1984 and 1985. However Machiavellian Siad Barre might have been, then, the United States itself diluted and distanced its support for Somalia to maintain a foothold in Ethiopia and, more broadly, the Horn. Because of Washington's own addled opportunism, Somalia stayed the remotest of allies, and a virtual stranger.

There were more innocent reasons for the Americans' lack of savvy. Unlike the Soviet Union, during its Cold War involvement, the United States did not suffer the painful consequences of the Somalis' political impermeability and manipulativeness. Moscow had experienced Somali double-dealing; Washington had not. For Siad Barre, allegiances to superpowers were taken on strictly to undergird his own strength and his clan's, just as the clan allegiances they mimicked arose to root the strength of the individual. Ideology was a matter of convenience. But at the time that Siad started grooming the United States, Jimmy Carter had just taken over the White House with a mandate for a nonimperial presidency that necessarily enervated executive power at its constitutional synapse—namely, foreign policy.

On top of that, humiliation in Vietnam had made Americans—and particularly Congress—reluctant to insinuate the American military into a conflict in Africa. Vietnam had also soured U.S. policy makers on the practice of intimately conditioning local governments to further American ideological interests without becoming formal colonies—called "Pax Americana" by its Western proponents, "neocolonialism" by its leftist detractors—in favor of propping up dictators from afar with guns and money. The disinclination to get close to Third World allies was an unavoidable feature of the realpolitik of the day, but as a result, any close American scrutiny of the Somali character was forestalled. Writing in 1985 in his book on Africa, Sanford J. Ungar aptly described the Somalis' dissembling Cold War attitude toward the United States: "But today Americans are treated as heroes—or, perhaps more accurately, as targets for aggressive affection. On the assumption that Americans will believe and accept almost any compliment, educated Somalis say coyly that they always liked the United States better anyway, that they simply went through a period of being foolishly enraptured by Soviet military aid."[18]

This coquetry reflected an ironic reversal of "ugly American" imperiousness, by which America's ignorance of foreign cultures was supposedly neutralized by its superior psychological insight and moral suasion. It worked in the Philippines under Edward Lansdale, faltered in Vietnam under John Paul Vann, and turned fully back on the United States in Somalia. There was probably some mild racial misapprehension at the root of the United States's casual approach toward Somalia. Its principal Cold War experience in Africa had been with Mobutu Sese Seko of Zaire (formerly the Belgian Congo), whom the CIA had helped install in 1965. He became the quintessential African "Big Man," an autocrat who ruled a seemingly anonymous people with ruthlessness and corruption. Thus, America's history in Africa suggested that if you pleased the Big Man, you controlled the people.[19]

The principle worked for a while with Siad Barre, then flamed out. In its pursuit of Aidid, the U.S. command seemed to be applying an equally invalid variant: Catch the Big Man, and you control the people, too. It didn't work. The Somalis' earnest-sounding laments of the predominance of warlords belied a populist resentment toward anyone who presumed to take their place. After seven years of living among the Somalis as director of SOS Kinderdorf's development operations in Mogadishu, Willy Huber summed up their manipulativeness: "They are such cunning people they deserve a compliment. They take the whole world for a ride."[20]

George Bush climbed on board. By the time Somalia needed hands-on American military help again, it was 1992. Siad Barre had been forced into permanent exile, which vindicated Washington's cancellation of military aid in 1989 following his cynical bombing of Somalia's northern capital, Hargeisa, with leftover Soviet aircraft. The Cold War was over. Bush was waxing triumphal from that and the Gulf War's acquittal of an impressive American military machine, built up over forty-five years of lantern-jawed apprehensiveness. Now a lame duck, Bush understandably wanted a military mission both doable and spectacular to unveil formally the new world order he had helped introduce. With its celebration of Somalia, the press gave him his mission. Only if Washington had twigged to the Somalis' mocking treachery—if some presidential aide had perused Ungar's book—would the White House have been able to forestall the rude shock it received four months after the propitious marine landing in December 1992.

In exterminating his own countrymen—Hargeisa and the northwest were dominated by separatists from the rival Isaaq clan, comprising the SNM—Siad had demonstrated vividly that his nationalism extended only as far as his own political advantage. But because of the Americans' obstinately shallow understanding of Somalis in general, they apparently believed this paralogism was merely a personal quirk of Siad's. Their perception of Somalia had always been panoramic rather than microscopic, as a segment of the geopolitical landscape. U.S. sponsorship came by default, as Siad's consolation prize. He had nowhere else to turn. As a result, the Americans had no need to be demonstrative or nurturing. They were able to avoid a strategically extravagant white-knight confrontation with the Soviet Union against Ethiopia on Somalia's behalf. For the sake of maintaining this political frugality, the Americans considered it inadvisable to get acquainted with the Somalis the way they got to know the South Vietnamese. In this sense, Vietnam was a lesson learned too well.

In another sense, Vietnam was a lesson unlearned. George Bush should have known from Lyndon Johnson that presidential conceit had a way of distorting overseas involvement—distance makes the heart grow bolder, or something along those lines. Bush insisted from the outset that Operation Restore Hope was strictly a humanitarian venture. The world's most powerful nation, he suggested, could not sit idly by while so many people starved to death—particularly when the immediate problem, security, called for an essentially military remedy.[21] That line wended its way all the way down to the grunts. "It needs to be done, we're the only ones who can do it, so it's an appropriate mission," said one marine after a week in Mogadishu.[22]

Nobody doubted the first two propositions. It was the third that seemed suspect. At best mutual self-interest, not altruism or ingenuous nobility, has long driven the United States's (and just about everyone else's) foreign policy. Why should that have changed in December 1992? Circumstances initially suggested a couple of ulterior motives—preserving oil interests and containing Islamic fundamentalism.[23] They turned out to be illusory.

The U.S. diplomatic mission lived in an air-conditioned house owned and maintained by Conoco. Since the U.S. embassy was evacuated in 1991, American diplomats based in Nairobi used that house exclusively when in Somalia. One political officer, John Fox, made it a habit of wearing a Conoco cap, T-shirt, or both.

Osman Ato, Aidid's one-man brain trust, lived right next door. For years he was the primary cut-line contractor for Western Geophysical Corporation, one of the world's largest oil exploration firms. Western Geophysical did virtually all of Conoco's seismic survey work in Somalia, so Ato developed close personal ties to Conoco's representative in Somalia.

After the Hunt family of Texas discovered oil in an unusual geological formation in Yemen in the early 1980s, other oil concerns found that the formation extended under the Gulf of Aden and into Somalia. Interest burgeoned. The U.S. Agency for International Development assisted Siad Barre's Ministry of Petroleum in parceling out drilling rights, which were quickly purchased by Chevron, Amoco, Phillips Petroleum, and Shell. Conoco purchased the biggest block of drillable land. Preliminary results were promising enough to move Chevron to increase its investment from twenty million dollars in two wells to one hundred million dollars in three wells before it had even capped the first hole. Oil exploration made Osman Ato a millionaire before he was forty-five. But war stopped all development cold by the end of 1990.[24]

It was Ato who convinced Aidid to welcome the American troops into Mogadishu. Ato also convinced Aidid to dig into Kismayu, which is not traditional Hawiye homeland, probably for commercial reasons. A good deal of the hardware used for drilling and pipeline construction would pass through the port. And Ato admitted in December 1992 that at the end of the day, "I will not disappear, but I don't want to be in the political forefront. I am a businessman, and that's all I want to be."[25] A quid pro quo between Ato and the U.S. government—first dibs on business in exchange for oil security, with Conoco and others the third-party beneficiaries—seemed at least a possibility. Mark Fineman of the *Los Angeles Times* reported as much, in a sketchy article.[26]

U.S. special envoy Robert Oakley convincingly refuted any such speculation. "There are no vital oil interests here, I assure you," he claimed. "The amount of oil here is miniscule. It's small potatoes. I've talked to no one in this country about Conoco. I intend to talk to no one about it."[27] And the United States had just finished fighting a war over oil resources that dwarf those of sub-Saharan Africa and was then enjoying its fruits: solid relations with Kuwait and Saudi Arabia, Qaddafi's inclination toward moderation, and the increasing isolation of Iran and Iraq in the Middle East. In any event, Somalia's reserves, even if considerable, were unproven then and remain so.

Presently it began to look as though Ato himself was more of an "asset" to be used than a "friendly" to be appeased. Before the American intervention, but after he had admonished Aidid to embrace it, Ato said that he did "not think any troops would be in Somalia until after Christmas," intimating that he had U.S. diplomatic reassurances. He also radiated confidence that the United States's principal aim was to help the Somalis (read: Aidid) "set up security" in the form of a reconstituted national police force.[28] Neither take was accurate.

The only source of genuine strategic fear for the United States was the potential spread of Islamic fundamentalism. The militant group in Somalia is known as Al Itahad—"the Unity"—and is backed by the usual suspects, Iran and Sudan. But most Somalis are Sunni Muslims of the Sha'afi sect, which is decidedly tame and nonfundamentalist. Aidid and Osman Ato are secular in their political outlook, as is their arch-rival, Ali Mahdi. These men had no reason to seek the support of the fundamentalists and every reason to oppose them. On the other hand, it made some sense to view Washington's precipitously hands-on approach to Somali welfare as a pretext for a new brand of containment. Immediately the U.S. military intervention in Somalia had a partisan impact—namely, scaring Khartoum's fundamentalist government into opening Sudan's southern borders so that aid agencies could resume relief to the Christian/animist south Sudanese rebels.

Again, Oakley's refutation on this score, though certainly obligatory from the State Department's point of view, was persuasive and replete. "The use of militant Islam against the United States for political purposes is a big problem," he admitted. "But we have to distinguish between political action and terrorist action. We don't disapprove of religious groups per se, but if political action is taken against us, we respond—though not with force unless we're dealt with violently." The fact that the United States was using force in Somalia, whereas Al Itahad was not, could have meant a propaganda coup for the fundamentalists if any American antifundamentalist intent were uncovered. "Militant Somali groups would like nothing better than Somali casualties at American hands," noted Oakley. "We'd have the martyr syndrome all over again." He had learned from hard experience in Iran, Iraq, and Afghanistan.[29]

Oakley insisted that the world was seeing what it was getting. "We're in Somalia for strictly moral, humanitarian reasons," he said. "As the world leader we got terribly embarrassed when the relief we were pouring in wasn't working." He acknowledged that it was U.S. policy to encourage democracy whenever feasible. But he also regularly cited the Vietnam experience as an object lesson in both why the United States should not attempt to take responsibility for the security of an entire country and why it should not try to impose democracy coercively on anyone. Having ruefully assisted the late Philip Habib in the drafting of the stillborn South Vietnamese constitution as a young Foreign Service officer in Saigon, he observed that either endeavor leads to a "totally artificial result" that invites retrogression once the U.S. departs. The American institutional wisdom was that Somalia ultimately must help itself to survive and decide how to govern itself.[30]

In keeping with these chastisements of recent overseas entanglements, American diplomats did not presume to outfit Somalia with some modular version of democracy. What they tried to do instead was provide their good offices to enable Somali political figures to arrive at their own form of government, while the soldiers made the people more governable by pacifying them and bringing them food. The obvious risk was that as the two processes converged, the United States would find itself immovably planted in the political driver's seat, even though political reconciliation in Somalia was nominally reserved for the United Nations. Oakley knew the pitfalls. "The clan system is almost impossible for a foreigner to understand," he conceded. "We cannot become a negotiator, arbiter or enforcer of bloody subclan disputes."[31] Somalia, in a word, had the makings of a quagmire.

And the Somalis, paranoid, insular, and unforgiving as they are, had some reason to be suspicious of the Americans. In fact, it was only at Aidid's scheming insistence—he expected partisan U.S. support[32]—that the Somali people gave the marines a warm reception when they landed. But, notwithstanding the Security Council resolution as a fig leaf, the Somalis perceived Operation Restore Hope as an essentially unilateral American effort. Over this Oakley suffered a tactical disadvantage. Somali political leaders, following their cultural template, sought the United States's partisan support. Most Somalis in positions of power still could not stomach the idea of a clan-neutral, egalitarian polity arching over the network of regional clans. Each clan wanted an advocate for its legitimacy, and down the road, a sponsor for its government, which would then become a conduit for development loot. If the United States were to submit to one of them—which Oakley vowed it would not—it might well have fallen into precisely the same blueprint for dictatorship that brought the world Siad Barre.

Ambassador Oakley knew enough about Somalia to understand that the key to precluding this result was neutralizing factional military power and skewing the Somali political idiom instead toward negotiation and balanced local control. He had some stroke with erstwhile dissidents like Aidid on account of his own expulsion from Mogadishu when, as U.S. ambassador in 1982, Oakley openly criticized Siad Barre's ruthless treatment of political opponents. And Oakley did edge the Somalis in the direction of reconciliation by getting the two principal warlords, Aidid and Ali Mahdi Mohamed, talking civilly and persuading Aidid to attend the U.N.-sponsored peace talks in Addis Ababa. In fact, thanks to Oakley's brokering, the two warring Mogadishu subclans staged an elaborate parade and a grinning public embrace as they opened up the "green line" that divided the capital city. A friendly soccer game followed.

But not even Oakley's deft touch could overcome the Somali zeal for the upper hand. The United States's muscular intervention had presented Somali political leaders with divisive and retrograde temptations of partiality that the United Nations neither would nor could have presented. The diplomatic task of forging peace reverted back to the United Nations when the United States officially handed over the command of foreign military operations in Somalia, but U.N. neutrality seemed inadequate consolation for the American friendship the Somalis had seen dangling before them. Despite Oakley's admirable stubbornness, a Somali political solution most likely would have been easier to achieve in the absence of U.S. intervention.

And Oakley's savvy was rare among Americans. Understandably eager to resume his interrupted retirement, in March 1993 he was replaced by another old Somalia hand, United States Information Agency officer Robert Gosende. Gosende's inclination was to "give Aidid what he wanted"[33]—a position that, dubious in March, became untenable in June, when Aidid orchestrated the massacre of Pakistani peacekeepers and had a bounty put on his head by the third player in the American franchise, U.N. special envoy Admiral Jonathan Howe.

This decision too was taken in ignorance of the collective Somali psyche. The move made Aidid a revered martyr. In any case, no one diplomat could counter the conceptual vulnerability of a large-scale U.S. presence to calculated Somali sycophancy or, failing that, provocation. In that light, Operation Restore Hope—in particular, the mythologizing of Aidid—looked very much like a Cold War mistake in the post–Cold War world.

# 3 Siad Barre's Ouster Somali Retribution Run Amok

The rumor is that Siad Barre literally drove General Mohamed Farah Aidid out of his mind. Aidid had been an early opponent of Siad. Once Siad took power in November 1969, he imprisoned Aidid and did not release him until October 1975. Supposedly Siad's henchmen subjected Aidid to electric shock therapy, for some time after which he would eat only Lux soap.[1] Any dietary abnormalities had apparently subsided by the time he was set free, and he served with distinction in the Ogaden war. Thereafter he was a presidential staffer and in 1979 became a member of Parliament. From 1984 to 1989, Aidid was Somalia's ambassador to India, but he was reportedly recalled because of a smuggling scandal. By then Aidid had had quite enough of Siad Barre and covertly helped organize the United Somali Congress (USC), becoming chairman of the party in July 1991.[2]

In December 1991, after Aidid and crosstown USC rival Ali Mahdi Mohamed had shelled Mogadishu back to the Stone Age with Soviet and American weapons glommed from vanquished government troops, *Newsweek* reporter Jeffrey Bartholet asked Aidid how he could continue to declare for peace while perpetrating mass fratricide. Above Mogadishu's white noise of artillery and small-arms fire, he replied cheerfully that in any war of liberation, "there is a tendency for what the Americans like to call collateral damage."[3] He sent all fourteen of his children out of the country—to study in Canada, Italy, Saudi Arabia, and the United States—for their safety.[4] One of his wives was a Canadian welfare queen until she got caught, when she fled Toronto—air fare courtesy of the United Nations—to be with her husband in Addis Ababa for the annual Somali national reconciliation conference.[5] The irony that Aidid has made Somalia uninhabitable for his own family escapes him.

Aidid was far from all good, but Siad Barre was probably just as far from all bad. Though broad concern for the economic welfare of the populace does not often reside in military governments, Siad Barre's was a modest exception. When he took over, Somalia's population was three-quarters nomadic and largely illiterate. Nationalization of agricultural industries focused and coordinated production, crowded out sleazy and inefficient middlemen, and nurtured foreign trade. Through largely inspirational government self-help programs Somalis built an operating health and education infrastructure from the ground up and inched Somalia into the twentieth century. In 1973, Siad instituted Somalia's first written language (a hybrid of indigenous argots and Arabic) and promptly brought literacy in Somalia up to a level that was in fact exemplary for the Third World.[6] By 1975, with his program of "scientific socialism," he had centralized the budget, nationalized land, and imposed wage and price controls. He conscientiously tried to ban khat, recognizing that it rotted the core of Somalia's work force by creating young addicts who spent the morning hours scoring the amphetamine weed and the afternoon hours chewing it. The ban didn't work—but Siad tried.

At the same time, Siad left the most lucrative industries in private hands and devoted 20 percent of his budget to the military. Private plantation owners, many of them Italian, continued to grow all of Somalia's bananas, and individualistic nomads remained free to trade their livestock on the Arab and Persian Gulf market. That Siad's economy was mixed, not dyed-in-the-wool socialist, reflected his intention to fund Somalia's economic progress eclectically, and not only from the Soviet Union. He recognized that Somalis were at heart mercantilist entrepreneurs, driven by profit. But there were ideological reasons as well. Siad could not square his people's strong Muslim beliefs with Moscow's prescriptive atheism. And he knew that the muting of clan affiliations that outright egalitarian socialism entailed just wouldn't wash with Somalis. In 1972, Siad admitted, with a prescience no doubt unintended, "Our nation is rather too clannish. If all Somalis are to go to hell, tribalism will be their vehicle to reach there."[7]

Back then, under Soviet tutelage, he knew the limits of even dictatorial power and harbored some genuine affection for his people. KGB-driven fortification of his security forces and Moscow's insistence that he make bloody examples of his foes, however, led to a policy of executions and fueled his megalomania. Washington's arm's-length approach to U.S.-Somalia relations provided no antidote. Rebellion and retribution spiraled as Siad neared eighty. For the sake of his own security and the perpetuation of his rule, he became increasingly insular and nepotistic. At Washington's invitation, he selected his son-in-law, Mohamed Said Hersi, to attend the U.S. Army's Command and General Staff College in Leavenworth, Kansas. The young man adopted the moniker "Morgan" during his matriculation, and returned to head Siad Barre's armed forces. In 1989 he precociously earned a second nickname, "The Butcher of Hargeisa," when he carried out the bombing of Somalia's northwest capital after the secessionist Somali National Movement besieged it. Although Siad Barre fearfully held the city, in the bargain he lost one thousand troops and forced one hundred thousand frightened and resentful Somali refugees into Ethiopia.[8]

By mid-1989, other Somali clans and subclans regarded the Marehans' lust for power as uncontainable. Siad's bombs had destroyed 80 percent of the buildings in Hargeisa, and government troops were slaughtering civilians wholesale in the northwest to prevent guerrilla alliances with the SNM from arising. About five thousand Isaaqs were killed in the latter half of 1988; one thousand of them were women and children bayoneted to death in cold blood. By early 1989, Siad Barre had gotten wind of the formation of the United Somali Congress in Rome by exiled Hawiye "to liberate their county from the clutches of Mighty Mouth." "Mighty Mouth's" reaction was unhappily nonverbal: He summarily dispatched his security force, the "Red Hats," to Hawiye towns in central Somalia, where they exterminated the men en masse and fed them to crocodiles in the Shibelle River. At the same time, Mengistu's expulsion of the SNM from Ethiopia as a result of a rapprochement with Siad Barre only made the northwest rebels more fervent, as they forged loose alliances with other rebel groups from south and central Somalia who smelled the blood of government troops coursing from Hargeisa.[9]

Africa is the prime breeding ground for the grandiose acronymic political organization. In 1989, that was the one commodity of which Somalia enjoyed a bumper crop. Several new political groups, all clan based, emerged: the Somali Patriotic Movement (SPM) in the south; the Somali National Army (SNA) in the central part of the country; the United Somali Congress (USC) in Mogadishu; and the Somali Democratic Alliance (SDA) in the northeast. In November, the USC joined forces with the SNM and the two briefly retook Hargeisa. The Somali Salvation Democratic Front (SSDF) was fronted by army officers from a Darod subclan, the Majerteen, and had existed since 1978, when Siad's defeat in the Ogaden prompted a failed coup attempt. Because of that attempt and their haughty preeminence in earlier civilian regimes in the 1960s, Siad Barre had a standing policy of systematic persecution. He sent the Red Hats to rape Majerteen women, abduct pubescent girls for concubinage, and decimate Majerteen livestock by obliterating their reservoirs. In the late 1980s, the SSDF staged guerrilla operations from Ethiopia in the area northeast of Mogadishu it claimed as its homeland. The new tone of rebellion revived the organization.[10]

By June 1989, civil order was breaking down in Mogadishu, prompting Siad Barre to impose a curfew. Early one August morning, Siad rounded up scores of Isaaq transients living in Mogadishu, and in retaliation for the SNM's incursions in Hargeisa, executed them in a previously dug mass grave at Jesira beach on the outskirts of town. The atrocity drove the citizenry over the edge. The Somalis' intolerance for Siad Barre became open and truly populist. Fearing the "three o'clock knock" that presaged executions, poets and singers led dissent. Siad muzzled an entire troupe after it performed "The Land Cruiser Song" for him at the National Theater. The song condemned his Nero-like propensity for collecting expensive foreign vehicles while his people perished. One hundred prominent Somalis signed a declaration, known as the Mogadishu Manifesto, calling for Siad's resignation, the appointment of a transition government pending elections, and the abolition of the government security apparatus.[11]

With political opposition to Siad Barre gathering momentum, the United States slashed aid to almost zero in September 1989. Now friendless, Siad Barre dismissed the government in January 1990 and offered posts to opposition leaders. Taking Siad's softening as a sign of weakness, to a man they declined. Ever a Somali, a Mogadishu restaurateur blamed his country's woes on other people. "The Americans are again driving Barre into the hands of the communists, which is not what we want," he declared.[12] But a crumbling USSR no longer had the time or energy for Somalia. In March, a desperate Siad launched a massive military offensive in the north and recaptured three towns on the Djibouti border previously held by the SNM.

Siad attempted appeasement by calling for multiparty elections, but by then, political opposition had reached critical mass. Italian and Egyptian efforts to bring the organizations to a peace conference were rebuffed. By December 1990, Siad's demiurgic countenance had become a spoof. When he sauntered out to the podium in Mogadishu Stadium to open a sports competition, decked out in a pinstripe suit and expensive sunglasses, he expected the crowd of thirty thousand to sing him the prescribed tribute, "Siad, Father of the Nation." Instead they jeered, "Murderer" and "Dictator."[13]

Somalia's political factions, like Siad before them, preferred better government through bloodshed. The SNM, USC, and SPM teamed up and advanced against government troops in the northern, central, and southern sectors of the country. In Mogadishu, hundreds of decaying civilian bodies demarcated the angles of crossfire. Teenage gunmen wiped out entire families belonging to Siad's Marehan clan. In a vain attempt to deter advancing guerrillas, Siad's troops had perforated city buildings from the presidential palace, Villa Somalia, with batteries of forty 122-mm rockets mounted on trucks, known as "Stalin organs." As mobile guerrillas converged on the palace, Siad the military man found out that passive defenses don't work very well. His capture by the USC imminent, Siad Barre was forced to flee Mogadishu on January 27, 1991, under heavy army protection, and hunker down near his birthplace on the Kenyan border.[14] He died in exile in Nigeria four years later, intent, to the end, on retaking Somalia.

Even through a lens of gore, the siege of the capital had a burlesque, banana-republic quality. Radio Mogadishu absurdly blared government victory. Marauding rebels painted the word *Guul*—"victory"—on the humps of camels. Like Idi Amin's digs, Siad's abandoned office was littered with thousands of unopened letters dating back fifteen years from human rights organizations and the friends and relatives of political prisoners. According to a Somali journalist, the CIA station chief searchingly asked a source from Siad's government whether he thought the rebels could take Mogadishu without reinforcements moments before they occupied the town.[15] On January 5 and 6, 1991, U.S. Marines from the USS *Guam* staged an amphibious rescue of 272 staff from the new $35 million U.S. embassy, just ahead of looting hordes who stole the ambassador's furniture, sinks, even his toilet. As he headed for the airport, Giuglio Marcchesi, the Italian cultural attaché, quipped, "Given the choice, I'd rather be home watching this on TV."[16]

Ali Mahdi was named interim president on January 29, 1991. Aidid was livid: as the liberator of Mogadishu, he considered himself heir to Siad's stream of skimmable foreign loot. Both the SPM and the SNM also opposed Ali Mahdi's appointment. In March, the SNM, as well as other nascent political groups, rejected Ali Mahdi's invitation to a national unification conference and declared an independent "Republic of Somaliland" in the northwest, with the same boundaries as the former British colony and Hargeisa as its capital. The nonseparatist Somali factions convened their own reconciliation conferences in Djibouti in June and July, signing a second manifesto resolving to eradicate the Siad Barre government unconditionally, work toward national unity, and keep Ali Mahdi as president for another two years. They also decided to resist the SNM's attempts to secede, establishing perhaps the single lasting point of agreement among southern Somali clans. Under the eventual government, stillborn though it was, major executive posts would be equitably divided among factions—that is, clans—and two-thirds of the seats in parliament would be allotted to the south and one-third to the would-be secessionists in the north.[17]

Meanwhile Somali leaders had been casting about for a folk hero and found him in Aidid—a Mogadishu native whose Hawiye clan had been dispossessed and politically abused by Siad, and a former political prisoner of the dictator. Aidid was a soldier of another vintage, trained not in Leavenworth but in the Soviet Union; it was an association that recalled better days for the Somali people. He was elected chairman of the United Somali Congress in July 1991. Though the USC feigned solidarity, Aidid himself rejected Ali Mahdi's new cabinet. After several months of skirmishing between Aidid's Habar-Gedir subclan and Ali

Mahdi's Abgal subclan, pitched battles began in November 1991. Over the next four months, cavalier shelling and looting killed over one thousand civilians and another four thousand subclan combatants. Although the warlords and their gunmen lived in relative luxury, the rest of Mogadishu became a wasteland of starving ciphers and child amputees. No diplomats were left, no businesses were open. Artillery fire kept meandering food ships from docking at the port, leaving an entire population dependent on small planes for food.[18]

Italy—southern Somalia's former colonial master, with heavy commercial interests in Somalia—tried to broker peace but was thwarted by Aidid supporters. The United Nations took notice only from a distance. The secretary-general's emissary to Somalia, James Jonah, the undersecretary for political affairs, did stop over for a few days in early January 1992. Squeamishly disgusted with the Somalis' unregenerate clan treachery, however, he failed to forge an agreement between Ali Mahdi and Aidid on a peacekeeping force. Ali Mahdi wanted bluehelmets on the theory that they would bolster his own ostensibly inferior firepower. The possibility of the United Nations's sending Italian soldiers also loomed. A Mogadishu hotelier backed by Italian businessmen, Ali Mahdi likely would have been delighted. But most Somalis regarded their present fight as a second quest for independence. The deployment of Italian U.N. peacekeepers would have been a twofold insult, because southern Somalis had been under a U.N. trusteeship administered by the Italians during the ten-year interim between Italian hegemony and statehood.

In fact, Aidid believed Ali Mahdi's "Manifesto" faction of the USC was underwritten in part by the Italian government and business community and amounted to "Siad Barre's government by self-appointment." Ali Mahdi, he said, "came into the picture out of nowhere. We are the ones who are trying to make Somalis love each other."[19] Osman Ato characterized Aidid as "political savior of the Hawiye."[20] All this, after Aidid's supporters in Kismayu executed a dozen Majerteen squatters like sick dogs. Later Aidid spread the rumor that Ali Mahdi was allowing Italian concerns to dump hazardous waste off north Mogadishu, though a cursory U.N. Environmental Program investigation turned up no supporting evidence.

The U.S. government did have an asset in Ali Mahdi's camp, a former protocol officer for Ambassadors Bishop and Crigler named Abdulkadir

Yahya Ali. He remained technically employed by the State Department throughout the civil war and clan battles and kept in touch with Washington by satellite phone. According to Yahya, in October 1991 Washington offered to broker peace if asked to do so by the Somali government, to which Ali Mahdi and his cabinet were then the pretenders. Yahya proffered the invitation but claims the United States never followed up, instead courting Somali politicians covertly through the Red Cross and the World Food Program. In any event, when the peephole of opportunity opened between Siad's ouster in January 1991 and the eruption of subclan warfare in Mogadishu the following November, nobody with any transnational clout stepped in.[21] Thereafter, Yahya went to work for the United Nations

By late 1991, the SPM had split into factions, one of them forming the Somali National Front (SNF) with Siad Barre's troops and the other joining Aidid under Colonel Omar Jess, an ambitious, charming, bloodthirsty Darod from a rival subclan. (This schism led to the ongoing battle between Aidid and Morgan for Kismayu that plagued the United States and the United Nations in 1993.) On January 23, 1992, the U.N. Security Council unanimously passed a resolution slapping an arms embargo on Somalia, calling for humanitarian aid, and urging a cease-fire. The United States, though, had vehemently expressed its opposition to Cape Verde's proposal that peacekeeping troops be sent to Somalia—as good as a decree in U.N. internal politics. Instead Aidid and Ali Mahdi themselves agreed to a cease-fire on March 3, signed and witnessed by the U.N. delegation in Mogadishu. So far, the United Nations had acted as little more than a notary public. But in late March, a U.N. technical team, twenty strong, arrived to "supervise" the cease-fire and get humanitarian aid projects started. A day later, four Somali gunmen killed a U.N. driver in a plainly marked vehicle. *Newsweek* asked sarcastically, "*This* Is the New World Order?"[22]

Given Somalia's runaway entropy, Jonah's meager efforts were laughable. The United States and the rest of the West looked better in sheer neglect. Rather than urging stepped-up relief on the heels of the cease-fire, Jonah simply recommended a technical assessment of Somalia's peacekeeping and relief needs and the deployment of U.N. observers. Then he threatened the warlords that the world would withhold food aid unless the cease-fire held, maintaining that it was they "who must bear responsibility for denying the starving population of Mogadishu this vital source of life."

Mohamed Sahnoun of Algeria was appointed the secretary-general's special envoy in April 1992. In contrast to Jonah, he immediately acclimated himself to Somalia, meeting with clan elders in the bush. In mid-June, just as political talks were starting to bear fruit, an Antonov plane with U.N. markings delivered military hardware and newly printed Somali currency to Ali Mahdi at his airfield in north Mogadishu. Although it eventually transpired that the Russian crew's contract with the United Nations had expired beforehand, the United Nations had no ready explanation. Ali Mahdi's disingenuous rationale was that he was implementing "monetary policy to increase the money supply and rehabilitate the economy." He skirted the weapons issue with Third World standard cant: "Aidid is one man destroying many Somalis." Aidid played into his hand by refusing to allow forty-seven of a planned fifty U.N. military observers into Somalia, withdrew the consent he had tentatively given for five hundred armed troops, and accused the United Nations of favoring Ali Mahdi. But Sahnoun deemed Aidid's suspicions of bias "understandable" and criticized his own organization for its "lack of vigilance" in policing its contractors. An invigorated Aidid's position was now that it was simply "not necessary to negotiate with Ali Mahdi."[23]

Even with the United Nations thus beleaguered and the warlords misbehaving, Sahnoun held, contra Jonah, that the United Nations was indeed responsible for feeding the starving innocents in Somalia. On July 20, the *New York Times*'s Jane Perlez wrote of walking skeletons dying every few minutes in Baidoa, the hardest-hit town.[24] But Sahnoun importuned donors to leap-frog a second U.N. technical assessment with food airlifts to Somalia's interior "because kids are dying right now."[25] The chief of the U.N. technical team, Danish political scientist Peter Hansen, cautiously admitted that U.N. employees had to "take into account more complexities" than those in New York and that Somalia's was a "situation not foreseen by the U.N. Charter."[26] But with Sahnoun's dervishlike activity, the feeding situation improved substantially, partly because his impassioned rhetoric drew press coverage that increased global contributions and partly because Sahnoun rallied warlords and elders to self-help.[27] Aidid had formed a coalition of political groups into yet another acronymic organization, the Somali National Alliance (SNA) and through it generated at least some semblance of cohesion in south-central Somalia. Weekly mortality in Baidoa shrank from 1,780 dead on September 6 to 336 dead on November 1.[28]

The engine of famine was flagging. But Sahnoun's tenure was a brief Camelot. Because of bureaucratic infighting Sahnoun was forced to resign in late October. Aidid lost the incentive to restrain his manchildren. Looting and shelling closed the port. General Morgan, now allied with Siad Barre loyalists from the SPM and SNF, ousted Aidid from his western stronghold in Bardera and advanced toward Kismayu. In November 1992, south-central Somalia was more dangerous and chaotic than ever.

The humanitarian aid culture in Mogadishu, in the meantime, had styled itself a uniquely tough and embattled corps. The cross-hairs and banana clips of the assault rifles their extortionate guards carried had become mythical emblems of "seeing the world." Aid workers tended to fancy themselves confirmed and proven do-gooders, but in candid moments they talked about the rush. It was an adrenal temperament, not a sense of duty, that drove them to do what they did. At the heart of their enterprise were adventure and camaraderie, catalyzed by being in a strange place away from home. It made for a heartening but, at bottom, callow college-dorm atmosphere. They were conscientious but inefficient, seat-of-the-pants.

In July 1992, a veteran CARE worker in Mogadishu, bathing in melodrama, beamed that it was "the most dangerous port in the world" and that getting food from the port into the city "was an achievement in itself."[29] Certainly he wanted to feed all those starving people, but his more immediate need was simply for some sense of accomplishment to show for his risk and someone to share it with who was gonzo enough to take the same chance. A French aid worker confided that it was not the distress alone that made Somalia so extraordinary, but the "distress and craziness."[30] Dealing with baleful, desperate people enriched his pride. The aid people probably did have the will to make their good intentions bear real fruit but had not figured out the way. The International Committee of the Red Cross was doing most of the feeding in seven hundred kitchens in south and central Somalia. It distanced itself from the rest of the aid organizations and cut its own deals for food security, draining the power of Somali "protection" cartels like the one terrorizing Mogadishu port. Kickbacks later tainted the effort.

But by giving in to outright extortion, other groups merely vouchsafed Somali payback once foreign troops made Somali security functionally unnecessary. In August, Irish Concern workers caved in to demands that they increase their drivers' compensation after being held hostage for two days; the following February a nurse who worked for the organization was killed by a sniper. Somalia's marquee-quality strife was the young guns' day in the sun, a Warholian moment in a life with dim prospects. The bad boys resented it when the Americans stole their thunder. UNICEF workers were murdered in Bardera and Kismayu by disgruntled Somalis who had lost their jobs. Nonetheless, the Somalis made redundant as port security guards had the nerve to ask the United Nations for back wages in March 1993.

Important aid mavens like Bernard Kouchner, then head of Médecins Sans Frontières (MSF), publicized the Somalis' strong-arm tactics to convince donors to give more money. Yet only one, SOS-Kinderdorf-International, toughed it out through all the shelling and looting with nary an evacuation, taking seventy-two artillery rounds in the compound through November 1991. More a rehabilitation and development operation (orphanages and maternity care) than an emergency relief provider, over several years SOS had established neutrality among the clans where less savvy parvenus in Somalia had become virtual shills for one warlord or another. In August 1992, for example, one of CARE's logistics experts justified his organization's co-optation by Habar-Gedir gunmen by lecturing journalists about how Somali clan culture actually condones looting as a mechanism of distributive justice. That, he said, was why half of the dry food that CARE trucked from Mogadishu port to distribution centers was stolen. Such behavior was inevitable, the reporters were told, in a nomadic society that exalts blood over community.[31] Sad to say, most journalists bought the rap—hook, line, and sinker—and cast Somali cultural peculiarities as impervious to any moral compunction whatsoever. MSF seemed to parrot Aidid when it recommended against even a small contingent of U.N. peacekeeping troops in September. Aidid ended up embarrassing MSF by changing his mind and letting the soldiers come anyway.

The interest of relief outfits in Somalia significantly waned once the food emergency was over in April 1993, even though the need for rehabilitation and development programs then became all the more acute. At bottom, tactics like Kouchner's were unscrupulous and cynical in imputing to all Somalis the evil of a few in order to mask the desultoriness of aid organizations. At the same time, the aid community's publicity campaigns did serve the purpose of airing salient generalizations about the Somali people: they do have a lower threshold for violence than most others, a primitive ethos, and mercenary tendencies—generalizations that in a more demure context would have been too politically incorrect, too countermulticultural, too Kiplingesque to gain the currency they warranted.

A fair number of journalists winced wanly through their own expensive sunglasses at masses of emaciated ciphers and cozied up to thugs on their "technicals" to cadge photo-ops and nasty quotes. In private they muttered profundities like, "God, why do there have to be superpowers?" It was a small miracle that so many journalists toured Mogadishu during the last six months of 1992 largely unscathed. The crux of the explanation was that they were the hired gunmen's meal tickets, at one hundred dollars plus per day. But it seemed that many of the hacks themselves failed to grasp the point. In one editorial, an American reporter suggested that Somalis be offered money for their guns, apparently unmoved by the fact that the revenue stream from keeping the gun and hiring out as "security" would dwarf any affordable one-time payment.[32]

But after the marines moved in, many of the armed thugs did indeed become employed. To add to their irritation, virgin television crews wandered around to places Somalia-seasoned hacks knew enough to avoid, brandishing their cameras as if somehow blessed. Early on, several were pelted with rocks and relieved of their expensive equipment. With the usual labored irony of the Western journalist slumming it in the Third World, in December 1992 one reporter suggested that a set of T-shirts be commissioned, the garment to read, "I was stoned in Mogadishu." The remark seemed even less funny on July 12, 1993, when three journalists did indeed get stoned (as well as beaten and hacked)—to death.

Eventually the press tired of on-scene horror—"You've seen one starving child, you've seen 'em all"—and instead looked summarily to a cadre of certain in-country relief gurus they dubbed "dial-a-quote." CARE's Rhodri Wynn-Pope, a recently retired Welsh major in the British Army's Grenadier Guards, was a particular favorite. The International Medical Corps' Stephen Tomlin was another, often characterizing Somalia as "the litmus test for the new world order." Boffo. The starving, of course, didn't care how interested in their unshared agony peripatetic reporters were. It was easy for the journalists to forget that the people were center stage.

A fair number of hacks fancied they could have a heroic episode, work a little salvation with a pat on the head and a candy bar, and exit, without seriously considering the bizarre politics or cultural viruses that got the Somalis into their mess to begin with. But the press corps did, at least, make the world take notice—in the revelatory heyday of fall 1992, Audrey Hepburn, Sophia Loren, and Somali supermodel Iman (Mrs. David Bowie) all made headline sojourns to Somalia. Irish President Mary Robinson also paid a visit. That was real spin. Still the only suggestion from journalists of any durability was simply to send more troops. Although it was not quite the place of journalists to dictate policy to the United Nations, that is basically what happened.

The Arab League, the Organization of African Unity, and the Organization of the Islamic Conference are to blame for the persistence of Somalia's problems, too. The regional organizations effectively ignored Somalia. Aside from attending a Valentine's Day meeting at U.N. headquarters in New York that merely confirmed that a cease-fire would be nice, they did nothing. Whereas the United Nations had both strong regional support and a reasonably accommodating host government in the Persian Gulf, it had neither in Somalia. Sub-Saharan Africa deserted it, and Somalia had no national government. Until long after Operation Restore Hope was under way, not a single black African leader had even visited Somalia or sent a lone grain of food. Neighborly help was limited to Kenya's passive acceptance of three hundred thousand Somali refugees inside its borders.

Several sub-Saharan countries did contribute troops to the UNITAF effort. These included Botswana, Nigeria, and Zimbabwe. Among North African countries, Morocco sent almost 1,400 soldiers, Tunisia a small contingent. Through June 1993, Sudan was the only African country to donate food to Somalia (in October 1992), and it was widely considered inappropriate for Khartoum to send food to foreign Muslims when non-Muslims in its own country were starving. On April 2, 1993, President Yoweri Museveni of Uganda met with Aidid in Kampala and offered to act as a mediator. In short, regional attention to Somalia remained minimal.

The concern vacuum, coupled with the international media's discovery of Somalia's live-ammo simulation of the postapocalypse in the summer of 1992, forced the United Nations to act in spite of its institutional inclination toward ostracism and avoidance. On July 27 the

Security Council resolved to send the second technical team, forty-eight cease-fire monitors, and eventually five hundred Pakistani troops. Through Sahnoun's yeomanlike efforts, Aidid came around and agreed to the five hundred. They began to arrive in late August. Their commanding officer, urbane and genially tough, was Brigadier General Imtiaz Shaheen. In his view, the soldiers' "proctorial presence" would resurrect the United Nations's damaged neutrality. Their function, he said, was that of "a truant officer."

But the United Nations as an institution, like the Americans months later, mistook the Somalis' military amateurishness for lack of guts. On September 2, the Security Council lurched from inch to mile, approving another three thousand Pakistani soldiers with Resolution 775. At the time, Aidid claimed to have a militia of over thirty-five thousand. Rather than generating hopeful solidarity, the Somalis' revolution had simply crystallized their native suspiciousness and bellicosity. Managing his clan's finances and enjoying the Trattoria's pasta in Nairobi, Osman Ato said upon hearing the news of more U.N. troops that he did "not think Pakistanis were ready to die," but if they did come he and Aidid "would fire the first shots."[33] There was a nine-month lag between that pledge and the massacre of June 1993, but in essence, Osman Ato was true to his word.

# 4 UNOSOM I AND II
## TWO SETS OF NOMENKLATURA

Although the aid community had stopped the momentum of the Somalis' hunger crisis, it was the American military intervention that actually contained the famine by securing food delivery routes and distribution points. But until June 5, 1993, many failed to understand that the work remaining for the second U.N. contingent (called UNOSOM II) involved far more than just soldiers mopping up. On that day, a month after the handoff, General Mohamed Farah Aidid's supporters, in a well-organized attack, killed twenty-four of the Pakistani U.N. troops who had taken over for the Americans in Mogadishu—by far the highest single-battle death toll since the U.S. Marines had arrived six months earlier. By prompting the United Nations to place a bounty on Aidid and brand him an outlaw, this singular incident turned what had been plausibly styled humanitarian intervention into overt military occupation—precisely the outcome that Sahnoun had sought to avoid. In short order Admiral Howe called in four hundred Rangers and Delta-force commandos and launched the hunt for Aidid. Absent the United Nations's abdication and the White House's grand intentions, the whole scenario could have been avoided.

Among the early U.N. players, Mohamed Sahnoun alone had been able to drive a wedge in the grinding gears of Somali perfidy.[1] During Sahnoun's heyday in August 1992, anarchy made the static case for a U.N. force in Somalia clear enough. Initially the United Nations dispatched only five hundred Pakistani troops to Mogadishu. But General Aidid warned that he would fire on any foreign soldiers beyond the token five hundred. The United Nations could not ignore the threat—at the time Aidid boasted of thirty-five thousand troops and had the fresh blood on his hands to back up the claim. The three thousand additional men for which the United Nations had secured commitments might well have been outgunned by a hostile Aidid. The Pakistanis' mission was to secure the port, safeguard food shipments going to and from the airport, and escort food convoys from the port to destinations within Mogadishu. But the soldiers stayed bivouacked in seclusion near the airport for months and never did clamp down the port. Their commanding officer, General Shaheen, knew he was outnumbered and refused to deploy his men. From a military point of view the five hundred were strictly symbolic, yet they seemed to have been assigned a task—replacing an economy actuated by armed extortion and outright theft with orderly martial law—that obviously required military muscle that Shaheen did not have. To make matters worse, the small U.N. force's rules of engagement allowed them to fire only in self-defense—a virtual death consignment for unfortunate point men in a jittery population armed with assault rifles.

Thus did Somalia's recalcitrant politics, the United Nations's own benign neglect, regional apathy, and internal turmoil distinguish Somalia as the place in the most dire need in the summer of 1992. These factors also severely limited Sahnoun's options. He had to make do strictly with the United Nations's own internal capabilities: supplying food (the World Food Program); administering relief operations (UNICEF); resurrecting infrastructure (U.N. Development Program); and mediating political disputes (the secretary-general's office). Conspicuously absent from the list was providing security services. Those the United Nations could not then provide, so it had to offer the Somalis an alternative to its growing "relief economy" grounded on extortion without compromising the safety of expatriate aid workers.

The approach Sahnoun adopted in Somalia in September 1992 stayed within those rough parameters. It was pointedly modest but also thoroughly attentive. Facing critical security problems without a police mechanism at his disposal, Sahnoun worked indefatigably to forge at least a semblance of accountability to the United Nations in the warlords—particularly Aidid, the predominant leader and the one most hostile to the United Nations. (Though he has been criticized for focusing too exclusively on Aidid, the other main players, Ali Mahdi and Mohamed Abshir Musa, needed far less convincing. Because they were militarily weaker than Aidid, they actually favored U.N. intervention as an equalizer by the time Sahnoun had been appointed.) Aidid finally agreed in August to allow the five hundred Pakistani soldiers into Mogadishu. At the same time, the United Nations was trying, with its one hundred–day plan, to improve the distribution of aid by tightening its logistical rein on the operations of its own and private relief groups. Even then, vague rumblings of "nation-building" could be heard from U.N. headquarters: the plan also called for U.N. agencies and nongovernment organizations "to assist in building a civil society, strengthening local capacity and working with indigenous NGOs."[2]

The idea behind the United Nations's quiet initiative was twofold. First, it sought to deploy a force small enough not to pose a territorial threat to the Somalis but big enough to deter them from attacking and, ideally, to exhort them to cooperate. Second, the United Nations wanted to show the Somalis in selected locales that if food aid were channeled in an orderly fashion, each person could get enough without having to steal. The hope was that inspired Somali warlords—and on a local level, clan elders—would convince the gunmen to help feed their communities of starving people rather than taking food from them.

Sahnoun's scheme in September 1992 was to put the clan system to work for Somalia. Back in August, he began to secure local elders' cooperation in preparing airfields to receive the U.S. Air Force Operation Provide Relief's food airlifts—staged from Mombasa, Kenya, starting August 9—to the interior. By the time he left in November, those airlifts were helping to sustain populations in Baidoa, Bardera, Belet Huen, and Hoddur—four of the nine sectors covered by Operation Restore Hope. The most crucial test was Mogadishu port, where over a thousand young gunmen staffed five subclan-based security teams that insisted that CARE and WFP pay them all for escorting food—which they often stole themselves—to distribution points. Sahnoun worked out a deal with Aidid and clan elders whereby they would be given food with which to coax the gunmen away from the port: the compulsion of Aidid's might and the elders' authority, in theory, would keep them out. Although the port was looted shortly after Sahnoun's consultations, his chastising response woke up the Somali leaders. Within a week the port had been purged, and food distribution was improving. Shortly thereafter, the U.N. troops secured the international airport, which enhanced the small-scale logistical capabilities (that is, the ability to deliver medical supplies and special nutrition foods and to transport personnel) of nongovernment organizations based in Mogadishu.

It is a pity Sahnoun wasn't able to oversee a complete trial of his ideas. He abruptly stepped down in November. Much of the blame lies with the U.N. bureaucracy. After he had tortuously cajoled and coddled Aidid into allowing five hundred troops into Mogadishu and started to nudge him toward allowing another three thousand, U.N. headquarters without Sahnoun's knowledge announced its intention to send the extra three thousand troops regardless of the warlord's wishes. Aidid threatened to send any unwanted U.N. soldiers home in body bags and lost interest in controlling the port and safeguarding relief operations. The situation deteriorated almost instantly—the Pakistanis were attacked at the airport, a food ship was shelled and turned away, and U.N. officials were mugged in Kismayu. Sahnoun's four months of arduous and fruitful diplomacy had been undone with one public statement from New York, and he was furious. He sent Boutros-Ghali a letter offering to resign and become a special envoy accountable only to the secretary-general. His idea transparently was not to quit Somalia but merely to circumvent an obstructive U.N. bureaucracy.

Boutros-Ghali accepted the resignation but not the alternative proposition. He and Sahnoun were old friends, and Sahnoun was anything but the good soldier. Although his public disgust over the United Nations's foot-dragging in Somalia had spurred the secretary-general to malign the Security Council for its ethnocentric concern over the "rich man's war" in ex-Yugoslavia and its ignorance of Somalia,[3] Sahnoun's criticism of U.N. agencies and middle-managers continued unabated. His maverick upstaging even after Somalia had drawn a crowd appeared to cost him Boutros-Ghali's esteem. He had sardonically characterized the United Nations as "civil servants who seem to need social accommodations that emergency situations won't provide."[4]

Sometimes he sided with the U.N.'s foes, as he did with Aidid on the Antonov incident. He publicly excoriated U.N. brass on several occasions, notably in a *60 Minutes* segment.[5]

Much of this vitriol was tactical rather than impulsive. Sahnoun said in an interview that the United Nations would have to work hard to "repair the damage" caused by the Antonov incident and hinted later that personalizing the United Nations's involvement in Somalia was the way he had chosen to do it. But the United Nations bureaucracy—especially Jonah—felt chagrined and complained to Boutros-Ghali. Sahnoun's effectiveness in an exhausting and thankless job was undeniable, so Boutros-Ghali kept mum through most of Sahnoun's stint. But in November, Sahnoun publicly refused to deal with "the bureaucrats and nomenklatura at headquarters."[6] Boutros-Ghali apparently felt he had no choice but to deal with them and dropped Sahnoun. His nuanced but quick demise smacked of headless bureaucratic payback rather than the secretary-general's personal reprisal.

Sahnoun's replacement, Ismat Kittani, an Iraqi Kurd who had served as Saddam Hussein's ambassador to the United Nations from 1980 through 1985, plainly lacked the Algerian's charisma and tirelessness, as well as his conviction that understanding the Somali mind was the key to solving the Somali problem. Even more importantly, Kittani was a twenty-five-year U.N. veteran, a loyal bureaucrat whose preoccupation it was to harmonize the United Nations and the rest of Somalia's benefactors in—and for—the public eye. But because many Somalis harbor a deep distrust of the United Nations in general, and Boutros-Ghali in particular, this attitude was counterproductive. The United Nations's earlier fecklessness and perceived tilt toward Ali Mahdi was one source of the problem. The other was Boutros-Ghali's alleged deal, as Egypt's foreign minister, to provide Siad Barre with arms in exchange for his allowing forty thousand Egyptians to farm some of Somalia's most arable land and displace Somali farmers.[7] Some Somalis saw him as a Siad Barre collaborator.

The United Nations indisputably needed a white knight to buy it time to resurrect its image. The media were nonplussed at Somalia's theretofore hidden atrocity and demanded an immediate response from the West. President Bush came through with twenty-five thousand soldiers and the United States's peerless logistical capabilities. Sahnoun had always sought the consent of the warlords and proposed only limited deployment at selected points because of the Somalis' fear of military occupation. But a relieved Security Council forgot about this caveat and gave Bush his U.N. fig leaf. Almost immediately Aidid began to stoke Somali misgivings about the United Nations in order to marginalize the United Nations vis-à-vis the United States, which he regarded as a more potent and corruptible backer. He was to some extent successful. On his New Year's visit, President Bush, dressed in desert fatigues, was greeted by adoring Somalis. A few days later, Boutros-Ghali's motorcade was pelted with stones and rotten fruit and denied access to U.N. headquarters during his visit to Mogadishu. In addition, the Addis Ababa peace talks in December had made headway only when the United Nations left the table. As it turned out, Sahnoun's very aloofness from his superiors and outspokenness had been the greatest asset of the United Nations in Somalia. In its place, the United Nations got two perishable novelties: camouflaged U.S. Marines and military hardware, and the prospect of American sponsorship.

In fact, the American initiative would have been both unnecessary and inappropriate had the United Nations not squandered its prestige and authority by firing Sahnoun and rendering a political solution temporarily impossible during the time of Somalia's most critical need. Ambassador Sahnoun a year earlier had envisaged precisely the conditions that Operation Restore Hope produced—locally sustained peace, functioning markets, and a population gainfully surviving—as the goals of an essentially diplomatic program with only an ancillary military component.[8] His program had a good chance of working and preempting Operation Restore Hope.

The competitive bidding programs for selling food and awarding transport contracts that the World Food Program and CARE "started" in February 1993 to help legitimize Somalia's economy were in fact initiated by Sahnoun and lost steam only upon his departure. The cooperation of clan elders in Baidoa and elsewhere that Oakley repeatedly vaunted was nothing new—Sahnoun had tapped it months earlier in Hoddur, where fines and jail terms dispassionately imposed by octogenarian elder Mohamed Nur Shoduk effectively deterred gunplay. And it is worth remembering that the original five hundred Pakistanis did secure Mogadishu airport. Another battalion might well have been able to secure the port and get convoys moving safely—particularly if it had been unleashed with the preemptive rules of engagement that the

Americans were permitted to employ. Finally, as of January 1994, the Somali peace process was not much farther along than it had been more than a year before under Sahnoun's more modest initiatives.

The United Nations faltered when it exalted bureaucratic propriety over the very results it was seeking. It might have seemed dishonorable to keep a cantankerous malcontent like Sahnoun on the payroll, but beyond appearances lay the reality that his minor indiscretions endeared him to the Somalis and let a stigmatized United Nations glide quietly along behind him. This would not have reached a point of institutional self-deprecation—it was not as if Sahnoun's cachet with the Somalis turned only on his flippancy and insubordination or came only at the expense of the United Nations. Substantively, his program was well conceived and becoming effective. He criticized "rich Arab nations" and the West for their neglect far more than he did the United Nations.[9] When Somalis stood outside UNOSOM headquarters in Mogadishu hollering epithets like "U.N. shit" and "Boutros-Ghali die," Sahnoun would calmly emerge and mingle. A gaunt, sallow man with wavy black hair, he would say, "Ah. Do you have something you wish to tell me? I am glad you are exercising your freedom of speech."

As time passed, by his very domination of the Somali political process, Sahnoun was slowly closing the gap between himself and his employer: to the Somalis, he was becoming the United Nations. Most important, he was able to moderate Aidid's calculated fickleness—something neither the Americans nor the United Nations has been remotely successful at doing. Humble pragmatism would have dictated tolerating Sahnoun for the sake of both the Somalis and, ultimately, the United Nations itself. By firing Sahnoun, enervating his initiatives, and desiccating his salves, the United Nations ratcheted the basic requirement for sustaining safe relief operations in Somalia all the way up to full-blown military occupation.

In the bargain, the United Nations's bureaucratic stiffness introduced a whole new host of difficulties—relief worker insecurity, military transition, and its own marginalization, to name a few—that otherwise might not have surfaced so obtrusively. The Americans, meanwhile, stepped right into the middle of the U.N.'s mess. Oakley's sanguine proclamation in March 1993 of the conclusive efficacy of overwhelming force can only be regarded as disingenuous. The show of strength improved the feeding situation but created a wholesale dependence on soldiers. To complicate matters further, the Somalis themselves had come to resent that dependence because it fell so far short of salvation. Now it seems a foregone conclusion that political progress in Somalia will have to be squeezed slowly through a bottleneck of low-intensity conflict like that in Kismayu, among a dozen different factions. It is bound to be painfully incremental and, despite the factions' showy agreement to form a provisional national government, has always had to proceed from the ground up. That is inevitably the case in countries plagued by civil war, since internecine conflict is caused by either excessive or ineffective central authority.

Sahnoun knew these considerations bounded the Somali problem. But as an organization, the United Nations was both too grandiose and too callow to let Sahnoun get deeply into Somali politics and culture. It was easier to arm the United States with a Security Council resolution and let it pave a highway for the United Nations, as it had done in the Persian Gulf. The move created unnecessary costs and burdensome expectations both inside Somalia and around the world.

The nature and degree of U.S. participation in this dissonant orchestration is not entirely clear. There have been some assertions that the Pentagon and Joint Chiefs were planning Operation Restore Hope in earnest in June 1992, but there is no available evidence that the consideration Washington extended to Somalia at such an early stage exceeded the abstract level of feasibility. Certainly the claim once bandied about Washington—that Sahnoun's ouster in October 1992 was engineered by Bush and Boutros-Ghali to remove the largest political obstacle to massive intervention—is illogical. At that time both were preoccupied with Bosnia. Moreover, had so glamorous an operation been given such early attention, presumably it would have been undertaken in time to help Bush's chances at reelection, rather than a month later. Surely Bush had not conceded Clinton's victory as early as June. As for Congress's inclinations, Senator Nancy Kassebaum provided the initial firsthand alert on post-Siad Somalia and did not even visit Mogadishu until late June 1992.

Given the United States's de facto primacy in U.N. internal politics, though, there were at least some unconscious parallels in the strategic thinking of George Bush and Boutros Boutros-Ghali. There is a raw irony in the fact that in a January 1992 Security Council meeting, after Cape Verde had proposed sending troops to Somalia, the United States discouraged the United Nations from sending even a small contingent of forces to Somalia for the limited purpose of distributing food. At that point as well as now, the United States enjoyed determinative power among the five permanent members of the Security Council. Witness the Gulf War. Whether by design or not, the unarticulated U.S. policy shift that Operation Restore Hope demarcated—namely, from not sending any force to dispatching a huge one—translated into an explicit change in policy on the part of the United Nations.

Although it is fair to say that the United Nations had institutionally ceded its responsibility to a superpower, Boutros-Ghali himself steadfastly apprehended the task in Somalia as one of nation-building. In a speech at the U.N. headquarters in October 1993, he asserted: "There was no government. There was no law. There was no order. There was death. . . . We, the United Nations, are rebuilding Somalia."[10] As far as it went, the statement was accurate. For Boutros-Ghali, Restore Hope was essentially a political exercise augmented by the military.

For Colin Powell and transitively President Bush, it was the exact converse: a military mission eased, if possible, by a little political spadework. The difference was one of emphasis, perhaps, but it was not insignificant. There were operational consequences. Just before the marine landing, Powell remarked, "It's sort of like the cavalry coming to the rescue, straightening things out for a while and then letting the marshals come back to keep things under control."[11] It followed that Robert Oakley's diplomatic efforts were programmatic at best. He himself pointed out in January 1993 that any diplomatic advances he had forged were but "ancillary benefits" in support of a limited humanitarian objective. If they led to a new civil government, "that is fine, but it is a Somali phenomenon we are not trying to determine."[12] The problem was that between the United States and the United Nations, the United States alone had the power and prestige to tame the Somali politic. America did not use it, as it was inconsequential to the Powell doctrine of overwhelming force. In *The New Yorker,* Sidney Blumenthal astutely observed the overwhelming irony. "In accordance with [the Powell doctrine's] strictures," he wrote, "intimidating means justified the morality play. Military capability was equated with policy. With the intent of avoiding another Vietnam, troops and armor substituted for strategy."[13]

And the marshals, in the form of civil authority, never really showed up. As a condition of keeping some U.S. forces in-country and under

U.N. command, Washington insisted that a retired American admiral, Howe, be appointed U.N. special envoy and a U.S. Army major-general, Thomas Montgomery, the U.N. forces' second-in-command. Perversely, it was the ostensibly civilian authority—Admiral Howe—who held sway over military operations. Despite Montgomery's objections, Howe put a price on Aidid's head, called in the elite troops, and hunted the warlord relentlessly. Tacitly reversing his own casting of UNOSOM II as a vehicle for nation-building, Boutros-Ghali backed Howe's quest for Aidid, seemingly in retaliation for Aidid's calumny and the rude reception his supporters had given the secretary-general in Mogadishu back in January 1993.

The foreign-policy players in the Clinton administration were even less familiar with the Somalis than their Bush administration predecessors had been. To them, Aidid's behavior was unambiguously renegade and the bounty hunt as naturally chivalrous as slapping down any other scoundrel. U.N. Ambassador Madeleine Albright, National Security Adviser Anthony Lake, Secretary of State Warren Christopher, and Secretary of Defense Les Aspin all approved the U.N. resolution sanctioning the hunt for Aidid and the deployment of the Rangers. With Boutros-Ghali and Howe, they had formed a new battery of nomenklatura that even President Clinton couldn't penetrate. It took October 3 and Jimmy Carter, after an appeal from a fugitive Aidid, to shift the United States's focus from military retribution to political reconciliation.[14]

At first, the Americans had looked like the busy superpower who had finally bent down to help the beleaguered Third World country, whereas the United Nations had seemed the fearful stepparent forced from the role of casual overseer to grudging babysitter. When Somalia operations turned sour, though, the two no longer seemed easily distinguishable. Congress castigated the United Nations over the October 3 Ranger debacle, while U.N. diplomats accused the White House of trying to sanitize its profile by making the United Nations out the incompetent culprit when in fact the United Nations is the United States. "When it comes to understanding the U.N., the Congress is on the moon," one such diplomat told *Newsweek*. "It's very easy for the U.S. to get the U.N. to 'say no.' All they have to do is exercise their veto in the Security Council."[15]

This view is an oversimplification, perhaps, but circumstantial evidence suggests some executive awareness in Washington of the perceived power loop. In August 1992, once UNOSOM I acquired some credibility with Sahnoun at the helm, the United States carefully stepped in with Operation Provide Relief, staged from Kenya with just a thirty-four-person military team, under which U.S. Air Force C-130 Hercules transport planes brought food and medical supplies to interior Somali cities inaccessible by road because of banditry. To some observers, the United Nations might have appeared to be nothing more than a cut-out for America's salvational, tangible action—a protracted airlift that fed the starving but nonetheless did not require the United States to commit a single ground troop to Somalia.

Arguably, the public-relations serendipity of Provide Relief gave President Bush an irresistible sip of painless Third World heroism, with no backwash. The hostilities encountered by the Air Force over the course of its food deliveries consisted of a few potshots fired at a C-130 tail assembly in Belet Huen as the plane took off. At the December 4, 1992, press conference in which Bush officially unveiled Operation Restore Hope, he celebrated the airlift's more than 1,400 sorties and dispatch of over seventeen thousand metric tons of food. The subtext of his statement was that a complementary ground operation "to get the food through" would be similarly easy to quantify and therefore to limit. "This is not an open-ended commitment," he promised. "We will not stay one day later than necessary." Yet the President also vowed, "We are determined to do it right." The pronouncement suggested a misplaced sanguineness about the ease of the mission. In its pre-Vietnam ingenuousness and cheerful confidence, Bush's press conference was the world's first fully seasoned taste of post–Cold War atavism. The fortuitous timing of the operation—it was launched just as world opinion cried out for redress of Boutros-Ghali's poor man's war—clinches the case that U.S. intervention in Somalia was at least designed to be politically costless. Beyond that rather effortless inference, the chain of events intimates that in December 1992, Washington still tended to regard the United Nations presumptively as a partisan adherent of its own foreign policy. It was in this light that much of the world cruelly viewed October 3 as the Americans' comeuppance.

# 5 Snafus on the Hope Restoration Detail

In north Mogadishu three weeks after the Marine landing, ten Somali gunmen hijacked a UNICEF car along a 150-yard stretch of road and robbed the UNICEF worker riding in it. The U.S. Marines were at one end and armed Somali UNICEF guards at the other. The marines were unaware of what was happening; the guards saw everything but hesitated to brandish their weapons for fear that the marines would shoot them instead of the thugs. The owner of the stolen car later returned to the UNICEF compound in south Mogadishu with grenade in hand, demanding compensation that his contract plainly barred.[1]

The episode cast the American military operation in a dim but poignant light. By then the United States had sent more than eighteen thousand soldiers to Somalia, yet they had failed to alleviate the need for relief workers and the nonpredatory population to display or carry weapons to protect themselves in Mogadishu. "I've been here since before the [March 3, 1992] cease-fire and this is the worst incident I've been involved in," said a quaking Nur Hussein, the victim of the north Mogadishu attack.[2] The troops had also failed to make any visible dent in the flourishing mutant economy, in which prices had been set by armed threat since myriad weapons began circulating randomly through the population.

Central Intelligence Agency estimates formulated long before Operation Restore Hope was launched projected a protracted urban guerrilla war waged by a ruthlessly unafraid populace.[3] The incident in north Mogadishu certified these reports. October 3 bronzed them. But the marines' initial approach had been so circumscribed that an armed hijacking within the plain view of a marine escort went unnoticed and undeterred. By its own admission, the United States had limited disarmament to "areas of positive control"[4]—a euphemism meaning any place where soldiers happen to be physically present at a given time. Even in those places persons carrying assault rifles were allowed to keep them as long as they didn't aim them at anyone. The fact is that save for eastern Mogadishu, where most of the U.S. forces had to live anyway, they provided precious little territorial security.

In western Mogadishu, only a few kilometers from the American headquarters, a pitched battle between rival clans raged on the first day of President Bush's visit, costing one faction seventeen dead and twenty-five wounded on New Year's Eve alone. Auld Lang Syne. The American-led forces did not intervene. A couple of weeks earlier a Somali woman suspected of selling herself to French soldiers was stripped and beaten by hundreds of Somalis on Mogadishu's main drag in front of the Sahafi Hotel, where journalists watched from atop the wall and roof. No gallantry materialized from nearby marines or French soldiers.

In Somalia in early 1993, as in post-Tet Vietnam in 1968, the U.S. military controlled only islands where its soldiers stood.[5] But unlike Westmoreland, Lieutenant General Robert Johnston, the marine commander, had no delusions about the degree of his control. He pleaded limited objective—namely, that of providing a secure environment for relief operations. But it took the Americans a full week to get two hundred miles northwest to Baidoa, the city hardest hit by famine, despite the entreaties of the Somalis and the press to move faster. So eager were journalists to see the dramatic rescue of Baidoa that a report circulated that the marines were on their way there four days after the December 9 landing. A number of reporters hightailed it to Baidoa, leaving Mogadishu relatively journalist-free for a day. It turned out the marines were merely going to Bale Dogle, a town between Baidoa and Mogadishu, to secure an airfield and reconnoiter for the Baidoa expedition. American commanders explained that logistical considerations necessitated the delay. "I am aware of the preoccupation with Baidoa, and I understand that," said General Johnston. "There is an assumption that it is benign, but it may not be. I cannot orchestrate everything that happens in Somalia. I am trying to get to Baidoa as soon as possible."[6]

U.S. officers above and below Johnston backed up his hesitant approach. General Joseph P. Hoar, Johnston's superior and General Norman Schwarzkopf's replacement as head of U.S. Central Command, told the press on a visit to Mogadishu, "What we're trying to achieve is arms control, not outright disarmament. To make boxloads of weapons in Somalia a measure of merit would not be appropriate. There are areas in which local militias are creating a relatively secure environment. They were prepared to turn in their weapons if we could protect them, but we don't have enough people to do it."[7] Major Rudy Wormeester, USMC, offered an elegant statement of the American philosophy: "There's a deterrent in sheer numbers, and you can't get sheer numbers without logistical support. That's just a sound tactical principle."[8] These explanations expressed the post-Vietnam style of projecting power: to establish a dominant military presence while subjecting soldiers to the smallest possible risk. But many observers saw the American approach as overcautious.

In fact, though, the Americans did make quick and serious progress in alleviating Somalia's hunger. By New Year's the port was operating at full capacity; three convoys carrying three hundred metric tons of food each were escorted to Baidoa, the city hardest hit by famine, each week; and seven other famine centers had been secured. "Our mission is not to take over the responsibility for the security of this country," said U.S. special envoy Robert Oakley, citing the folly of such an effort in Vietnam.[9] But servicing the humanitarian relief aims of the American mission took only a small fraction of the troops then on the ground. Although the operational plan—to secure the "hub" of Mogadishu, then the eight "spokes" of Baidoa, Bardera, Bale Dogle, Belet Huen, Kismayu, Jalalaxi, Merca, and Hoddur, and finally the convoy routes extending from the capital along each radius—sounded extravagant in terms of manpower, in fact it probably called for no more than ten thousand soldiers. The remaining fifteen thousand or so remained in base camps near the old military airfield in Mogadishu and in ships offshore.

The American military, in keeping with the Weinberger-Powell doctrine, made much of the extraordinary level of logistical support needed to mount an operation in a country devoid of infrastructure. They stressed the deterrent effect of sheer numbers and "an overwhelming show of force." And they brought with them a tacit but distinct tradition, amplified by the adverse Vietnam experience, of extreme stinginess with the lives of their soldiers. But the Somalis had no interest in the sorts of pitched battles that would call for a massive deterrent or produce heavy casualties on their side. Those who menaced with guns were fighting not to hold onto their country but rather to keep the stream of money and material they had liberated with the extortionate power of the AK-47 flowing into their own hands and those of their clans. Like it or not, Somalia did not need a military force as such. It needed a police force. Essentially for this reason, the CIA had sternly recommended against intervention.

The UNITAF command eventually caught on. By then it was too late to pull out. But instead of controlling the damage by changing its approach—by blanketing broad areas with frequent patrols and aggressively searching for weapons to confiscate, for instance—U.S. commanders tentatively decided their troops were simply the wrong people for the job. Before the Americans had been in Mogadishu even a month, a French colonel leaked the Americans' plans to turn over the command of the Somali operation to a mostly African and Arab U.N. force headed by a Muslim and begin a slow phase-down of U.S. troop strength on January 20.[10] The colonel was promptly muzzled, reassigned, and told not to speak to the press. But the move he let slip was perfectly consistent with the view long espoused by the United Nations and the United States—and, for that matter, most Somalis—that the only true solution to Somalia's chaos was a Somali solution. "I personally am confident that the United Nations will come up with a force and a command structure that will earn the respect of the Somali people," Colonel Fred Peck, the marines' spokesman, commented hopefully. "Otherwise I don't get to go home."[11] And in fact, UNITAF personnel dropped from over thirty-eight thousand (two-thirds of them American) in mid-January to twenty-four thousand in early February.[12] Simultaneously, Oakley accused the United Nations of "dragging its feet" in assuming control from the United States.

But there was a clear difference between encouraging Somalis to help themselves—the United States's official approach as set forth by Oakley—and telling them to sink or swim. The initial overkill produced great expectations among civil, peaceful Somalis that could not be easily dashed. Hussein Mursal, a Somali doctor with Save the Children, explained, "They did invade us and we don't mind. But now that they've done it, let them do their business."[13] The United States's lumbering presence did manage to upgrade the condition of Somalia from outright anarchy to sporadic, patchwork disorder. If its pullout were to cause a relapse, reasoned Somali intellectuals like Mursal, the United States would have turned a noble gesture into an act of betrayal. The right approach, said Mursal, was for the Americans to stay for a while and tailor a remedy to fit Somali culture.

As it happened, of course, the Americans did not leave. But they did not study Somali customs and lifestyles, either. Instead, UNITAF promoted the idea of forming a Somali police force, which the Germans and the Italians had offered to train, pay, feed and clothe.[14] From the outset it was highly unlikely that Aidid would have accepted any foreigner-backed law enforcement contingent theoretically superior to his own militia. In any case, U.N. lawyers ultimately balked at the project. At the time of this writing, Mogadishu still had no effective indigenous police force. From day one, therefore, some form of conscientious liaison between Western culture and Somali culture remained an obvious need in an environment of long-term occupation. The task of cultural buffing was left to the U.S. Army's psychological operations division—"PSYOPS."

"The slave of the troops (United Nations) came here to help the people," began 860,000 Somali-language flyers dropped from helicopters and C-130 Hercules cargo planes over Mogadishu, "to help the Somali people." Portraying the United Nations as the servant of the United States was hardly the Americans' intent in sending their first formal message to the Somali people in December 1992. PSYOPS had meant to say that the American troops had come to Somalia under the U.N. flag, and to denote a relationship of sponsorship rather than servitude. The idea was to temper the Somalis' mistrust of the United Nations with their current adulation of the United States by equating the two. Given the precipitous loss of prestige of the United Nations in Somalia, embarrassed PSYOPS personnel could only hope that the

Somalis laughed at the malaprop, along with the cartoon picture of a U.S. soldier and a Somali civilian shaking hands on the flip side. The bungled translation was just one reflection of a wide gap in language, religion, and culture that separated the American rescuers from their Somali hosts. The most powerful military machine in the world could tell a big missile to hit a tiny target and ferry millions of tons of equipment and supplies to a faraway land. But for most American soldiers, just saying "hello" to a Somali was impossible.

The potential for misunderstanding between two such diametric cultures was enormous. When American marines issued orders to Somalis, they often yelled louder and louder as perplexed locals, unable to understand English, didn't respond. The marines also failed to realize that Somalis regarded argument as an end in itself, even when they knew they would wind up on the losing end. Innocent encounters got rough. Dr. Mursal was shocked to see marines grab a Somali from his car one rainy afternoon and push him to the pavement. "What are you doing?" Mursal beseeched the soldiers. "Are you mad?" The man, the marines explained, had refused to get out of his car. After Mursal helped the Somali up from the street, he informed the marines that their victim didn't speak English and was lame. The soldiers dutifully apologized.[15]

Noncommissioned soldiers received language cards with basic Somali phrases before they landed; officers were given an eleven-page pamphlet of background notes about the country. Written before the civil crisis, it contained morsels of obsolescence like: "Visitors are strongly advised to obey all laws regarding currency controls and declaration, for local officials enforce these laws quite strictly."[16] What laws? What currency? What officials? These features of the infrastructure had largely perished in the civil war. Officers also got detailed intelligence briefings, including information about specific warlords and clans, before deploying, but many line soldiers said they weren't informed in any detail until they got to Somalia. Little more would have been needed if the soldiers were simply being dispatched to kill the opposition rather than befriend its victims. "In a normal combat environment, you dehumanize the enemy. That's your job: to eliminate him," said Corporal James Moore. "But this is a unique mission."[17] The military's objective in Somalia—a Muslim country with no black-and-white demarcation, literally or metaphorically, between the good guys and the bad guys—was much more subtle. A key element of the task was simply to avoid creating enemies. The technique, one sergeant half-joked, was "to win hearts and minds."[18] The entity directly responsible for that daunting task was again military intelligence—which in the early stages of Operation Restore Hope unfortunately proved itself the oxymoron it is often accused of being.

Obviously, upsetting Muslim sensitivities was a potential hazard of the American mission. But many soldiers knew little about Somali beliefs. One marine thought the Somalis were partly Hindu; another believed Islam was a Christian sect. There was a general lack of awareness about Muslim social modesty—marines skinny-dipping in Merca, an Islamic fundamentalist stronghold, offended the locals. The fundamentalists, mindful of the party-animal reputation of American grunts, warned that U.S. soldiers were there to change Somalia's culture. "Most of our people are illiterate, and the Americans will do bad deeds against our religion," said Abdulsamad Abdulahi of the militant Ittihad group. "They will encourage prostitution, like in the Philippines."[19]

This was not just idle talk. Recall the attempted lynching of the unfortunate Somali woman, who had apparently accepted chocolate from a U.S. soldier and was later seen in the company of French Foreign Legionnaires. The crowd beat her with sticks and tore her clothes off, believing she had sold herself to foreign soldiers. Other Somalis spirited her away to a local security office before the mob could kill her.

To be sure, some American soldiers did venture out on their own to bridge the culture gap. Captain Tom Imburgia, an Air Force intelligence officer, found himself sitting in the shade of a thorn tree near Bale Dogle airfield with a group of Somali men one afternoon in December 1992, shortly after the marines had secured the area. One of the Somalis had an English language primer and prevailed on Imburgia to give him and his friends English lessons. "They were thrilled that I took the time to read them English," said the Air Force officer. The Somalis were even happier when he asked them to reciprocate with a Somali lesson. "If you treat people like people, they'll treat you that way back," counseled Imburgia.[20]

The American public relations task was also eased by the brooding presence of the French Foreign Legion, whose abrasiveness initially absorbed the largest portion of Somali xenophobia. "The Marines are doing a hell of a job," boasted one U.S. diplomat. "They are soft-spoken and courteous, quite a contrast with the Legionnaires, who are threatening and alienating."[21] The Legionnaires, composed largely of non-French volunteers who are given aliases upon joining the force, have a fierce and nasty reputation on the battlefield. They are not known as model citizens. Within the first few days of their deployment, they fired on a truck as it ran a checkpoint, killing two Somalis. Many Somalis saw them as hostile mercenaries. "My men are uncomfortable with this mission, that is true," said Colonel Jean-Paul Perruche, the Foreign Legion spokesman in Somalia. "We are here for peace, which is an apparent contradiction." Of his soldiers, with a wink, he proudly added, "Aggressive tendencies, yes; criminal tendencies . . . I hope not."[22]

But enterprising officers and the French soldiers unwittingly running interference did not completely insulate the Americans. As the operation proceeded, the room for distrust between Somalis and GIs actually widened. Again PSYOPS was involved. PSYOPS had been used in benign missions before—like getting information to people in Florida during Hurricane Andrew—but a fair number of Somalis interpreted their efforts as brainwashing. One of Mogadishu's newsletters ran their own version of the U.S. flyer dropped on the city. It reproduced the picture of the American soldier with outstretched hand greeting the Somali, only in this rendition, the Somali was not reciprocating the gesture. "If you are not interfering with our religion and our sovereignty," read the balloon from the Somali's mouth, "we will help you."

PSYOPS did start a free Somali-language newsletter called "Raji," meaning "hope," containing information on the activities of the international force, as well as an independent radio station to broadcast public-service announcements. PSYOPS officers hoped to avoid any impression that they were in Somalia to impose alien ideas. "Our intent," said Lieutenant Colonel Charles Borchini, 8th PSYOPS Battalion Commander, "is merely to relate to the people what the task force is doing."[23] That mission was unobjectionable, indeed laudable, as far as it went. But Somalis didn't only want to be informed; they also wanted to be involved. Nonetheless, during the period of wholesale American involvement in Somalia, Somalis were largely sidelined from decision making on the overall relief operation. The body created by the United Nations to coordinate the activities of relief organizations and the military had no Somali members for months. Squeezing the Somalis out of policy decisions hardly squared with U.N. special envoy Ismat Kittani's declaration that "our number one priority is to get Somalis to help themselves."[24]

U.S. forces wanted to help without getting too close. To avoid any cultural misstep, officers hoped to keep social contact between their troops and the Somalis to a minimum. "There is no liberty time here," said Colonel Peck. "I don't see a lot of social interaction on the horizon."[25] One sullen marine guarding the port muttered, "We don't want to talk to anyone. We didn't come here to talk to anyone. We came here to do a job."

Perhaps the most complete information American soldiers received about Somalia concerned the potential for contracting diseases like malaria, hepatitis, and cholera.[26] Some grunts appeared wary of touching people and wouldn't think of eating local food or drinking local water. Naturally the soldiers were not allowed to partake of khat, but many didn't even know the nature of the drug. It is now a controlled substance in the United States, but in Somalia it is an unabashed and legitimate part of the culture. "I guess they've got their own kind of dip [chewing tobacco] that I understand looks kind of gross," drawled Lance Corporal Brad Vawter. "We don't accept anything you got to eat or put in your mouth."[27] (The young man was misinformed. Khat does not look gross; it only tastes gross.) Early in the operation, a marine major noted that Somalis had been offering marines khat as a gesture of friendship. "It's being treated as an illicit drug," he said stolidly. "If Marines see it, they'll confiscate it."[28] The policy was so flagrantly alienating that it was never carried out. But the fact that it was even under consideration reflects the Americans' initial attitude of peremptoriness and disgust, which was incongruous with the supposed humanitarian character of their mission. The tactical foxhole between them and the Somalis soon became a cultural gulf. American soldiers never came to appreciate fully that despite its antisocial consequences, chewing khat was a perfectly respectable activity in Somali culture and did not indicate behavior that was unacceptable in Somali terms; in August 1993, they mistakenly arrested eight U.N. employees partly on the strength of finding khat in their house.

The glancing treatment the military gave Somali culture created "the image of a Somali as a khat-chewing thug lying under a long-hauler," commented Mark Stirling, UNICEF's representative.[29] It was an image that ill-served the objective of providing humanitarian relief, for which it helps if you have at least guarded respect for the people you are trying to save. Moreover, the military's derisive characterization of Somalis led to a severe underestimation of their fighting ability. The result was the October 3 firefight, like the Battle of Ap Bac in miniature. Americans in Vietnam in 1963 had regarded the North Vietnamese as "raggedy-ass little bastards" who couldn't fight and misinterpreted their guerrilla tactics as desperate measures rather than what they turned out to be: the execution of a military philosophy of attrition prescribing underdog victory in spite of a high "kill ratio" on the battlefield.[30] In much the same way, Americans thirty years later in Somalia saw their opponents as disorganized cowards. Just as Brigadier General Frederick Karch admitted in 1965 that in rating the North Vietnamese quitters he "made a miscalculation,"[31] the special operations commander in Somalia, Major General William F. Garrison, conceded in October 1993 that in hitting the Somalis where they live, "we'll win the gunfight, but we might lose the war."[32]

The Pakistani command, by contrast, gave soldiers detailed cultural briefings and a thick book about Somali customs. "We also allow them to be open with the Somalis—to eat with them and play with them," said General Shaheen. "It is not enough to give someone a book to read."[33] Shaheen also did not presume to deprecate the Somalis' valor or spunk, even before they had shown their mettle. In August 1992, he remarked that the typical young Somali gunman was "brave and proud" and "not afraid of getting killed."[34] Marginalized by the inappropriately small force he was given and then by American upstaging, on the eve of the marines' landing Shaheen told the BBC that saving Somalia was not as easy as saying, "Bring in the Marines, bash up the blackies."[35] It was an angry remark but an astute one, for certain Americans evidently had thought it was precisely that easy.

The Pakistanis did have Islam in common with the Somalis, and certainly that gave them a leg up on community relations. Out of perfunctory respect for local customs, the U.S. command did ban alcohol and pornography in the early days of Restore Hope, though a New Year's Eve party at an American relief agency definitely produced some creative exceptions to the one restriction and probably a few to the other as well. In the early going, with little entertainment in one of the most miserable places on this earth, the soldiers acted with admirable restraint. Perhaps it was the natural exuberance of American youth that accounted for their initial enthusiasm. "The basic grunt doesn't care what he does, deep down," said one marine corporal. "He likes to go overseas and, for lack of a better word, see some shit."[36] But in the muggy, alien climate of Somalia, homesickness and frustration set in quickly and wound down a tense honeymoon. Soldiers looked for someone to blame. They did not have to look hard. On January 14, 1993, after Aidid complained that American forces were unfairly disarming his forces and warned they would resist, Somali gunmen killed their first marine in Mogadishu. If the Somalis began to view the Americans as an occupation force, "all of a sudden, we won't be here on a humanitarian mission," warned Captain Imburgia, the Air Force intelligence officer. The Somalis would "become gooks or dinks or gooners."[37] Basically, he was right.

Until Private First Class Domingo Arroyo was shot and killed on foot patrol at Mogadishu International Airport on January 14, 1993, the Americans and the Somalis had enjoyed a shy courtship. Small wonder. The marines had let all but the most threatening Somalis roam Mogadishu with all but the most threatening weapons in the name of their "limited objective" of providing only humanitarian assistance. Ongoing violence convinced the U.S. command that disarmament in some form had to become part of the mission. Oakley persuaded Ali Mahdi and Aidid to relinquish some of their technicals, which were dismantled and placed in "cantonments" (secured pounds). Aidid naturally whined that he had yielded more of the armed jeeps than Ali Mahdi had, stirring up his boys in south Mogadishu. During the ten days before Arroyo was killed, the marines raided Aidid's arsenal, swept north Mogadishu's largest gun market, and swarmed the Bakhara gun market in south Mogadishu, the largest in Somalia.

The arsenal foray was prompted by hostile gunfire, but the two other actions were not. The marines broke into buildings, searched them, and seized small arms. Operationally, the raids verged on house-to-house door-kicking, which UNITAF had earlier sworn off. Thirty Somalis were reported killed. Only weeks earlier, Lieutenant General Robert Johnston, the marine commander, had said, "I think the belief that we can disarm Somalia is totally naive."[38] In the meantime a global rumor had circulated that Washington had secretly agreed with Boutros-Ghali, in fact, to disarm Somalia.[39] Now it was the Americans who looked like dissemblers.

To make matters worse, Aidid's supporters accused the Americans of targeting only his forces. Mohamed Jana, youth leader of Aidid's faction and all-around zealous toady to the warlord, proclaimed, "We will not accept this. We are getting organized and are preparing several things that we cannot divulge." These were ominous words, given that Private First Class Arroyo's eleven-man squad had been attacked by a slightly larger Somali squad "in an L-shaped ambush formation near the airport," according to Colonel Peck.[40] Previous attacks from Somalis had come from unorganized bands.

The marines themselves confirmed that their collective mood had turned dark. "Last week, after the big firefight, all the little kids were saying, 'shoot the Americans,'" reported Corporal James Evans. They also chanted "I love Saddam Hussein!" and "Down with Bush!" he said. The marines were forced to become even more cautious and less friendly. Guarding the entrance to UNITAF headquarters, Private First Class John Berrest shook his head ruefully, remembering that the marines had "thought the airport was the safest place in town."[41] Seconds later he spotted a Somali teenager advancing toward him with a long dagger and coolly confiscated it.

The relief community saw the same picture. "I don't like the looks on people's faces," warned Dennis Walto, then Operations Director of the International Medical Corps. "Somali smiles are disappearing." Walto said most of his Somali employees viewed the killing as an isolated incident but smirked that "there may be a series of 'isolated incidents' about to occur."[42] Others argued that security had unambiguously worsened since the marines had arrived. "There were only two dead relief workers during [more than a year of] the 'anarchy,' and they were caught in crossfire," noted Gemmo Lodesani, Deputy Director of Operations for the World Food Program. "Now two relief workers have been murdered in fifteen days."[43]

The marine command did its best to keep the grunts under control. Major General Charles C. Wilhelm, the Operations Director, issued a bulletin warning, "If we're not careful we will start thinking that we're at war and we may forget that our mission here is one of peace and humanitarian assistance." He counseled that marines were to continue to wave at Somali children, show patience in traffic jams, respect aid workers and their Somali guards, and refrain from pointing their weapons at unarmed Somalis—"or be pulled off contact with those whom we are here to help." General Wilhelm's message closed: "The people of Somalia need a friend—not just another oppressor in desert camouflage utilities."[44]

Regrettably, Wilhelm's thoughtful exhortation didn't fully register. Many marines, perhaps the majority, felt privately that they were not trained to be anyone's friends. Corporal William Hutchings, frustrated but contemplative, commented, "Sometimes guys get a little edgy. I have to tell them there's a time to be aggressive and a time to be respectful. This is their land, and we're acting like an occupying force." Most marines outwardly confronted their comrade's death with the Marine Corps's standard-issue game face. "We try not to let it happen, but with so many guns it's bound to happen," said Hutchings. "Still," he added, "within his unit, I'm sure they feel worse."[45]

Indeed they did. Lance Corporal R. E. Duarte, Arroyo's best friend, forgot about the marines' mission altogether and could think only about setting his pal to proper rest. He was so angry, his superiors had to confiscate his ammunition. Duarte walked distractedly around the marine compound, his M-16 looking toothless without a clip, occasionally straying to the gate and peering at and then over the clamoring, buzzing Somali children, who had turned so petulant. He had been trying to call Arroyo's mother by satellite phone, with no luck. He pivoted away from the gate and started to trudge back to the phone for another try, then turned around and said quietly, "I want the world to remember him."[46] Maybe it would, but by the grunts' own admission, only as the first casualty of a misguided adventure. "He was just like most other Marines," said Corporal Evans. "Nobody really wanted to come here."[47]

By February 1993, the American soldiers had become as uncomfortable with their mission as the Legionnaires had been at the beginning. Within three weeks of Arroyo's death, skittish marines had killed two unarmed Somalis and wounded three more. One of those killed was a twelve-year-old boy who had rushed toward the marine's vehicle holding a "suspicious object." It turned out to be a toy. Both of the soldiers involved were court-martialed for use of excessive force. "Other Marines will take the news of the Article 32 [of the Uniform Code of Military Justice] proceedings solemnly," Colonel Peck assured reporters, "in appreciation for the seriousness of deadly force and the weapons they possess."[48] The unventilated tension of peacekeeping without disarmament affected other Western troops as well. In March

1993, two Canadian soldiers in Belet Huen took turns beating and burning with a lit cigar a sixteen-year-old Somali thief they had taken into custody, then killed him. The prime culprit tried to commit suicide and ended up brain damaged; nine others were court-martialed, and one of them has been found guilty of manslaughter and sentenced to five years in prison. A dozen soldiers casually watched the young Somali's ordeal.[49]

The American troops simply got cynical. Early on American officers had complained with rigid sanctimoniousness of the Italian troops' lax attitude toward joint security operations in Mogadishu and even accused them of drinking on duty. A few months later, SOS-Kinderdorf's Willy Huber visited the Italian barracks, only to be told that the Americans had traded the Italians a shipment of SOS beds for beer. Huber had to laugh when he found himself perched on a cot stencilled with the SOS logo. According to Huber, the Americans had promised to deliver the beds, but later claimed that the shipment was unauthorized and therefore had to be dumped in the ocean.[50] Less humorously, in early 1994, the Americans intercepted a shipment of SOS's fencing on the suspicion that the relief agency was running guns to Aidid. The matériel was discovered months later by SOS personnel when they spotted it piled at a construction site inside the UNOSOM II compound. The U.S. and U.N. commands, it seemed, had lost sight of not only the humanitarian aim of the original mission but the expanded aim of nation building as well. UNOSOM II's approach had become punitive and petty.

As time went on, the short-timer's preoccupation with comfort, and dismissiveness of mission, took hold. On August 8, four more GIs were killed by a land mine. Two weeks later, six more American soldiers were wounded. Though the Ranger deployments in August and September may have boosted morale momentarily, the October 3 firefight dropped it several levels below even the status quo ante. Helicopter pilot Michael Durant, traumatized, bruised, and fragged during his twelve days as Aidid's hostage, told *The Guardian*'s Mark Huband that all he wanted from the Red Cross was "a pizza . . . and a plane ticket home."[51]

That summed up the general mood. In November 1993, in the *Washington Post,* Rick Atkinson wrote from Mogadishu: "There are two worlds in this tormented city, increasingly separate and utterly unequal." He went on to describe the UNOSOM II compound as "an 80-acre replica of America" complete with reserved parking, take-out pizza, liquor, and erotic movies. The PX carried Oreos. The navy had installed a $60,000 shark net on the beach to protect tanners looking for relief. Operation Desert Dorm. Atkinson scripted the other world, separated from the $160-million U.N. compound by a ten-foot wall crowned with broken glass and concertina wire, as follows: "There is no electric power, no telephone network, no sewerage. There is no law, no order, no shark net." Enlisted men rarely mentioned the humanitarian aims of Restore Hope anymore. The perquisites accorded U.N. personnel had helped ostracize the primitive Somalis, whom GIs had come to call "skinnies" or "Sammy Somali." They were now a disdained enemy. "It was Jerry for the Germans and Charlie for the Vietnamese," commented one marine. "We first called them Billy. But now it's Sammy."[52]

The new nomenclature seemed a crass form of retro-chic. It reflected disaffection foreshadowed by operational mistakes. The American approach to disarmament, amorphous going in, took shape only gradually and erratically. The American forces enjoyed far more aggressive rules of engagement than did the UNOSOM I Pakistani troops—the GIs were allowed to shoot first. Yet their original brief was to disarm only when directly threatened. Although this directive was consistent with the limited objective of Restore Hope, in a matter of weeks it became evident that food distribution could not be stabilized even in the medium term unless territorial security were established. That necessitated a more aggressive disarmament policy and broader physical occupation. All of a sudden the slouching Americans stood up and flexed their muscles. By the same token they became bigger targets.

The abrupt shift angered many Somalis and supported their suspicion that the United States was simply a new colonial master. Dr. Mursal, an early supporter of the intervention, by March was lamenting, "It's sad that the country in the vanguard of democracy and human rights would show no sensitivity to killed and wounded Somalis."[53] It had become the United States's official policy not to keep track of Somali combat deaths. "This is inconsistent with the view that this is a humanitarian mission," muttered Mursal.[54] By the time the Americans pulled out in March 1994, U.S. and UNOSOM II troops had killed or wounded hundreds of Somalis.

The undulating intensity of American disarmament efforts also suggested troughs of opportunity down the road to savvy Somalis. General Shaheen, by now marginalized and a bit resentful, barked: "Disarmament must be universal or not at all."[55] Intrusive measures sporadically applied, he said, would simply impel people to bury their weapons. (Baidoa markets ran out of plastic bags the day before the marines showed up in late December 1992.) "And when they reappear," Shaheen prophesied, "they will reappear with a vengeance."[56] So they did.

Once the Somalis stopped perceiving the Americans as humanitarian saviors, most U.S. soldiers gave up the pretense of being any such thing. By the end of 1993, the goal of territorial security had been effectively abandoned. In late January 1993, jumpy U.S. Marines fired on a crowd in a Mogadishu street and killed eight Somalis after snipers had shot at their convoy. Once again young Somalis were permitted to carry loaded weapons, poised on "automatic" with safeties off, as long as they were registered. Somali men in their twenties and thirties considered themselves old soldiers, and Somalia in a perpetual state of war. "These young men, they do not know what it means to kill," remarked an SOS driver in January 1994, a few days after gunning down a teenage bandit.[57] (Five months later he was shot dead by members of his extended family over a dispute involving stolen cars.) An entire generation of Somalis had rejected government of any kind—indigenous or U.N.-imposed—in favor of exclusionary clans. "People look to clans because there is no government to help, and because of Siad Barre they don't trust central authority," said Omar Ibrahim Salah, SOS Project Director.[58]

Frustrated by this double whammy of the Somali mind-set, most U.N. troops were hunkered down in their comfortable digs behind The Wall. Their resignation was also a natural outgrowth of the devolved psyche of the short-time line soldier, in which the natural compulsion to survive prevails over that of performing a duty on a mission whose purpose has become obscured. In performing a humanitarian mission in a land rife with plainclothes snipers and mines, 30 were killed and 175 were wounded. There were 6 noncombat deaths, and 7 soldiers perished when an AC-130 Specter gunship crashed off the Kenyan coast. Under U.S. military guidelines, only the few killed or hurt returning enemy fire were eligible for medals; sniper and land-mine casualties didn't rate.[59]

As the last of the one hundred thousand American troops who served in Somalia, save for fifty marine guards for the diplomats, prepared to leave in March 1994, people from all quarters had axes to grind. Lieutenant Joe Frescura, an army platoon leader, said defensively, "All the soldiers here are trained to fight, not to sit."[60] Lieutenant Colonel Dave Young, a marine, frankly told his men, "Nobody really cares that you've done this."[61] Somalis, jeering at departing American soldiers and starting fistfights with them, verified Young's claim. But a senior U.N. official explained that "the Americans and the United Nations came in with a kind of arrogance. Their psychological operations were naive, their intelligence very poor." And, he concluded, "they didn't speak the language."[62] Mohamed Jirdah Hussein, the urbane Somali who runs the Sahafi Hotel, claimed, "The Americans should have known better. They set deadlines. In our society we have no deadlines. . . . There was a misperception of cultures."[63] Finally, Ahmed Hussein Fidow, a Somali who watched the marines land in December 1992 and leave fifteen months later, observed, "It looks like the Americans are slipping out quietly. It's a strange way for a superpower to act."[64]

# 6 Building the Perfect Beast

As late as winter 1994, the East Africa press corps were fond of saying that General Aidid had no real power base, that most of "the people of Somalia" were in fact against him, that his days as a popular leader therefore were numbered. This chant missed several points. First, Aidid's power base consists of a nucleus of loyal gun-toters, the guns themselves, and his own brass. Because Somalis respect tough guys, he doesn't need to be liked. Indeed, his popularity derives from the fact that other Somalis share his haughty barbarity. "What's the use of killing Aidid?" asked Ali Gulaid, his U.S. representative. "Everybody is Aidid. If he goes tomorrow you will have a million Aidids around."[1] For ninety-seven days he hid from thirty thousand troops, U.S. Rangers, and the CIA. To the Somalis he has nothing left to prove.

Second, even if he did have to qualify for leadership, Aidid might win by default. Rivals like Mohamed Abshir Musa haven't got his vast territorial ambitions. Ali Mahdi simply lacks Aidid's military strength and popular following. Nobody has come forward to offer the Somalis a viable foil. The U.N. pipe dream—that an indigenous political solution would naturally devolve power to traditional local and regional authorities—hasn't panned out primarily because these rustic institutions don't want the kind or degree of power that might supplant anarchy with order. Aidid does.

Finally, "the people of Somalia" is a fiction. There are dominant clans and dominated clans. That's all. Aidid maintains his constituency by inspiring fear and awe. Like Siad Barre, Aidid is just the type of charismatic leader to which Somalis traditionally respond. Neither the United States nor the United Nations could project an image durable or dangerous enough to match that of the bulletproof nomad. Aidid stands above all of Somali candidates because it is American and U.N. bullets that he has repelled. When the United Nations finally called off its bounty hunt in October 1993, Aidid emerged from his hibernation looking robust and sounding cocky. "I have been bombarded at my house at the beginning," he told *The Independent*, "but after that I was always in Mogadishu and they never came close to me."[2]

Aidid's public relations problems came mainly from outside Somalia, but by early 1994, even they were on the wane. On January 18, as a gesture of peace, the United Nations released the eight Aidid lieutenants it had detained. Such deference from Howe and Boutros-Ghali, so close on the heels of persecution, amounted to a joint American-U.N. concession that Aidid was still the man to see in Somalia. How did he do it?

In late 1992, a prominent head of a nongovernment relief organization casually remarked that Somalis represented "the stupidity of human virility." The Somali mindset is indeed baleful machismo bootstrapped from attitude into ethic. During the fall before the Americans showed up, a Somali guard who worked for the International Medical Corps was shot in cold blood, waiting for an IMC plane at the international airport. It turned out that the clan controlling the outlying K-50 airport, used primarily for khat shipments, wanted to discredit the security at the larger airport and glom the landing fees. The relief economy had made Somali lives especially cheap. The dead man's family got sixty-four dollars from the perpetrator's clan. The traditional recompense—one hundred camels—would have cost ten thousand dollars on the distorted Mogadishu market. The murderer went free, presumably to earn one hundred dollars a day guarding journalists with his Kalashnikov; he was able to pay back his elders on his first day back on the job before lunch was over. And the game worked. IMC boycotted the international airport for months in favor of K-50.[3]

On reflection, Aidid's methods were airport tactics writ large. He was crazy like a fox, alternating cloying acquiescence to American majesty with bullheaded defiance of American status. His apparent fickleness made the Americans critically underrate his single-mindedness, and with it his guile, his competence, and his support.

In early December 1992, Aidid relaxed initial jingoistic tensions over the United States's offer to send its thirty thousand troops with a broadcast endorsing Acting Secretary of State Lawrence Eagleburger's reassurances that U.S. soldiers would be deployed only to protect relief efforts. His influence was pervasive and immediate. "Suddenly everybody's attitude changed," said Stephen Tomlin of IMC.[4] Somali economic indicators proved it. Gun merchants dropped the price of an assault rifle 75 percent, from two hundred dollars to fifty dollars, in response to slackening demand.

From the outset, Aidid's conciliatory stance was contingent on the United Nations's functional disengagement from the operation and on the Americans' willingness to allow Somalis as much self-regulation as possible. The two other principal warlords, Ali Mahdi and Mohamed Abshir Musa, applauded outside intervention without qualification, but Aidid claimed to believe that only the Americans would be impartial. What gave him some element of credibility was, again, the firing of Sahnoun. "Sahnoun was a man who tried hard to help Somalis solve their problems, but Kittani does not have our respect and trust," postured Osman Ato.[5] Aidid also publicly blamed the rise of Somalia's extortionate and licentious "relief economy"—in which nongovernment relief organizations were effectively paying ten thousand dollars to have one thousand dollars' worth of food delivered—on the United Nations's preference for paying armed thugs rather than resurrecting a trained police force for security. But he did not want the assistance offered by the Germans and the Italians. Instead, the American forces were to help Aidid to reconstitute the Somali police force under his control.

This position, ostensibly utopian, enabled Aidid to resist wholesale disarmament with maximum plausibility. "We will surrender weapons only after Somali police can protect Somalis," Osman Ato warned ominously, pointing to an M-79 grenade launcher and a G-3 assault rifle in his plush bedroom.[6] Aidid and Ato carried their minions by linking the sentiment of self-protection to Somali nationalism. "My gun is to protect myself, my family and my property," proclaimed twenty-seven-year-old Abdulkadir Isse Faraadde, a college-educated former Somali Air Force lieutenant: "I bought my gun in the open market, and it belongs to the Somali people. I will not give it up to an American because it would no longer protect Somalia. I will give it up only to a Somali."[7] American officers, at least at first, found it difficult to knock Somalis off this stance—it sounded very much like the National Rifle Association's position on the second amendment's right to bear arms. The propaganda wasn't far from American sloganeering: This car insured by Smith & Wesson; you can take away my gun when you pry it from my cold, dead fingers. Colonel Peter Dotto, the marines' chief disarmament officer, became enough of a believer to profess at the Addis Ababa conference in March 1993, "It isn't fair to disarm everybody."[8]

The upshot was that Aidid's Somalis would accept some guidance in materially rebuilding their country but none in disciplining themselves. Dr. Mursal put it this way: "Somalis have expectations, and they want security and opportunities. If the Americans don't fulfill them, they will rebel."[9] The unspoken reality was that Aidid could and would inspire violence but would not and probably could not impose restraint. As Osman Ato vowed that Aidid's thirty thousand men were "prepared to shoot Somalis who disrupt any process that serves the best interests of Somalis,"[10] Steve Tomlin dispassionately observed, "Aidid has never really had control of his people."[11]

Aidid had manifested so much heartless bellicosity throughout 1992 that merely symbolic gestures at the end of the year made him look plain conciliatory. In August 1992, for his headquarters he took over Bardera, a farming city on the Shibelle river, about two hundred miles west of Mogadishu. While its thousands of inhabitants rioted that September for the scarce food that was flown in, Aidid offered a group of journalists a pasta lunch in his villa as he told them, "We are trying to make Somalis love each other." Even then he tried to predetermine American sponsorship with skewed but statesmanlike proclamations about the Somalis' victimization. "The world has an obligation to help Somalis because the world supported the regime that put the country in this mess," he said. "Only the United States said, 'Enough is enough.'"[12]

Three months later, at Oakley's urging, Aidid embraced Ali Mahdi at the leprous "green line" that divided their respective territories in

Mogadishu and joined his rival in preaching peace. But Oakley's bipartisan sponsorship was suggestive enough for Aidid to take it the wrong way. The American had made an inadvertent pass that Aidid took to heart. By the time UNITAF was preparing for President Bush's New Year's visit, Aidid was bragging that the president was coming to Somalia to hash out a plan for an interim government that Aidid would head. Ato puffed superciliously that Aidid's faction had been "trying to involve the United States and western Europe in Somali problems discreetly."[13] Aidid enjoyed a stagy reunion with one of his expatriate sons, Corporal Hussen Farah—ironically enough, a U.S. marine who did a two-week hitch in Somalia.[14]

Washington quickly disabused Aidid of his hopeful notions. "It is a misimpression," said Oakley pointedly, "that the United States would support a reunified USC against all other factions."[15] Oakley made it clear that he regarded efforts by Somali factions to gain preferential treatment by the United States, rather than dialogue with other factions, as the prime obstruction to political progress in Somalia. "I'm sure many Somalis will be let down, particularly those who believe that using Somali tactics will get us on their side."[16]

Aidid's response was in essence, "Who, me?" On December 20, 1992, a diplomatic source indicated that the impending American and Belgian landing in Kismayu had been discussed and cleared with the local strongman, Colonel Jess, Aidid's ally. The source offered reassurances that Jess was "shrewd enough to cooperate demonstratively" and that he was "on his best behavior." The landing itself did proceed smoothly, but soon afterward it became apparent that Jess had ordered the mass execution of two hundred men from an opposing clan, the Majerteen, because they had been agitating against the USC. Although this atrocity nominally fell short of a spurning of U.S. authority, it showed that no outside entity, however powerful or prestigious, could tame Aidid's vindictiveness. Only Somalis could. "We're encouraging them to solve their bloody disputes," Oakley insisted.[17] His dilemma was that Colonel Jess thought that was exactly what he was doing. Jess's brutality provoked General Morgan to advance on Kismayu at the end of January; Belgian and American troops turned them away, but forty-two Somali casualties fueled the growing public relations problem for UNITAF.

Once Aidid's men inaugurated the list of dead GIs with the killing of

Private First Class Arroyo on January 14, Aidid went into denial. His preposterously named Somali National Alliance issued the following press statement: "The arrival of the U.S. Marines–led multi-nationals was . . . basically to open the pipelines of food supplies to the needy people. This encouraged us to welcome their arrival and to commit to collaborate with maximum efficiency, yet there are irregular elements of no men's control backed by irresponsible figures [who have] . . . made use of the general chaos in Somalia." After expressing sorrow over Arroyo's death, the release waxed peaceful: "We warmly welcome the disarmament of the free-lance group and confiscation of the weapons being marauded [*sic*] by the inciters." Finally, the punch line: "However, these weapons would be preserved for the coming legitimate government of Somalia, as long as they're owned by the Somali people."[18]

There had never been any doubt in Aidid's mind who would front "the coming legitimate government of Somalia." Months earlier in Bardera, faced with the fact that it was not "the world" but rather Somali gunmen who were stealing donated food, Aidid responded that putting a halt to the looting was "simple: if the SLA [Somali Liberation Army, what he then called the military wing of his faction] is given food for itself, we can guarantee security." He also blithely suggested that the money the United Nations would use to finance the three thousand additional troops it had proposed be given instead to him so that he could outfit a six thousand–man Somali police force. He thought he could run a game on Oakley and the marines because they were temporary visitors, willfully ignorant about Somalia and Somalis and disinclined to inconvenience him just as Washington had been blandly indifferent to Siad Barre's assortment of moral lapses. He was far more worried about the United Nations, which had ambitions, in fact a mandate, to stick around and rebuild Somalia into a peaceful nation. It was no surprise that in advance of the marine landing, Aidid had flyers strewn through Mogadishu reading, in both Somali and English, "NO UNOSOM!" "UNOSOM IS BANDIT," "USA DEMOCRACY," and "USA IS FRIEND." Much to the general's chagrin, in early January 1993, the United States warned that by the end of the month the marines would start the gradual process of passing their job onto U.N. troops. The United Nations, in turn, pressed the Americans to extend their areas of control in Mogadishu and above all to disarm Aidid's rag-tag militia. From this point forward, Aidid played both ends against the middle, courting the United States and scorning the

United Nations, or vice-versa, to suit the moment.[19]

But by then the UNITAF command had adopted the view that universal disarmament unfairly penalized a cross section of peaceful people who still needed guns for self-protection in a predatory, unregulated society. "It is very difficult to take weapons from people who have traditionally kept them as you would a rake or a lawnmower," remarked Lieutenant Colonel Andre Leroy of the Belgian Army, Colonel Dotto's U.N. counterpart.[20] Yet with militias dispossessed of heavy weapons, it was just such people whom the warlords persuaded to do their bidding. The Majerteen "troops" loyal to Morgan that infiltrated Kismayu in mid-March were in fact ordinary citizens seeking to reoccupy their residences who smuggled weapons in under the skirts of their wives and used their children as human shields to stymie Belgian UNITAF forces. UNOSOM II planned to offer seeds and tools to Somalis who registered their side arms, but unless they could be sure their respective clans would not need their firepower they would be disinclined to tip their hands as potential guerrillas.

The disarmament quandary, then, was a bequest of sorts from UNOSOM I to UNITAF, reverting back to UNOSOM II. Other operational problems UNOSOM II simply bought new. The fresh U.N. force comprised twenty-eight thousand troops from thirty different armies—some cool and experienced, others callow and untested. Brigadier General James Cox of the Canadian army, Chief of Staff of UNOSOM II forces, diplomatically remarked that there was "a variation in the level of training of the different armies."[21] The administrative job of melding units of disparate skills, experience, indeed languages, into a cohesive force was itself a daunting task. Cox also noted that "uniform control exerted a better grip than a joint collegial army under U.N. command."[22]

Different peacekeeping philosophies also became a problem. When U.S. intelligence revealed that in June 1993, Aidid was successfully smuggling weapons cached outland in December back into Mogadishu through French and Italian checkpoints, a U.N. source complained, "The Italians are playing traffic cops when the arms come down the road." This may have been an exaggeration, but it was true that the Italian commander, General Bruno Loi, had a more conciliatory attitude than the Americans toward Aidid and proposed suspending combat operations with an eye to burying the hatchet and ending the bounty hunt. Aid agencies, the O.A.U., and the Kenyan government, among others, agreed with Loi, but the United Nations was immovable and asked that Loi be relieved. Italy refused and announced in mid-August that it would redeploy its troops.[23]

Even at full strength, the U.N. force would be 20 percent smaller than the American-led UNITAF's but responsible for pacifying all of Somalia—an area at least twice the size of that encompassing the nine humanitarian relief sectors covered by UNITAF. Yet, in its institutional determination to avoid the taint of intelligence operations, the United Nations refused to authorize the pooling of military intelligence among UNOSOM II's constituent armies, making centralized command-and-control all the more difficult. Operationally, UNOSOM II was far easier pickings for Aidid than UNITAF had been.

His propaganda would take hold more easily as well. Former U.N. special envoy Mohamed Sahnoun managed to arrest runaway famine and win the warlords' respect by coaxing and nudging. But from the moment Boutros-Ghali unceremoniously dismissed him, Somalis apprehended the United Nations itself as a distant bureaucracy repelled by Somalia's lack of glamour and its inscrutableness, reluctantly compelled to offer help only by its charter. By contrast, when the Americans arrived, the Somali in the street took perverse pride in having attracted the steadying armlock of the biggest guy on the block. But unlike his Cold War predecessors, Oakley (who resigned in early March 1993) refused to be seduced into partisanship by Aidid. The general cried breach of promise and portrayed the United States as a sneaky neocolonizer. In February 1993, Majerteen clansmen attacked 450 of Aidid's men in Kismayu. In a radio harangue, Aidid accused U.S. and Belgian troops of complicity in the attacks and called on Somalis to "defend your freedom, your honor, and do not allow yourselves to fall under colonial rule." During the two days of unrest that followed in Mogadishu, rioters looted the French and Egyptian embassies, tossed two hand grenades into the Egyptian compound as GIs tried to retake it, and attacked relief workers. February ended with anti-American riots in Mogadishu and jumpy UNITAF soldiers pasting downtown buildings with heavy machine-gun fire.

Short of exaltation by acclamation, Aidid did not have any interest in reconciliation except within his own clan, the Hawiye. Even that, he implied, would be coerced. "There is no comparison between Ali Mahdi's forces and my forces," Aidid boasted, adding that he "controlled 11 of 18 districts in Somalia." Candidly, he considered Ali Mahdi's Manifesto Group to consist of "a bunch of fatcats who got rich during Siad Barre's regime, intent on pre-empting all the revolutionary groups."[24] Although "we have dispatched representatives to reconcile the Habar-Gedir and the Abgal, and to unify the USC," said Osman Ato just before the marines walked ashore, "we will have nothing to do with Addis Ababa. People who go there have no mandate from the people."[25] Aidid did attend the U.N.-sponsored conference in early January, but saw to it that none of its objectives—not the scheduling of a full-blown national reconciliation conference, not the setting of its agenda, not the creation of a permanent liaison committee to coordinate input from a dozen factions—were fulfilled until U.N. representatives left the table and he could dominate the proceedings.

The March summit in Addis started auspiciously, with an elderly Somali man unfurling a Somali flag on the mezzanine of the conference center and rousing tearful countrymen to sing the national anthem. "I want to remind the Somali people of something they have forgotten about," the man had cried. But his exhortation was short lived. Secessionists filibustered for the first two days, and the national reconciliation talks foundered. By the time the conferees had turned their attention to the issue, Morgan's people had infiltrated Kismayu. Aidid stalked out, angrily brandishing his hand-tooled silver walking stick. The players chanted the usual litany. Aidid's people accused Morgan of cynically using the lull occasioned by the conference for his foray. Ali Mahdi accused Aidid and Jess of deliberately provoking Morgan to derail the talks. The United States, after sending a quick reaction force of five hundred men and thirteen helicopters to restore order and flying a Somali fact-finding team to get to the bottom of the incident, reported that it couldn't figure out who started it. With Aidid and his followers no longer at the table, most committees could not muster the quorums necessary to take binding action. For two weeks the conference twisted slowly in the wind, until Aidid dramatically whisked in for what he thought was a statesmanlike finish.[26]

The move did nothing more than salvage appearances, just as the United Nations's money for the conference ran out. The factions agreed to set up a provisional government in the form of a three-tiered quasilegislative, seventy-four-member Transitional National Council that would subsume both discrete regional authorities and an inchoate national government. The hard numbers and elegant terms-of-art sounded promising, but knotty and essential details—such as how membership in the council would be determined (by vote, appointment, ordeal?), how geographical boundaries would be drawn, how to resolve the secessionist claims of the entire northwest quadrant of Somalia—remained undecided. No timetable was set for the actual emplacement of the new government. The accord ambitiously called for disarmament by the end of June.[27] Somali factions agreed to impound weapons and isolate their militias at "transition sites," but they insisted that those moves be simultaneous—a tricky proposition in the best of times made even more so with American and U.N. troops distracted by the handover of administrative, financial, and military control in early May 1993. To this date no government has materialized, and the world knows how June 1993 shaped up. By January 1994, so-called militias mingled seamlessly with the general population; as long as they displayed a red gun-registration card and a yellow carry-permit with their locked-and-loaded weapons, nobody cared.

Given the divisive behavior of most participants and the unrealistically programmatic outcome of the conference, it seemed to be little more than an opportunity for the Somalis to live high on the United Nations for two weeks. Talks among Somali women's groups, often extolled in feature stories as the hope of the country, broke down irretrievably along clan lines. Unaffiliated Bantu groups had to beg for the limited participation they were ultimately allowed. One personal incident is particularly illustrative. I was covering the conference for *Newsweek*. Most journalists and many of the Somali participants stayed at the Addis Ababa Hilton—by East Africa standards, a luxurious hotel. One evening shortly after Aidid and his group had made their dramatic exit, I encountered the press officer from a rival faction as he entered the lobby from the bar. Though a Muslim, he was quite drunk. He stood teetering belligerently in front of me and said, "You journalists are just like the Hawiye. You have no respect for the Darod. I say we kill [the chairman of his own faction], kill [the president], and start our own independent country. We will call it the Land of Punt." (Punt existed centuries ago, and encompassed the tip of the Horn of Africa.) The man then took a loopy swing at me. I ducked, and said good night; he stumbled off to his room. The next day I saw him at the conference. He smiled at me and winked, tendering me a proposal for

Somali political rehabilitation with full knowledge that the private briefing he'd given me the previous night had completely disavowed national unity.

After the conference, UNITAF tried to make lemonade. "Disarmament is going forward," insisted Colonel Dotto. "And the next guy to be disarmed is going to be Aidid—the hard way or the easy way."[28] But behind the scenes the American attitude was not so blustery. The new U.S. special envoy, Robert Gosende, talked timorously about "giving Aidid what he wanted."[29] The hope was that UNOSOM II would now look like the better alternative. "The U.S. will suffer by being a Judas goat, but that will favor UNOSOM II," said CARE's Rhodri Wynn-Pope.[30] Like an amiable psychiatrist, Kittani remarked that the slander leveled by Aidid in leaflets distributed in Mogadishu was "not against the U.N., but UNITAF, so we need to take the shifting moods into perspective."[31] It wasn't to be. Aidid showed nothing but contempt for the U.N. operation. Although at less than twenty thousand a ripened UNOSOM II that June numbered scarcely more than half UNITAF's peak, Aidid continued to use radio messages to characterize the U.N. soldiers as an occupation force. His hyped broadcast on June 5, 1993, portrayed the Pakistanis' inspection of a weapons depository near the radio station as an attack on the station itself. Disinformation got Aidid the bloodbath he wanted.[32] Mohamed Abshir Musa of the relatively peaceful SSDF had explained Aidid's motivation aptly: "The warlords only dominate when there's war."[33]

At the end of March 1993, Colonel Dotto had admitted, "As we keep peeling the grapes in Somalia, we see the conflict is over territory that we have not yet secured."[34] The prerequisite of territorial security is disarmament, and the Americans' efforts were selective and incomplete. They eliminated the threat of pitched battles by impounding heavy artillery and the notorious gun-mounted "technical" vehicles that once ruled Mogadishu, but left well over one hundred thousand small arms in circulation—enough to support guerrilla conflicts indefinitely. Guns are money, so disarmament didn't get much community support. On the Somali gun market in June 1993, concealable weapons, like the 9-millimeter Beretta, sold for over two hundred dollars, and an assault rifle still brought fifty dollars.

The point that in practice escaped the United States (ergo, the United Nations) was that an overwhelming military presence would not spell security. The Weinberger-Powell doctrine, in fact, had virtually no penumbral effect in Somalia; artillery battles were waged, relief workers ambushed and killed, and compounds robbed, only a few miles from UNOSOM II headquarters in Mogadishu. After the June 5 battle, Admiral Howe, then green, confessed with bright-eyed surprise that the United Nations "certainly didn't anticipate this kind of major assault."[35] More seasoned relief workers said it had been only a matter of time. "Without a political resolution and with all the weapons still around, everyone knew that the U.N. would be tested at some point," remarked one. Short of a sustained territorial dragnet, some degree of indigenous cooperation was essential to maintaining peace and stability.

But the Americans' large-scale intervention had effectively squandered any prospect of teamwork. The broad stroke made Somalia immune to any solution but a military one. Even as late as June 1993, no Somali political renascence had yet crystallized from Operation Restore Hope. The Addis conference was supposed to help, but its outcome was far too tentative to make a substantial difference. In 1993, the only proposal that emerged was that the sharia become the basis for all Somali laws—not exactly encouraging, given the Somalis' heritage as moderate Sunni Muslims and stubborn individualists.

American and U.N. efforts did bring some leaders closer together—notably Aidid and intraclan rival Ali Mahdi Mohamed—but Aidid and his disagreeable sidekick, Colonel Jess, remained at odds with General "Morgan," their common enemy. Until they are co-opted, there is little hope for progress. At the root of their conflict, of course, is Byzantine clan rivalry. Aidid is the Hawiye who ousted Siad Barre, Morgan the Darod who ran Siad Barre's army and married his daughter. Aidid spent seven years in prison agonizing over the Darods' encroachment on Mogadishu, traditionally a Hawiye stronghold. He wanted the southern port of Kismayu as a Hawiye redoubt. He thought he had it—until Morgan took it back from Jess in early 1993. He and Aidid claimed that UNITAF had emasculated Jess and that now UNOSOM II was finishing the job. Aidid wouldn't rest until he controlled both Mogadishu and Kismayu. Morgan wanted what was his—Kismayu—and had the tacit support of his SSDF clansmen in the northeast. Together they encircled the Hawiye.[36]

This is old news now and was in June 1993. Gothic as the Somalis' enmities are, obviously they are too basic and deeply rooted to be beveled. Yet the United Nations's approach remained to get Kismayu clan elders to declare for peace and to disown talks between Aidid's group and Morgan's sponsors. The theory was that weary compromisers will eventually break away from clan hardliners and leave them isolated, weakened, and ultimately becalmed. The approach was fallacious. The Somalis with clout showed they could prosper in an inferno indefinitely, and that quality lent durability to the people's admiration for strong and intransigent leaders like Morgan (whom Oakley branded a "war criminal" in December 1992) and Aidid. It took but a mere suggestion from Aidid to send his followers into battle against the far better equipped and trained Pakistanis in June.

Forced to react decisively, the Security Council condemned Aidid, and the United States mobilized gunships and more Marines. They battered his arsenals and destroyed his headquarters and the infamous radio station, but he did not become politically marginalized in the least. In fact, the retaliation enhanced his status. Once a mere strongman, he was now an outright martyr. Foreign troops killed at least twenty-eight more Somalis, and Aidid continued his protests of U.N. colonization with vocal and abundant support. Admiral Howe called for his and Jess's arrest and trial when feasible. Aidid stayed at large throughout the summer and early fall, whereabouts unknown and protected by a sizable contingent of brainwashed militiamen. He clandestinely spewed still more anti-U.N. broadcasts by short-wave radio.

In a criminal trial, the United Nations thought it might have a plausible way of taking Somalia's biggest troublemaker off the board. A publicized trial before an accepted tribunal—perhaps with respected Somalis co-presiding—the theory went, would parade the warlord's demonstrable atrocities before Somalis by unimpeachable means and showcase the United Nations's unsentimental resolve to pacify the recalcitrant country in spite of itself. It might then be possible for more peaceable leaders to come to the fore.

The obvious difficulty was to fish out from the political detritus a rule of law and a legitimate forum. Even the United Nations's legal team, headed by international law scholar Tom Farer, was skeptical. He later ragged to *Newsweek* that he might write a book titled, "My Summer in Somalia; or, I Have Seen the Future and I Don't Think It Works."[37] Although it was a neocolonial conceit that the West had to undertake the burden of exporting justice to Africans, Admiral Howe's alternative suggestion that Aidid be tried in a Somali court under Somali law[38] was ridiculous. Somalia's civil infrastructure was fossilized and, since it was a Siad Barre remnant, commanded little respect. Unlike the U.S. constitution, the U.N. charter does not empower military forces to set up judicial tribunals in occupied territory. Under the charter, the United Nations's "principal judicial organ" is the International Court of Justice, which has the power to prosecute only nations, not individuals. In any case, its very jurisdiction is not mandatory but consensual, and the court has no inherent power to enforce its judgments.[39] Legally, not even the dubious "Noriega solution" was available to the United States—Aidid had not violated any U.S. laws.

There was a tenuous argument that the United Nations had the power to form its own criminal tribunal and try Aidid for violations of international law under chapter 11 of the charter, which permits it "to further international peace and security" in non-self-governing territories.[40] But the provision plainly contemplates places that have never been U.N. member nations, as opposed to those, like Somalia, which have descended from statehood into anarchy. The Security Council already finessed the charter once in authorizing "humanitarian intervention" in Somalia under chapter 7. Any additional ad hoc straining of the charter would probably have upset lawyers and some member nations—and established another burdensome precedent the United Nations would be hard-pressed to follow. Imposing judicial authority might also have been an inexorable step toward trusteeship, a protracted responsibility that no nation capable of fulfilling it wanted.

With Aidid in hiding, the legal issues could be deferred. Howe's biggest problem, as he saw it, was world opinion. The West was running out of patience with Somalia, and with Aidid in particular. In early March 1993, donors gathered in Addis Ababa fell almost $40 million short of the $166.5 million requested by the United Nations for Somalia and warned that further aid would hinge on political progress.[41] The United Nations, however, had no choice but to accept the challenge of resurrecting Somalia. Howe settled for a Security Council resolution calling for Aidid's capture and trial, again based on preservation of international security under chapter 7; a $25,000 bounty on Aidid; and Task Force Ranger, composed of some four hundred Rangers and Delta-force commandos, to track him down. The manhunt was dubbed "Operation Continue Hope," and the name indicated its plenary importance in UNOSOM II thinking. From the outset, the plan was an ominously radical precedent. Saddam Hussein had presented a far greater global threat but had never drawn a resolution aimed at his personal incarceration. Panama's Noriega, on the other hand, had elicited precisely that from the U.S. government. In effect, Howe and Boutros-Ghali had infused U.N. procedures and dictates with Noriega tactics.[42]

Unfortunately, Howe's insistence on a military solution with legalistic window-dressing was precisely the wrong approach. He simply missed the probationary message of Restore Hope: that military force could do little more than suppress percolating hostility while the politicians and diplomats figured out a way to defuse it. Ismat Kittani, Boutros-Ghali's caretaker representative and Howe's immediate predecessor, recognized Restore Hope as a "temporary police action."[43] When Howe replaced Kittani in March 1993, his experience in Somalia having then amounted to a few days' orientation in Mogadishu, he saw "a new opportunity to make progress in Somalia."[44] That misnomer reflected the United Nations's systemic flaw: The "new opportunity" had actually come when James Jonah, the first of Boutros-Ghali's four special envoys, was appointed in January 1992. What Howe faced as he began was a tragically old problem perpetuated by the United Nations's consternation over one vengeful warlord.

Despite the failure of Western policy that dropped in his lap, Aidid did not seem harried or complacent. Frighteningly, he showed some flair for political correctness. Holed up at the Serena Hotel in Nairobi in January 1994, afraid that the Americans would snatch him if he returned to Mogadishu, Aidid asked Mohamed Ibrahim Egal, de facto president of breakaway Somaliland, to plead his case with the United States. Egal graciously declined, loath to sour the prime backer for a new state.[45] But as Aidid's stock rises he may be able to cut a power-sharing deal with Egal that makes Aidid president, at least, of southern Somalia. No doubt he was mindful that Siad Barre's downfall ultimately stemmed from the fight over northwest Somalia—Somaliland—and that resolving differences between Hawiye and Isaaq best be done soon. In a characteristically Somali departure from the rehearsed secularism he flashed to the Americans in December 1992, Aidid began to court Islamic fundamentalists in Somalia and elsewhere, and after the October 3 conflagration dispatched Colonel Jess to Iran to cadge more weapons in case of a

U.S. escalation. On May 19, 1994, after six months in exile, Aidid returned to a hero's welcome in Mogadishu. At the rally that greeted him, he praised his supporters for repelling "foreign aggressors."[46]

Beyond the savvy backroom activity and public swagger, Aidid has orated, "The U.S. and U.N. troops in Somalia should be reduced and the money spent on development."[47] That too is disturbingly shrewd. The swords-for-ploughshares shtick tends to play well with Western donors, whose money Aidid naturally welcomes. At the end of the day, as with many African leaders, the donors are his real constituents.

The process of Aidid's empowerment began when Robert Oakley arrived in December 1992 as U.S. special envoy. A hardnosed Vietnam hand, Oakley remembered the litany of mistakes made in Saigon and was determined not to repeat them in Mogadishu. He resisted both Aidid's and Ali Mahdi's sidling for partisan American grooming. Although Oakley backslapped the two into a tenuous rapprochement, when Aidid found himself unable to gain special status as steward of Somalia's future body politic, he directed his wrath toward the United States and convinced his followers it was looking for a puppet.

Inadvertently strengthening Aidid's propaganda were American insistence that a U.S. military officer be made second in command of UNOSOM II; Washington's apparent installation of another Yank, Admiral Howe, as the new U.N. special envoy; and the nearly five thousand U.S. troops left in-country and seaborne as an ominous quick-reaction force. Once Howe put a price on Aidid's head, after Aidid's men had killed twenty-four Pakistani peacekeepers, Aidid became a genuine folk hero. The prevailing image was of Aidid, a Third World underdog, scrapping gamely with the world's most powerful nation. He was able to capture a Nigerian soldier and an American helicopter pilot, kill eighteen Americans and wound seventy-seven others in a single engagement, and drag a dead and denuded GI through Mogadishu for his own video crew to capture for posterity—not merely with impunity but with the consequence of having his official status transformed from criminal to embattled statesman. After he emerged from hiding, he continued to insist on wholesale U.N. withdrawal from Somalia. A few weeks after the October 3 battle, American soldiers politely ferried him from Mogadishu to Addis Ababa on an American plane for reconciliation talks. Airport tactics had worked.

# 7 Nonchalance Redux

By transforming Aidid from parochial bully into international fugitive, Operation Restore Hope shifted the United Nations's focus away from local politics onto global diplomacy. The particular mechanism of change was military magnification, which made the picture bigger and the details fuzzier. The principal actor was the United States. Starting in August 1992 with Operation Provide Relief, the food airlift, Washington fell victim to an old Third World seduction: Simple people, simple problems, simple solutions.

In Vietnam, the United States had disregarded the corrupt history of South Vietnamese "republicans" and President Ngo Dinh Diem's bizarre culture of pompous autocracy because it saw all communists as part of a single evil movement and all its opponents as deserving recipients of American support. Thus, Washington failed to entertain the possibility that underpinning North Vietnamese communism were grassroots nationalism and a veneration of Ho Chi Minh that may have been less susceptible to Soviet or Chinese suasion than the government of South Vietnam and might well have been receptive to conciliatory American overtures.[1] It took Einstein to show the likes of Newton that the status of the participant reflexively skews any experiment. So it took Restore Hope to remind the United States that its very involvement complicates even the most ostensibly easy riddle.

Once the United States made the Somalia situation part of its own, for the media Somalia became an American story rather than an African one. All Somali political figures, even the few peaceful ones, became "warlords." The niceties of Somali clan culture were too esoteric for the name-brand defense buffs that the Gulf War had so mesmerized, so journalists settled for a single buzzword—*tribe*—to denote the genealogical web in which Somalis found themselves entangled, moving on apace to Cobras and Blackhawks, RPGs and APCs, Abramses and Humvees. A common peg was the Somalis' compulsion for "ethnic cleansing," hardly an accurate take on their racial and cultural homogeneity, and their unanimous relish of the double-cross and of revenge savored cold or warm.

The humanitarian story still had some resonance, but even that became bleached. One story that received great attention was that of ABC correspondent Donald Klaedstrup. At the peak of the famine in summer 1992, he toured Baidoa and found a little girl standing in a hut surrounded by the rotting bodies of her parents, brothers, and sisters. Klaedstrup was deeply affected, brought her to Mogadishu, and inquired about adopting the girl and taking her back to Johannesburg. While Somalis claiming to be her relatives clamored for adoption fees, clan elders said they couldn't allow a Christian to raise a Somali Muslim. The little girl was placed at the SOS orphanage, where she remains today. To his credit, Klaedstrup keeps up with her progress and visits often, even though Somalia is no longer on his beat. "He really loves the child," confirms Willy Huber.[2]

By contrast, journalists with household names came to Mogadishu for a few days, got their fast take, and went home. *Newsweek*'s Colonel David Hackworth came in on a C-130, spent Christmas with some old pals from the army's 10th Mountain Division at an isolated airfield in Bale Dogle—pinpointed by Rhodri Wynn-Pope as being "between nothing and nowhere"—and then filed a story deriding the Somalis' battle-worthiness and the army's waste of prime manpower.[3] P. J. O'Rourke did a creditable gonzo piece for *Rolling Stone*, but since it played up the Somalis' bizarreness and inscrutability, it didn't do much for deeper global understanding.[4]

Neither did Aidid or the U.S. State Department. The general was angling to be a certified strongman among Third World leaders. Uncle Sam was looking, in the abstract, to blueprint the new world order. For both players, local political bottlenecks were avoidable inconveniences. In December 1992, Osman Ato set the tone for Aidid's serenade, hawking the tired line, "Somalis are one nation, one blood. Clan divisions have no major effect."[5] Publicly anyway, Oakley bought it. As he bid Somalia farewell in early March, the veteran diplomat assured journalists that "clan warfare is virtually gone. The last attempt, I think, was down in Kismayu last week."[6] Two weeks later came the clan battles in Kismayu that interrupted the Addis conference. Colonel Dotto admirably came forward with his candid admission that the conflict involved clan turf at bottom, but the U.S. and U.N. commands did not let the awkward facts get in the way of public relations.

The Americans and the Security Council artificially deleted mending clan rifts from the set of priorities by maintaining that the problem was not political diffuseness but lack of security. The fact that the latter was caused by the former they willfully overlooked. According to the U.N. Security Council Resolution 794 itself, the objective of UNITAF was "to establish as soon as possible a secure environment for humanitarian relief operations in Somalia."[7] Boutros-Ghali interpreted that mandate as calling for a U.S. handover to the United Nations "as soon as the irregular groups had been disarmed and the heavy weapons of the organized factions brought under international control."[8] Post-Sahnoun, the United Nations was well-nigh phobic about using the word *clan*. Save for Aidid's SNA and USC, the Somali acronym political organizations got camouflaged and forgotten amid marquee alphabet entities like UNITAF and UNOSOM. Analogously, the official U.S./U.N. position subordinated the political reconciliation process to the task of controlling Mogadishu militarily. After the nutshell of initial interest in internal Somali politics had cracked, what grabbed the attention of the policy makers—and through their spin-doctors, the journalists—were American blood and combat.

Between March and June 1993, there was no gore or fighting to speak of. Somalia dropped out of the international news. *Newsweek*, whose prehype coverage had far surpassed that of the other news weeklies, ran a feature on Oakley called "The Father of All Warlords" three weeks after he announced his resignation.[9] The *Washington Post* published a story on Somali women's groups.[10] Reporters joked that what they needed was "Operation Restore Hype." From the perspective of the United States and the United Nations, no news meant victory. A few days after the marines landed in Mogadishu, Walter Isaacson had written magisterially, "By taking the unprecedented step of embarking on a military operation for altruisic reasons, the United States may once again show how idealism can go hand in hand with realism."[11] Three weeks later Oakley confidently said, "The Weinberger-Powell doctrine has succeeded beautifully in Somalia."[12] As he left Mogadishu in early March, Oakley triumphantly announced to the press that the American military initiative had "allowed Somalia to come back from the brink of self-destruction."[13] Complacency continued through the United States's handover of operational control to the United Nations on May 4, 1993. Then came the reality check on June 5.

Aidid's massacre of the twenty-four Pakistanis betrayed the rhetoric. The general spent more than three months on the lam as the United Nations's public enemy, while Howe and Boutros-Ghali drew hundreds more elite American troops into their ad hominem quest for Aidid, which culminated tragically in the October 3 firefight. Only then, wrote Blumenthal, did "events . . . reveal the Somalian political morass which, though present from the outset, had been all but invisible to the top decision-makers."[14] When the dust settled, President Clinton acknowledged that the vendetta "never should have been allowed to supplant the political process."[15] With what *The Economist* snidely called "a chutzpah level high even by American political standards,"[16] Clinton, Congress, and the press tried to shift the blame to the United Nations, the president claiming that diplomatic rebuilding was "ongoing when we were in effective control up through last May."[17] It was a spurious retrenchment. Though by acquiescence rather than studied affirmation, Washington had sanctioned the chase all along.

Although Boutros-Ghali eventually jumped on the bandwagon, U.S. pressure initially moved the Security Council to certify the hunt for Aidid in a formal resolution—not the other way around. (Resolution 837 did not name Aidid at the behest of African members but called for "the arrest and detention for prosecution" of "those responsible" for killing the Pakistanis and "the disarmament of all Somalian parties." Washington made public its view that Aidid fell into both categories.) On authority of the U.N. resolution, U.S. gunships and attack helicopters pounded Aidid's arsenals and strongholds in late June and July. The attacks wiped out both Aidid's Mogadishu house, which had stood a mere block from the Conoco house used by Oakley and the U.S. diplomatic mission four months earlier, and the notorious radio station.

President Clinton himself deemed the operation "a complete success."[18] But the United States and the United Nations were not winning hearts and minds. On June 13, angry Pakistani soldiers fired on a crowd in Mogadishu, killing twenty and wounding fifty. UNOSOM II began door-to-door weapons sweeps; during one of them, three Italian soldiers were killed. After a helicopter raid on Aidid's command center on July 12, in which more than seventy Somali civilians died, incensed Somalis killed three photographers and a sound man—Hansi Krauss of the Associated Press; Dan Eldon and Hos Maina of Reuters; and Anthony Macharia, also of Reuters.[19] In August, Somalis killed four American soldiers in an ambush. By September 9, Aidid had achieved a degree of martyrdom sufficient to impel his Mogadishu supporters to attack en masse American and Pakistani soldiers attempting to clear a roadblock. U.S. Cobra helicopters fired 20-millimeter cannon into the crowd, killing scores of Somalis, many of whom were women and children. President Clinton and General Joseph P. Hoar, who headed the U.S. Central Command responsible for Somalia, were appalled. Both the president and the Pentagon began to reconsider the manhunt directive but refrained from revoking it during the ensuing month.

Howe, it is true, requested the Rangers and Delta-force commandos, but never without at least the tacit agreement of General Bir and General Montgomery (respectively, the U.N. and U.S. commanders in Somalia) and civilian Washington's rubber stamp. Administration officials initially rejected Howe's call for the high-profile special-ops soldiers on the theory that their presence would be inflammatory, but they were cowed by Howe's incessant pleas and slick networking and soon caved. The program in early summer, deemed "Operation Caustic Brimstone," called for only fifty commandos and a quick insertion-and-extraction to get Aidid. As Aidid proved himself increasingly wily, however, Howe decided he needed 350 more soldiers, including Rangers. In late August, with Aidid continuing his guerrilla and propaganda campaign, Howe got his first installment of Rangers. No longer really covert, the hunt reared its head; it was renamed "Operation Gothic Serpent."[20] The elite GIs didn't smoke out Aidid, but did capture several of his more malignant lieutenants (including Osman Ato) and commandeer large caches of his equipment.[21] These small successes encouraged Howe to ask for more Rangers. This time U.S. special envoy Robert Gosende, having reversed the position he had taken six months earlier, backed him up vigorously—his September 6 cable to the State Department, entitled "Taking the Offensive," advised, "Any plan for negotiating a 'truce' with General Aidid should be shelved" and "We should not deal with perpetrators of terrorist acts."[22] By then, Boutros-Ghali's miasma over Aidid had come to match Howe's, so he supported the requests for the bloodhounds. Howe got still more crack troops. The October 3 raid was executed by the American field commander on the basis of his standing orders, derived from Resolution 837, to capture Aidid; Washington was not directly involved.

To be sure, General Montgomery had stridently opposed the bounty hunt as plain bad strategy. At the tactical level, General Hoar fervently wanted to nix the second request for Rangers, believing the chances of catching Aidid were about one in four.[23] But after weeks of fielding intense lobbying from both schools, General Powell finally approved of the "snatch mission" as the only alternative to being "nibbled to death."[24] Furthermore, Montgomery had asked for tanks on September 9 and artillery on September 23—qualitatively radical leaps in ground ordnance that made the elite personnel requests look incremental and modest. These two factors turned the tide. Final executive authorization was given by a subcabinet level deputies committee. This committee was a puzzling buffer institution by which the administration negligently allowed top executive policy makers to be "not sufficiently attentive," Secretary of State Warren Christopher later admitted.[25]

The tail wagged the dog. Military capabilities determined political goals. The policy makers themselves were complicitous. According to an aide of former Secretary of Defense Les Aspin, Admiral Howe had "adopted Aidid as his Great White Whale" and revealed his fanaticism with "frenetic and obsessive" lobbying for more forces.[26] Likewise, Boutros-Ghali, long vilified by Aidid as having sold out Somalia as Egypt's foreign minister and the U.N. secretary-general, had settled on making an example of Aidid rather than making peace with him. Ironically, it was Hoar, a military man, who offered the only political wisdom of the moment. Urging denial of Howe's second Ranger request in a classified message to Undersecretary of Defense Frank G. Wisner, General Hoar wrote: "A coherent plan which involves the political, humanitarian and security needs for the country has yet to emerge. Control of Mogadishu has been lost."[27]

To the extent that Washington conceded its culpability, the CIA was a leading scapegoat. The agency had counseled—wisely, it came to pass—against military intervention way back in late 1992, before the marines hit the beach. With intervention a fait accompli, strategically the CIA had ostensibly backed up the United Nations's and the Clinton administration's position that Aidid was a prime obstacle to peace—not exactly a flagrant misreading of the situation. (According to a *Washington Post* article, once Delta-force snatched Aidid, the agency planned to try him for murder before a panel of African judges it had assembled aboard a U.S. Navy ship off the Kenyan coast.[28] Assuming the CIA was not operating in complete ignorance of international law, it contemplated nothing more than propaganda value from this inane scheme. Silly as it was, however, the plan never came to fruition and had nothing to do with actual intelligence collection. I recount it here only as an illustration of how warped American perspectives on Somalia, and particularly Aidid, actually got.)

On the ground the agency had been embarrassed over the inability of its sophisticated electronics to intercept the propaganda messages Aidid transmitted on his primitive low-power radio.[29] Moreover, CIA's human intelligence had given rise to at least two futile Task Force Ranger operations. On August 30, operations officers informed the Task Force commander, Major General Garrison, that Aidid was hiding out in a house off Via Lenin. The next day the commandos, having first found khat on the premises and presumed criminal activity, arrested eight Somalis who turned out to be employees of the U.N. Development Program. On September 14, Delta-force snatched a man reported to be Aidid, only to discover that he was Ahmed Jilao, Siad Barre's former security chief and an American asset. Notwithstanding these embarrassments, CIA's network of about twenty Somali agents operating inside Mogadishu did produce the intelligence about the meeting of October 3 at the Olympic Hotel. It turned out to be all too right—the place was radially fortified because, as suspected, Aidid was there for a meeting with his capos. But the agency failed to figure out just how competent, determined, well armed, and organized Aidid's militia was.[30]

In the postmortem of the October 3 battle, it transpired that Aidid's militia divided Mogadishu into eighteen sectors, each with a tactical commander. Although the Somalis offered no pitched opposition to the five Task Force Ranger operations during September in which Aidid himself was not in peril, what they did do was reconnoiter. They learned that the Americans always used the same tactical "template": Delta commandos would blitz the target building to take prisoners; Rangers would ring the building to protect their Delta-force compatriots; and helicopters would hover overhead to control crowds and provide an umbrella of cover fire. Colonel Harif Hassan Giumale, the commander of the Somali force that engaged Task Force Ranger on October 3, had attended a Soviet military academy in Odessa for three years. His subordinate, Colonel Ali Aden, summed up his commander's perspective on U.S. tactics: "If you use one tactic once, you should not use it a third time. And the Americans had already done basically the same thing six times."[31] Moreover, an American chopper was shot down and its three crew members killed on September 23—a mere ten days before the disaster.

The Americans did try to offset the loss of surprise caused by repetition by varying ancillary operational details such as the time of day of a given mission, and by sending out decoys. But to the Somalis one irrepressible lesson shined through: to thwart Task Force Ranger, the helicopters had to be neutralized and the attacking force had to be surrounded. These objectives required, respectively, rocket-propelled grenades and, to offset superior U.S. skills and firepower, a lot more Somalis than Americans. In an eerie reprise of Ap Bac thirty years earlier, military intelligence did not realize that Aidid had plenty of both and knew how to use them. On October 3, Somali RPGs downed two Task Force Ranger choppers. Just as Somali commanders had predicted, neutralizing air support completely discombobulated the American operation. After the first crash, the U.S. point of attack shifted three hundred yards west, from the building where prisoners were taken to the wreckage, where a swarm of militia ambushed the Americans. In the ensuing fifteen hours, as American reinforcements flanked the Somalis and Task Force Ranger survivors clawed their way north to safety in the stadium on 21 October Road, Somalis killed eighteen GIs and wounded seventy-seven. Master Sergeant Gary I. Gordon and Sergeant First Class Randall D. Shughart, both of Delta Force, had each died defending helpless comrades; posthumously, they were awarded the first congressional Medals of Honor given since the

Vietnam War. Somali casualties numbered over one thousand, including more than three hundred dead.[32] In the abstract, the ratio seemed acceptable—ten Somali casualties for every one American. It was about the same as the ratio in Vietnam. Roughly a third of the Somalis killed or hurt, however, were women and children.[33]

That fifteen-hour span will most likely influence American military policy for years to come. More immediately, it broke careers in Washington. Clifton Wharton, number-two man at the State Department, was cornered into resignation by targeted press leaks. Gosende and David Shinn, head of the Somalia task force at the State Department, were summarily fired. Finally, Les Aspin resigned largely because of the beleaguered countenance cast upon him by failures in Somalia.[34] Howe was the most tunnel-visioned of all the players, and therefore probably the most to blame. For the time being, he remained untouchable for Machiavellian reasons. The Clinton administration had pushed his appointment as U.N. special envoy as a condition of keeping its hand in the peacekeeping effort and, especially, subjecting American troops for the first time to U.N. oversight. For the United States now to insist on his ouster would have made it appear even more capricious and befuddled. As it happened, after the smoke cleared Washington brusquely replaced Howe with Richard W. Bogosian in February 1994; Howe first heard about his dismissal on the BBC World Service and faxed his Mogadishu staff farewell from the United States.[35]

Transitions between outgoing and incoming administrations in the United States are notoriously ragged and politically fickle. The cathartic thrust of spoils—"Happy days are here again!"—makes White House handovers anything but seamless. The prospect of tactical friction between Mogadishu and Washington was intuitively obvious even to Somalis. In December 1992, Dr. Mursal had averred, "It's safe for Bush—he's leaving. If the plan works, he takes credit. If not, it's Clinton's fault."[36] Sure enough, after the October 3 mess, in a speech to the California Grocers Association, Bush laid out a disclaimer. "Our mission was to go into Somalia, open the [food] supply lines, then to withdraw and have the United Nations handle the peacekeeping function," he commented. "For reasons I'm not sure of, the mission has been redefined."[37] As Aidid peddled his videotape of the dead GIs being hauled naked through Mogadishu debris to the networks, Senator Phil Gramm quipped, "The people who are dragging around bodies of Americans don't look very hungry to the people of Texas."[38] And *The*

*Economist*, remembering Vietnam, concluded, "Once again, television images are shaping American foreign policy."[39] The informed consensus was that it was Clinton's fault.

Congressional pressure forced the president to rethink American foreign policy extemporaneously, with Somalia the test case yet again, only this time for new insular restraint instead of the new world order. Republicans, led by Robert Dole, distanced the United Nations and preached virtual unilateralism, whereas Democrats reminded Clinton that his popular mandate was to fix domestic problems and not to swashbuckle overseas. The president roused Robert Oakley out of his brief retirement to reprise his original role of U.S. special envoy. Oakley's immediate task was to secure the release of the American pilot and Nigerian soldier being held captive by Aidid, which he promptly did. Then he was to secure a political solution to the Somali problem.

The White House, though politically unable to instigate Howe's removal, intentionally marginalized him. Oakley was explicitly permitted to leap-frog standing U.N. operational orders, and did so. To ferret out Aidid, Oakley spread the word that Howe's extemporized arrest warrant for Aidid, though technically still in force, would be ignored by the American command. The president sent another 5,300 troops and four AC-130 Specter gunships but also announced that virtually all Americans would be out of Somalia by March 31, 1994. The obvious inference was that the reinforcements and hardware were supposed to bolster American, not Somali, security: the Pentagon, and not the U.N. deputy commander, General Montgomery, retained tactical control over the new troops and the Rangers already on the ground.[40]

In September 1993, vague noises had emerged from Washington about "nation-building" rather than military coercion in Somalia. Jimmy Carter, having been solicited for his conciliatory voice by a fugitive Aidid, had won over Clinton with the idea of changing the idiom of reform from the military back to the political. The plan was to use African leaders—ideally the presidents of Ethiopia and Eritrea, which had recently enjoyed renascent democracy—to fertilize Somali self-renewal. But these musings did not crystallize into official policy. The hunt for Aidid proceeded apace. No U.S.-driven political initiative occurred before the ill-advised Ranger operation of October 3. Aidid continued to overshadow all other Somali political figures.[41]

That raid squandered any chance for a decent military interval that might have paved the way for a new run at political reconciliation. All a panicked White House could do was control the damage. It didn't even do that very well. Sidney Blumenthal's account in *The New Yorker* incisively recapitulated all the others:

> A closed briefing of about two hundred members of the House and Senate by Secretary of Defense Les Aspin and Secretary of State Christopher on October 5th was a spectacle worthy of Abbott and Costello. These two pillars of national-security policy volunteered to expose themselves as utterly bereft of direction. The senior policy-makers had come humbly to ask if anyone knew what their policy should be. The reaction to their bizarre performance was a combination of dumbfoundedness and anger that worked like a slightly delayed fuse on a thunderous explosive. Senator after senator, congressman after congressman, Republicans and Democrats alike, now demanded United States withdrawal. Calls for Aspin's head on a pike were heard from corners of the Capitol.[42]

As a matter of political reality, the trauma of October 3 had forced America into the cloisters. Sad to say, the episode was an avoidable consequence of casualness at the top, which started with the United States's Cold War backing of Somalia, twisted Operation Restore Hope from a humble humanitarian venture into a sexy military exercise, and finally atrophied UNOSOM II into a small, ugly grudge match. Earlier, the United Nations's institutional uneasiness with ascetic, workmanlike political programs like Sahnoun's shaved Boutros-Ghali's options down to humanitarian intervention. Now American proclivities for military flash over ground-level negotiation engulfed and suffocated any multilateral movement toward political reconciliation among Somali factions. And in turning Somalia's most potent—and, like it or not, its only indispensable—player into an inaccessible fugitive, Howe sabotaged for as long as Aidid was hunted (over three months) any political program that might have resurged. Both the United States and the United Nations, it turned out, preferred lancing to surgery to remedy tumors. By the time the policy makers had seen the folly of this treatment, the United States had lost Somalia, and vice-versa. It cost both countries.

# 8 High-Concept Foreign Policy

In theory, of course, Operation Restore Hope couldn't help but benefit both Somalia and the United States. Like most high-concept enterprises, though, the project got bogged down in the execution. Top management forgot to sweat the details. But even had it done so, the Somalia plan might never have worked.

Richard Nixon watched *Patton* for something like the third time before deciding to bomb Cambodia in 1970.[1] Ronald Reagan talked over Libya's punishment with a major league baseball player and apparently was not around to give congressional leaders a final briefing before American planes bombed Tripoli in 1986.[2] Presidential agony it seems was reserved for Truman on Hiroshima[3] and Johnson on Vietnam,[4] for George Bush was happily assured of fast success when he made up his mind to launch Operation Restore Hope.[5] Despite a compelling pastiche of concentration camps and the vestiges of genocide, he had opted out of intervention in Bosnia because a recession-battered electorate was tired of his administration's overseas focus. But once defeated, he appeared unprincipled for his forbearance. Journalists and governments alike juxtaposed his exalted new world order with the growing chaos on earth and mocked the notion as a turgid fantasy. Somalia looked like sure-fire redemption, for the sake of the Bush administration's place in history.

Immediately before Operation Restore Hope, the United States's interest in Somalia had been conspicuously slight. President Bush appointed Peter deVos in August 1993 to act as a special envoy, but his brief was merely to support Sahnoun's political initiative. He did little aside from helping to negotiate the return of a Kenyan helicopter and crew—alleged by Aidid to have been reconnoitering for Siad Barre—from Bardera to Kenya. DeVos soon moved on to become ambassador to Tanzania. John Fox, the foreign service officer who had been dealing with Somalia from Nairobi, was transferred to a hard-earned NATO post in Brussels. His replacement, Donald Teitelbaum, barely had time to get acclimated before Restore Hope was announced.

The president's sense of noblesse oblige passed into soaring rhetoric: Not only was the humanitarian mission "in the finest traditions of service," it was "God's work" as well.[6] At the same time, the project reified the concept of the new world order, which until then had remained obscure lip-service to "the vision thing," a platitude. With Restore Hope as his finale, President Bush could relax. Even though he left Somalia politically worse off than he found it, the people weren't starving anymore. The revisionists might nitpick, but at the start and the finish the first-drafters and the retrospectors would vindicate at least his initiative, if not Clinton's uptake. George Bush could well have thought, like Robert Stone's co-opted political scientist in *A Flag for Sunrise,* that "a man has nothing to fear . . . who understands history."[7]

But history might not make Somalia itself all right, and neither did it make Restore Hope necessary. Although the conventional wisdom has enshrined a happy coalescence of Somalia's need and Bush's sense of posterity—the zeitgeist is that by November 1992, Somalia had become so unruly that only massive military intervention could save it—a closer look raises serious doubts. Recall that the United States provided substantial airlift support to Somalis for months before December 9. And had Sahnoun been permitted to continue his painstaking but palpably efficacious tenure as the secretary-general's special representative, there might well have been no need for large-scale intervention. A former Bush national security official admitted to

*The New Yorker* that even the White House viewed the situation in Somalia as a golden opportunity rather than a call to duty. Between Somalia and Bosnia, he said, "there were two differences. In Somalia, there was really no vital interest remotely at stake. The other difference was that we could do something about it."[8] In any event, it is unlikely that so many were needed for such a concededly small objective, or that the awe the United States's grand display of might may have inspired was worth the eventual provocation of Aidid.

Whereas the nation-building needs of Vietnam were starkly ignored and the enterprise there cast as an essentially destructive one, those of Somalia were fully acknowledged and the task there apprehended as basically constructive. The problem, put simply, was that the Somalis needed far more help than the Americans had thought going in. Again haunted by Vietnam, Washington seemed to think that the less Americans were involved in pacification the better. Given intervention, though, that view made little sense. By virtue of having sent twenty-five thousand troops, the United States was just about as fully committed as it could get. For as long as the troops were in-country, the key consideration became the nature of the involvement rather than the degree. The United States opted not for active and close but instead for passive and distant, which played to the strength of overwhelming force. But merely awing the Somalis with tons of ordnance and a few arsenal raids was never enough to set the country back on course. Oakley's parting suggestion on March 2, 1993, that might had made right was both premature and wrong. In parallel, the U.S. military was in a hurry and reluctant to confront Clausewitzean "friction" directly.

Bush's original intent, however unrealistic, was to end U.S. involvement before Clinton's inauguration—a mere six weeks after the marine landing.[9] His aim was simply to secure ports, airports, and food distribution routes and points, and fell far short of nation building or pacification.[10] Accordingly, Resolution 794, passed by the Security Council on December 3, 1992, simply authorized the use of "all necessary means" to establish "as soon as possible the necessary conditions for the delivery of humanitarian assistance." Although officers in-country toed the administration line—that a humanitarian endeavor was an appropriate use of American troops—grunts generally disagreed. They were trained for hostile military engagements, they said, and were uncomfortable in more tentative peacekeeping roles. All this suggests a regrettably inorganic and distant relationship between the military itself and the civilian chain of command.

In September 1992, when U.S. military participation in the taming of Somalia was limited to airlifting food and the first five hundred Pakistani peacekeeping troops, the marines involved were classically gung-ho. Unused to cooling his heels in a hot zone, one marine standing on the landing strip at Mogadishu's military airport smirked disdainfully at the idea that under standing orders, he would be the escorted rather than the escort if he went into town. "Our unit [a 2,100-marine amphibious assault group] is perfect for this situation," he said. "The Cold War may be over, but the world needs us more than ever."[11] He could tell that the Pakistani troops would not be able to do the job; an internal U.N. memorandum later described them as "lightly armed and forced to operate under very restrictive rules of engagement" and "simply . . . not sent as a fighting force."[12] The outspoken marine's commanding officer, Colonel Michael Hagee, commented that in 1969, most Vietnamese just wanted to return to their humble way of life and reflected aloud that the Somalis would be happy if they could just get rid of the teenagers with the guns.[13]

That ended up being Washington's working assumption. Some of the political officers on the ground realized that the idea of popular unanimity on the disarmament question was unrealistic. "At some point the honeymoon will end," said one U.S. diplomat shortly after the marine landing, "but because of the bona fides that have been established, when people see coalition forces they'll realize they're societally important, even if inconvenient to the individual—like seeing a cop in the rear view mirror."[14] Then it sounded like good, measured analysis, words cribbed from a conscientious white paper. In the end, though, even that kind of hedged optimism turned out to be misplaced. Somalis would not respect marines as Americans might respect police officers. Once the enlisted men realized that, the contours of the mission—combat soldiers keeping peace—started to look distorted to them. They lost faith.

Washington also failed from the outset to realize that the so-called warlords had learned from Siad Barre how to manipulate superpowers. In a painfully real sense, the massive American military presence was a tease to Aidid and Ali Mahdi and ipso facto prodded them to vie for U.S. sponsorship. The U.N.'s power, by contrast, was and remains far too diffuse, too difficult to marshal on a single country's behalf, to be a serious enticement to Aidid or his ilk.

Finally, and perhaps most profoundly, the Americans in charge, in their determination to avoid a Vietnam-like quagmire, permitted caution to back them into corners that allowed only awkward means of escape. In March, Oakley pronounced Restore Hope's limited objective accomplished; Aidid's attacks in Kismayu seemed timed precisely to prove Oakley wrong, and U.S. troops had to return there to support the Belgians. Washington insisted on turning the operation over to the United Nations on May 4; a month later Aidid took advantage of a politically and militarily vulnerable United Nations by killing the twenty-four Pakistanis, and eventually an American quick-reaction force had to be mobilized and the Rangers sent in.

Then, in the wake of the Rangers' disastrous mishap on October 3 and morbid images akin to Vietnam's, Clinton faced a Hobson's choice. He could either escalate the battle for Mogadishu into an outright urban guerrilla war by continuing the hunt for Aidid, or pull back and declare for peace. Only the latter option made sense. Still, by revoking the contract on Aidid and calling for U.S. withdrawal by March, Clinton effectively certified Aidid the military victor and aroused a weird nationalism in the Somalis. They were now determined to face down their own problems but no longer willing to take the advice of great powers, which they now expected to misunderstand and undermine them as the United States had done. With the general lionized, all of the United States's Western partners—France, Belgium, Italy, Germany—were disinclined to stay in Somalia thanklessly and soon announced plans to withdraw as well.

In *Newsweek*, Michael Elliott likened the videotape of the dead American soldiers being dragged to the infamous photograph of the Saigon policeman shooting the kneeling Vietcong in the head.[15] The October 3 battle itself was even more audacious from Aidid's point of view, conjuring an elusive Somali patriotism in support of the resistance of occupiers as Ap Bac had done for the North Vietnamese. "It was a military disaster to rank with Desert One or the bombing of the Marine barracks in Beirut," wrote Elliott.[16] Senator Gramm cracked wise and pithy about the vigor the supposedly starving Somalis displayed in killing Americans and pulling the hog-tied body of one GI through the streets. Under such intense public and congressional pressure, Clinton's determined pull-out, like the Saigon evacuation of 1975, may have afforded the United Nations and innocent Somalis only an indecently short interval in which to rally. Perversely, the Americans appeared to have behaved like "the best and the brightest" of yore.

The uplifting American victory in World War II imbued American leaders with a sense of triumph that led the United States into Korea, and then Vietnam. That false sense of infallibility, in turn, gave rise, as Neil Sheehan put it, to "professional arrogance, lack of imagination, and moral and intellectual insensitivity" in the military leadership and intelligence services.[17] Eventually that spelled failure in Vietnam and a graduated period of tentativeness, lack of confidence, and calculated overmatching in the projection of U.S. military power. The Gulf War understandably delivered the rebirth of American triumphalism, but with it came the same negative by-products in the military and the intelligence community: a misplaced ascription of omnipotence, an oversimplified formula for military success, and an underappreciation for the operational ramifications of unfamiliar turf. As General Norman Schwarzkopf made immortally clear after Kuwait had been won, Saddam Hussein was hardly "schooled in the operational art." But the larger point got lost: The Iraqi army had challenged only the American military's pure technological might and not its capacity to outfox a clever and competent enemy.

For this reason, General Powell and his contemporaries became enamored of force at the expense of maneuver and failed to grasp, at least at first, that the overwhelming force doctrine and Somalia were far from an exact fit. In certifying Operation Restore Hope to President Bush, Powell played to what he thought was his strength—namely, pure military action—just as General William Westmoreland had done when he insisted on the deployment of his U.S. expeditionary force in Vietnam.[18] As a decorated veteran of the last popular and classical war, Bush, like fellow war hero John Kennedy in the early days of Vietnam, wanted to believe simply that American might would make right without getting into the nuances of its attainment.[19] The Gulf War let him do just that. Restore Hope did not.

Nevertheless, George Bush and General Colin Powell have argued persuasively that the duty undertaken was a limited one, that it was indeed fulfilled when food was delivered, and that American involvement spilled over from humanitarian intervention into the United

Nations's province of policing and nation building. That view squares with their original conception of Operation Restore Hope and with Ambassador Oakley's initial brief, which called for neither coercive disarmament nor proactive political brokering on the part of the United States. The day after Resolution 794 was passed President Bush wrote Boutros-Ghali reminding him of the modest objective of the American mission, but on the day of the landing itself the secretary-general wrote Bush angling for disarmament and mine-sweeping.[20] The Bush administration resisted a heightened commitment. The incoming Clinton administration, however, did not. With the new president's encouragement, on March 26, 1993, the Security Council passed Resolution 814, which effectively called for nation building and pacification in Somalia. Two weeks earlier, Admiral Howe had been appointed U.N. special envoy. Clinton's U.N. ambassador, Madeleine Albright, characterized the United Nations's new goal as "nothing less than the restoration of an entire country as a proud, functioning and viable member of the community of nations."[21] Some nine thousand American troops remained in Somalia, pending the handover to the United Nations on May 4. On June 6, a day after Aidid's massacre of the Pakistanis, the Security Council passed Resolution 837, authorizing the hunt for Aidid. The U.S. soldiers, who had been slowly withdrawing, returned to their posts. Functionally, this inaugurated the "two-track" approach, whereby American-dictated military pacification and U.N.-sponsored political reconciliation proceeded in tandem—a truly wholesale departure from Bush's and Powell's earlier notions.[22]

At the same time, the United States's more enterprising role was quite consistent with Bush's vision of Somalia, such as it was, as a proving ground for the new world order. So what was Operation Restore Hope? Empirical confirmation of Powell's prescription for the acceptably safe projection of American military power, or the long-awaited substantiation of Bush's airy sloganeering about making the world a better place? Now it is evident that the president could not have it both ways. A day after the marine invasion, an American political officer in Mogadishu noted in the same breath that "the helicopters were a big hit" and "the U.S. wants to scrupulously stress neutrality."[23] Helicopters alone wouldn't do it. If the United States was to be the political architect of the new world order, then it had to supervise its construction, wherever the building site happened to be. Bush's simple conceptual marriage of Powell's doctrine of overwhelming force, on the one hand, and the projection of a new world order, on the other, was specious. Even leaving aside the matter of subsequent long-term development aid, military flexing without finely coordinated policing and mediation proved to have no intrinsic constructive properties. If the United States was to be the new-world guru that Bush hoped it would be, the two-track policy could hardly have been avoided.

That policy was not inherently misguided, but analytically it carried rather obvious operational risks. The gravest was that the availability of two distinct avenues of approach presented the opportunity for policy makers to diverge. Also looming was the possibility that somewhere along the line, one track would lag the other. As it happened, in Somalia both risks kicked in. The military track splayed out from the political track, then left it in the dust.

Although Secretary of State Christopher pushed for moderation in dealing with Aidid, Howe and Boutros-Ghali maintained that military defeat of Aidid had to take precedence over political reconciliation. In their defense, they believed that none of the more palatable Somali leaders from other acronym organizations (like Mohamed Abshir Musa of the SSDF) would come to the fore unless Aidid were forcibly removed from the playing field.[24] The glacial pace of the Transitional National Council initiative that started fitfully in Addis in March 1993 provided some fodder for this view. Les Aspin, like Christopher and General Hoar, was uncomfortable accelerating the disparity between the two tracks and turned down Montgomery's requests for tanks and artillery and Garrison's requests for AC-130 Specter gunships.[25] Under Howe's and Montgomery's orders, the Rangers and Delta-force commandos undertook the October 3 operation with no heavy armored support.[26]

In retrospect, such support might have turned the tide of battle and saved American lives. Montgomery (though not Garrison) contended as much in Senate hearings on May 12, 1994.[27] But recriminations over tactics do not get to the root of the failure. The fundamental problem with the version of two-track policy that took hold in Somalia was that the person who was supposed to be spearheading the political initiative—Admiral Howe—had abandoned that track and proceeded down the other. So had Boutros-Ghali himself. Yet the standing assumption of the May 4 handover had been that whereas the United States would effectively control military operations in Somalia by virtue of its logistical domination of the in-country operations, the United Nations would manage the political program. The leading U.N. players' frolic-and-detour left a huge gap between the Washington policy makers tangentially involved in Somalia's political resurrection and their plenipotentiaries in Somalia. The gap wasn't filled until Oakley's return visit in mid-October 1993, when he informed Aidid, in effect, that as far as the United States was concerned he was a viable political player and no longer a wanted man. Because of a U.N. obsession in which Washington had acquiesced, virtually no other Somali leaders had been groomed or encouraged. General Montgomery admitted, "We're back at square one with Aidid."[28] The only alternative figure that had emerged was the Imam of Hirab, the traditional religious leader of the Hawiye clan, which counts the subclan of both Aidid and Ali Mahdi as constituents.[29] He rose up essentially on his own, however, with little resort to the good offices of either the United States or the United Nations.

Washington had almost casually placed Task Force Ranger, as the elite force sent to Somalia was designated, at the disposal of UNOSOM II, on the strength of its chief diplomat's being a retired American admiral. Because of the officially secret nature of Ranger and Delta-force activities, Howe was not publicly accountable for his use of the army contingent.

The lack of coordination led to a nonpolicy of mere damage control. Although President Clinton nobly proclaimed that "we must leave on our own terms" and "do it right,"[30] a Congress institutionally haunted by the false promises of light at the end of the tunnel would allow him no more than token face saving. As a result of October 3, Clinton had no more political currency to spend on Somalia. He sent in more troops and armor, but after some reactive braggadocio about "retaking the streets," even U.S. military officials conceded that the new troops came only to protect those soldiers who were already there, pending wholesale withdrawal in March.[31] Although the president publicly regarded six months as a decent interval, Third World leaders to whom he hoped to pass responsibility saw the United States as a bullying "Rambo."[32] In any case, after March 1994 there would be no U.S. military support for Somalia and most likely only passive political support.

Overall, the American approach smacked unmistakably of wishful thinking—in particular, the idea that the simple, scalar weight of benign power can transform anarchy of mysterious causes into a cooperative, self-perpetuating rebuilding package. It isn't so. As Ambassador Hempstone noted before Operation Restore Hope even began, "It will take five years to get Somalia not on its feet but just on its knees."[33] Even had the U.S. military been able to pacify Somalia and control Mogadishu, without money to spin entrenched emergency and rehabilitation programs into genuine development ventures, Somalia would remain highly susceptible to relapsing into the same moribund state that it was in when the marines landed in December 1992. Collectively, the nongovernment aid organizations that have toiled there have neither the cash nor the mission to rebuild infrastructure from rubble.

As the Americans prepared to leave Somalia in January 1994, most of the aid groups were already gone. CARE, in Mogadishu since 1981, was down to a skeleton crew. Its principal activity was to administer food monetization programs with food supplied by USAID. (In sadly typical U.N. fashion, the U.N.'s World Food Program functioned as a superfluous intermediary.) About 60 percent of the food sold at retail in Mogadishu was sold by CARE through public solicitation of competitive bids. The program was well conceived. Although Somali merchants could get the food at a cheaper price than they could in other wholesale markets, CARE took pains to confine its produce to nonindigenous foodstuffs so as not to discourage Somali farmers from vigorous planting and harvesting. To help them, CARE was distributing seeds and tools. But M. A. Khan, the project manager, freely admitted that absent a concerted development effort, Somalia would retrogress. The proceeds of CARE's food sales were earmarked for reinvestment in development projects, but USAID's umbrella grant totalled only $6.5 million and would soon run out.[34]

The massive military intervention and the famine before it had also transformed Somali society from pastoralist to urban and created a wholesale dependence on employment by the United Nations and aid agencies and on the relief dole. The United States and United Nations employed some twenty thousand Somalis. In 1993, forty-six aid agencies operated in Mogadishu, versus fewer than a dozen in March 1994.[35] This situation severely retarded the process of indigenous economic recovery and the development of self-sufficiency, somewhat as the massive U.S. military presence in Saigon had disoriented South Vietnam's agrarian economy.[36] Between twenty and twenty-five nongovernment organizations planned to come in with development programs in 1994, but with banditry on the rise, many were having second thoughts. The downsizing of UNOSOM II, on top of the earlier NGO pull-out, would create a whole new class of unemployed who would dig up their weapons, either to rob outright or to extort.

As the Americans withdrew in March 1994, they left neither a government nor a viable police force. In 1993, the United Nations said Somalia needed $148 million in aid, but donors contributed only $37 million. To appease the contributors, on March 24, Aidid and Ali Mahdi signed a perfunctory eleven-point agreement in Nairobi—a day after other Somali leaders walked out. No agreement was reached on the fundamental issue of whether Somalia was to be governed by majority or by consensus. As of March 25, local initiatives and a U.S. Justice Department training group had managed to collect only 1,100 Somalis and five vehicles to police a territory almost as big as Texas. Despite more than $50 million contributed by the United States, factional resistance and U.N. lethargy hindered the effort.[37] The bandits were free to emerge from hibernation. On March 20, 1994, Somali gunmen killed two Italian journalists, Ilaria Alpi and Miran Kroyatin, as they hijacked their car near the former Italian embassy.[38] The U.N.'s official line was simple banditry; the story on the street, and the more likely explanation, was that the journalists' bodyguards cowered as their predecessors, angry over being fired, exacted revenge. Although more active, mobile security measures might offset the shrinkage in manpower, said Khan, "I don't think the Somalis will have much fear" of a UNOSOM II force composed mainly of Africans and Asians. "Eventually it will go back to the way it was before December '92."[39]

In late February, several relief agencies were bombed throughout Somalia, including World Concern in Mogadishu. Some expatriates thought Muslim fundamentalists were the culprits, whereas others fingered bandits who were trying to extort one last bit of money out of the agencies before they left with the troops. The agencies naturally grew wary. Clay Burkhalter, project administrator at SOS-Kinderdorf, said his personal entourage of Somali bodyguards grew from two to five.[40] By March 27, Somalis were cutting holes in the fence around the U.N.-controlled airfield, siphoning gasoline out of U.N. storage tanks at the seaport, looting office equipment from abandoned command posts, and prying tires from U.N. vehicles.[41]

April came, and small clan battles became daily occurrences in downtown Mogadishu. In addition to registered assault rifles, high-caliber machine guns, bazookas, and RPG launchers were now openly carried in the streets—especially on October 21 Road, the site of the battle of October 3. Aidid's subclan (the Habar-Gedir) overran Merca. On April 16 and 17 in Mogadishu, they engaged the Hawadley subclan in a vicious firefight at the traffic circle near the Sahafi Hotel; each subclan sought control of the international airport, which is lucrative. Burkhalter, in country between January and July 1994, offered the following firsthand assessment: "Somalia is basically the same old dump with the same old fools flexing their muscles. Aidid seems to be enjoying his role as statesman—luxury hotels, Mercedes limos. . . . As far as the third-world troops go, the Somalis have fun toying with them."[42]

By June, Somali drivers and bodyguards, angry over being fired, had kidnapped Associated Press reporter Tina Susman, holding her for three weeks and demanding a hefty ransom before losing interest and letting her go. In late July, two Malaysian troops were killed and eleven other UNOSOM II soldiers detained. Washington decided to withdraw its twenty diplomats and their fifty-eight marine guards. Most of the ten thousand UNOSOM II troops in Mogadishu stayed inside their compound as Somalis died by the score in clan battles. With idiosyncratic logic, Boutros-Ghali noted that the fighting had made UNOSOM II unable "to justify its present size and cost," which in turn made it "feasible to commence a reduction in the level of troops."[43] Meanwhile, Aidid resumed anti-U.N. and anti-American broadcasts, and his clansmen fired on U.N. convoys. On August 22, about seventy Somali militia ambushed Indian troops seventy miles southwest of Mogadishu, killing seven and wounding nine; nine days later, on August 31, three Indian doctors, all civilians, were killed in an attack on a U.N. field hospital in Baidoa.[44] Intraclan battles in Mogadishu resumed.

Notwithstanding its internationalist bureaucratic trappings—namely, the International Monetary Fund and the World Bank—development still depends largely on the unilateral initiative of developed nations.[45] The United States, though the wealthiest, naturally must select the hardest cases as aid recipients. But a military undertaking of the time, expense, and risk of Operation Restore Hope seems folly, simply a bad investment, absent a deeper, softer civilian commitment to preserve any peace the military might make and to counteract any economic dislocations visited by the military intervention itself. And, like the Good Samaritan in the common law of torts, the United States should not undertake a duty it cannot or is unwilling to carry to a sound resolution or, at minimum, a modus vivendi.

This did not happen in Somalia. The nation has not been rebuilt, nor is a blueprint in place. Instead, the United States left a bloodthirsty folk hero astride a large territory run by Third World racketeers behind the turned back of a loose confederation of second-rate U.N. armies. To make matters worse, a rift in Aidid's Somali National Alliance has developed and widened. Osman Ato apparently had been swayed during his captivity and appeared ready to mediate a detente between Aidid and the United Nations. But Abdi Hassan Awale, Aidid's U.N. liaison man, took the position that the United Nations wanted to colonize Somalia but the United States had seen the light; he asked for more American buffing, but the United States remained disinterested.[46] As its parting gesture, Washington donated five thousand M-16s, five thousand handguns, and nearly three million rounds of ammunition to outfit the new Somali police force. A few diplomats merely fretted that now they just had to trust the Somalis.[47] The searing irony that it was precisely superpower profligacy with weapons that had greased Somalia's skid into hell to begin with was lost on Washington.

The United States came into Somalia like a lion and went out like a lamb. On January 27, 1994, the *Washington Post*'s Keith Richburg wrote from Mogadishu: "Few here like to talk about a possible nightmarish ending—a hasty U.S. retreat, armed Somalis leaping over the walls of the U.N. compound, a panicked evacuation by a helicopter to ships offshore—in the tradition of Saigon in 1975. But they are planning for it just in case."[48] For all Washington's fears about another Vietnam, it managed to replicate that war's worst features in miniature.

# 9 Lessons Learned

"Portrait of men at war: the infantry is dug deep into the couches and chairs and holds strategic positions on the linoleum. The perimeter has been secured by Sasquatch, while you man the observation post by the windows with Video and Rothfuss. Right now you are on alert status, beverages at port arms."[1] Thus Robert O'Connor describes U.S. soldiers during peacetime. Yet the wry passage could well have portrayed, aside from Task Force Ranger, the GIs in Somalia in late 1993 and early 1994: thousands of enervated cynics, safely inside the UNOSOM compound, a large body at rest keeping a fragile peace by inertia.

That image encapsulates the unfortunate wastefulness of the United States's military and political efforts in Somalia. It also reflects the Bush and Clinton administrations' expenditures of political capital, of which Congress and the American public are the rightfully stickling fiduciaries. Writing in the *Washington Post* in March 1994, Robert Oakley commented, "Plunging so deeply into Somalia's internal affairs inevitably brought the peacekeepers into political confrontation and then military conflict." Even so, he concluded, "Somalia has been an invaluable lesson for the United States and the U.N. in what is likely to work and what is unlikely to work in complex politico-humanitarian emergencies that have become all too common."[2]

The unavoidable vicissitudes of armed conflict make the prevention of some miscues impossible to guarantee. For example, by denying Montgomery's heavy armor requests, the Pentagon deprived Task Force Ranger of a basic element of support but also inhibited military enlargement for the sake of a neglected political track. Except under a crude argument from the consequences of the October 3 operation alone, it is impossible to judge whether that decision was appropriate. But there are lessons to be drawn from the United States's tussle in Somalia that if taken to heart would minimize the likelihood of repeat mistakes.

## FIRST LESSON: MILITARY INTERVENTION IS THE LAST RESORT

Somalia's first message is that military intervention in the service of humanitarian objectives should not be ordered cavalierly. Political brokering by the United Nations (or some other internationalist agency) should remain the preferred avenue of nation rebuilding, and it tends to work best without unilateral kibitzing from third-party nations, including the United States. When the softer methods unambiguously and irretrievably fail, however, military measures should be considered. In some situations, they may be infeasible or of such speculative value as to be unwise. In other circumstances, they may make sense. If so, intervention should be structured so as to be both limited and bold. It is essential that it be accompanied by vigorous efforts at political reconciliation and social reform. As one American soldier said as he left Somalia, "You can't solve social problems with a military force."[3]

Even with a military commitment, negotiation should be preferred. Washington and the United Nations got thrown off the political track when it refused to finesse Aidid and instead turned him into a criminal. That might have worked with Che Guevera or Patrice Lumumba back in the 1960s, when potential constituencies could be swayed by anticommunist information campaigns. Not anymore. One of the unfortunate by-products of the resurgence of grassroots populism wrought by the Cold War's end is that terrorists become statesmen. Hence Aidid's success. When a thug is likely to have considerable power even after he is stonewalled, an absolute refusal to deal may end up costly (or at least embarrassing) if he later forces capitulation.

Again, the general is a case in point. After weathering a summer and an autumn of Aidid's mocking evasion and the loss of a score of American soldiers, UNOSOM II was forced to let Aidid emerge from hiding exculpated and more viable than ever as a political player. On the heels of Aidid's helping forcibly liberate them from a propped-up dictator, Somalis weren't about to join the United Nations in censuring Aidid over the killing of a couple of dozen Pakistanis. As difficult as that is to stomach, it is a reality the United States bought on December 9, 1992. It will be difficult not only for Aidid but for the Somalis as a people to end their violence: these are people born and immersed in a culture of treachery and reprisal. The United States and the United Nations, though, convinced themselves that Aidid was the problem.

In fact, the Somalis were and are the problem. Insofar as Aidid could be seduced by American prestige (as, evidently, he could), co-optation could have turned that problem to best advantage and probably would have been a better approach than ostracism. That is perhaps a Cold War solution but one with a difference. Any decision to massage Aidid would have been informed by a knowledge of the Somali people and an assessment of how best to achieve the objective of political resuscitation on their behalf. Unlike support of Siad Barre, such a decision would not be based on the dismissal of cultural idiosyncrasies for the sake of geopolitical ends.

Aidid admittedly wanted (and continues to want) the same absolute power Siad enjoyed. Although U.S. policy should have been to deny him such power, Washington based its program of persecution merely on its recognition of his ambition and treachery. The constant it failed to work into the equation was the Somali people's acceptance of those qualities. In demonizing Aidid, Washington made the United States seem even more alien to the Somalis and Aidid even more powerful. The more sensible approach would have been to take decisive steps to neutralize Aidid militarily after the twenty-four Pakistanis were killed and then offer him a face-saving deal that he, thus weakened, would be loath to refuse. Aidid might have been receptive, for example, to the idea of partial disarmament in exchange for a direct voice in the governance of Somalia through the United Nations. Indeed, in June 1993, he intimated he would be.[4] In retrospect, one Pentagon official lamented the missed opportunity. "He sent us a message and we sent him a message," he said. "Then we should have invited Aidid to lunch and talked things over."[5]

Should wholesale intervention prove necessary, regional forces should be preferred, consistent with article 52 of the U.N. charter.[6] There are four reasons. First, international neighborliness should be encouraged to promote free trade and regional stability. Second, purely as a matter of logistics, local solutions to political problems will be the cheapest. Third, historical, economic, and ethnic links make it likely that neighboring countries will be more familiar with the problems of a nearby country. Fourth, if regional efforts fail and further intervention is necessary, any local opposition will generally have been short-circuited.

Encouraging international neighborliness is complicated by the fact that Somalis tend to disdain black Africans. But the fact also remains that Africans can win them over more easily than others. The Somalis loathed the Nigerians to a large extent because they were petulant and standoffish. The Botswanans in Bardera, though, were friendly and forthcoming and earned the Somalis' cooperation.

A substantial case in point for the use of regional forces for intervention is Liberia, a former tribal anarchy where fifteen thousand African peacekeeping troops, led by Nigerian generals and sponsored by the Economic Community of West African States, have successfully enforced the U.N. embargo against rebel leader Charles Taylor, defeated him on the battlefield, and started disarming his troops. To counteract Taylor's distrust of the Nigerians over their support of Samuel Doe, Ugandan and Tanzanian troops were brought in to collect arms. African U.N. observers were able to quell a destabilizing power struggle within another faction by brokering talks between tribal elders. Although elections scheduled for September 1994 were cancelled because of resurgent unrest, the fact remains that the peacekeepers' regional interest gives them staying power that the United Nations lacks.[7]

Concededly, regional intervention was not a viable option in Somalia. By December 1992, the failure of the United Nations had created conditions calling for intervention. With the exception of Kenya, Somalia's East African neighbors—Ethiopia, Sudan, Uganda—were too bogged down in their own internal strife to put together a regional peacekeeping force. The Organization of African Unity and the Arab

League issued hortatory statements but failed to reach any consensus on action. The United States was the alternative by default.

Military compulsion may be appropriate with particularly recalcitrant players—again, Aidid probably qualifies here—but it should be subsidiary to political initiatives. In other words, a two-track policy, notwithstanding its disastrous incarnation in Somalia, in theory is not only sound but necessary. As the experience in Somalia has shown, such a policy in itself is not self-executing and offers no guarantees. Military and diplomatic decisions must be coordinated extemporaneously. From the outset the decision makers must be expected to ad lib. Indeed, in light of Somalia, they should be acutely aware of the dangers of one hand not knowing what the other is doing.

## SECOND LESSON: KNOW YOUR ENEMY

The second lesson is simple and ancient. The American command believed the Somalis to be intellectually primitive, culturally shallow, and militarily craven. All three beliefs proved expensively incorrect. Aidid's commanders were sufficiently schooled in the military art to find and exploit the soft spots in Task Force Ranger's standard tactics. The militia had the moxie to carry out their commanders' studied counterstrike and take their lumps. More than three hundred of them died on October 3; as many as five hundred were killed protecting Aidid over the course of the previous summer.[8] To a true student of the Somalis, the guts and resolve would have computed. Somalis side with the strongest group, but their opportunism generally stops at the border: forced to choose between the strongest Somalis and a stronger opposing force, they will pick the former.

A more searching approach to intelligence would have explored the ramifications of Hawiye officers' having been trained extensively at the Soviet military academy in Odessa and in Italy. Such an approach also would have assigned far more inferential gravity to Somalis' inbred readiness to die in the Ogaden in the 1970s and, indeed, fighting alongside the Italians in their conquest of Ethiopia in 1935. When the CIA's most valuable Somali asset shot himself in the head playing Russian roulette in late September, the agency should finally have clued that there was something more dangerous animating these people than the blood lust to which the cocky architects of Operation Restore Hope reduced their motivation.[9]

But U.S. intelligence services, civilian and military, tend to devote their energies to tactical details at the expense of deeper background. Following is just one modest example of the maladroitness of U.S. intelligence practices. In early 1994, U.S. intelligence officers learned that an American civilian working for an aid agency in a remote section of Mogadishu had not been provided for in evacuation plans. The agency had put word out on the street that he was Canadian. The government officers suggested to the worker that they survey the layout of his compound to come up with the appropriate procedure for extracting him, should it prove necessary. Because Mogadishu had by then again become dangerous for expatriates traveling on open roads, the intelligence officers proposed arriving in armored personnel carriers with marine escorts. Such a display would have obviously tipped off the Somalis that a Very Important American was living at the compound and might have given them notions about kidnapping him (as they later did the Associated Press reporter) or worse. The aid worker politely declined the offer.

In 1992, Strobe Talbott, now deputy secretary of state and then writing for *Time*, reflected the operative view when he dismissed the threat faced in Somalia as "Toyota Land Cruisers mounted with recoilless rifles manned by boys."[10] And the Viet Cong were peasants who used pongi stakes. Shortly after arriving in Mogadishu in December 1992, Oakley himself commented, "The more you know here, the greater the risk," and noted, "Somali clans are almost impossible for a foreigner to understand."[11] These assessments appeared realistic but turned out to be self-defeating. At minimum, military personnel from general to private should be thoroughly and topically briefed on the cultural peculiarities of the people native to the country to which they are sent.

More broadly but in the same vein, the United States should be particularly wary of military involvement in ethnic or sectarian conflict. In today's tribal world, that is tantamount to cautioning against military involvement altogether. So be it. Where strife is born of ethnic or sectarian differences, the inherent risk of treachery to any foreign force is multiplied by the number of different factions at odds. Simply as an ethical matter, it is incumbent on the commander-in-chief, through the intelligence services (for example, CIA) and intellectual resources (for example, the National Security Council) available, to protect any troops that might be committed by anticipating any lurking sources of hostility they may encounter overseas. Obviously, fulfilling that duty will pay tactical and strategic dividends as well. Knowing what quarters to expect fire from makes military objectives all the easier and cheaper to take. And knowing the enemy surely topples barriers to converting the relationship to one of friendship and tolerance.

In confronting sectarian conflict in radically different cultures, the United States's knowing its enemy dictates a wholesale overhaul of its traditional Cold War approach. In his article "Containing Ethnic Conflict" in *Foreign Policy*, Charles William Maynes sagely pointed out that American biases in favor of individual rights and federalism are peculiarly inappropriate to all but Anglo-American problems. American diplomats, he suggested, need to offer "greater accommodation to group rights" and to avoid "federal solutions because they tend to promote secession or partition or even greater intolerance toward the minority groups that are left behind."[12] This advice tends to disfavor large-scale interventions, like UNOSOM II, by virtue of its emphasis on broad accommodation over defeat.

Moreover, Maynes's prescription lays great stress on anticipatory, preventive diplomacy. That, in turn, requires thorough and early intelligence about the people in question, as opposed to the jarring lurch from procrastination to siege mentality that the United States, in the event, actually manifested. Intelligence agencies should digest the little morsels as well as the big entrees. To take just one example: in February 1994, two British members of Parliament visiting an aid agency in Somaliland were kidnapped by some Somali clansmen. They released the MPs after twenty-four hours of good food and smiling politeness and wanted nothing from the British government. The Somalis had snatched the VIPs simply to gain the respect of a rival clan, in order to improve their bargaining position in a local political dispute. The gambit worked, and once the disagreement was resolved the Somalis had no further use for their captives. An account of these events appeared in London's *Independent* as a wry, colorful feature,[13] but intelligence agencies should not just salt such stories in some clipping file. Rather, they should be incorporated prominently into intelligence estimates and briefing papers as illustrations of the slow and attenuated Somali bargaining style.

The larger implication is that ongoing intelligence should seek to eliminate the need for intervention in all but the most flagrant cases.

The United States cannot afford to offer up its forces as long-term stewards of a potential U.N. trusteeship. "In turn, clearly the U.N. cannot intervene in every ethnic conflict around the globe," wrote Maynes. "The world must find other ways to address the problems of tribalism and group conflict before the hatred and mistrust are such that only outside military intervention is likely to succeed, yet is unavailable."[14]

## THIRD LESSON: ESTABLISH TIGHT COMMAND-AND-CONTROL

Having made the effort to plumb the psyche of those it wants to tame, if intervention just has to be, the United States squanders the knowledge unless it follows a third imperative—namely, to maintain control over the methods by which it engages its adversaries. This lesson has broad, and in the context of the international community, somewhat antisocial implications.

Senator Robert Dole has proposed limiting by statute U.S. participation in U.N. military operation to areas in which the United States has a direct interest and outlawing outright the service of American troops in a standing U.N. army.[15] His so-called Peace-Powers Act presents a cramped, neoisolationist view of U.S. foreign policy and implicitly brands the idea of helping Somalia and countries in like straits bad per se. The isolationism that held Wilson back in World War I and resurfaced to inhibit Roosevelt in World War II derived from nostalgic ethnic biases, first of German-Americans for an avuncular Kaiser, then of Irish-Americans against an oppressive Britain.[16] But Dole's isolationism is based mainly on U.S. failure in Somalia, and perhaps remotely on the Vietnam experience. Against the backdrop of intervening history—a proactive Cold War foreign policy spearheaded by NATO, Bush's new world order, and the Clinton administration's expansive but confused approach to internationalist diplomacy—Dole's approach appears small-minded and exclusionary. Potentially, it polarizes the available options between intervening alone or not at all. The ends he seeks—greater protection for American soldiers and more containable military commitments—could be attained by less restrictive means. Assuming the United States will continue to lead global reform, informed changes in operational policies rather than absolute legislative bars seem better suited to problems that are by nature fluid.

The Somalia operation illuminates several sensible changes. For one thing, it highlights the importance of centralized command and control not only over U.S. forces seconded to a multinational operation but also over the entire operation. A peacekeeping group composed piecemeal of contingents from different armies, like UNOSOM II, suffers enough inherent disadvantages because of linguistic barriers, methodological differences, and varying capabilities. Different UNOSOM II contingents had different rules of engagement, which jangled the Somalis' expectations and left soldiers uncertain as to how effectively their foreign comrades might defend them.[17] On October 3, a failure of communication caused two Malaysian drivers to turn their armored personnel carriers right instead of left, into a Somali ambush that killed one driver and waylaid several GIs dispatched to rescue Task Force Ranger.[18] U.S. soldiers reportedly also had to use an awkward nonverbal method—a gun to the head—to get an uncomprehending Pakistani tank commander to mobilize.[19] When Montgomery asked the Italian commander for backup tank assistance, he had to contact Rome for approval.[20]

James H. Smith, whose son, James Smith Jr., was among the Rangers who died in the October 3 battle, undertook his own investigation of UNOSOM II. In testimony given before the Senate Armed Services Committee on May 12, 1994, he said: "Although the concept of a U.N. multinational peacekeeping force appears to be the appropriate direction for U.S. involvement in conflict situations, the conditions is Somalia resulted in the Rangers being placed in a situation without reliable allies and, in certain cases, U.N. peacekeeping forces actually supporting the enemy." With remarkable equanimity, Mr. Smith, an ex-Ranger lieutenant, went on to identify three specific problems: the fragmenting of forces by confining each one to a specific geographic area; correspondingly inconsistent disarmament and weapons-screening policies that varied according to geographic sector; and penetration of U.N. headquarters by Aidid.[21] Better command integration and coordination could have ameliorated or eliminated each of these three shortcomings.

According to the final report of a U.N. investigation of peacekeeping force casualties in Somalia, in June 1993, General Montgomery had been told by Aidid's representatives that inspecting the arsenal near Aidid's radio station "would lead to war." But Montgomery failed to disclose the threat to the Pakistani commander when he ordered the inspection on June 5, 1993. As a result, the Pakistanis went in without armored personnel carriers, and twenty-four of them were cut down in the subsequent ambush.[22]

The U.N. report also points out that insofar as the Rangers and Delta-force soldiers acted independently of the U.N. chain of command, as they did, Aidid's men had substantial legal and moral justification in resisting the capture of their leader, which had been authorized only by a Security Council resolution.

From the comfort of the armchair, it is easy to say merely that these are matters that should have been thought through before actual combat, but with over thirty countries contributing forces during staggered intervals, beveling every potential edge is an impossible task absent decisive central authority. When, as with UNOSOM II, the United States is providing the logistical capability that drives the peacekeeping force, it is not out of line for it to insist overtly on overall command. In fact, it seems both ethically and operationally preferable to manipulating the United Nations behind the scenes in an effort to acquire de facto command, as Washington appeared to do when it installed Howe and Montgomery. Moreover, centralized supervision vested in people familiar with the designated channels of authority would tend to ensure more conscientious coordination of any two-track policy. General Montgomery attributed the military shortcomings of the Somalia operation to the fact the command structure had to be built up piecemeal and continually readjusted to the redeployments of different contingents. At the inception of UNOSOM II in May 1993, he noted, only sixteen thousand of the ultimate twenty-eight thousand troops were even in-country; the largest eventual contingent, the Indian army's, had not even arrived.[23]

The simple, a priori answer is a standing U.N. army, but the financial and political obstacles to conjuring up such an entity are considerable—due in part to Congress's own reluctance, led by Senator Dole. A more realistic alternative, at least in the near term, would be to revive the hibernating U.N. Military Staff Committee.[24] Granted, the United Nations is now facing a crisis of confidence both within and without the organization,[25] having dropped the ball in both Bosnia and Somalia and at least bobbled it in Cambodia. Any suggestion that some of the United Nations's institutional shortcomings might be cured by recourse to yet another U.N. organ therefore deserves a high degree of skepticism. But the fact is, the end of the Cold War did open the door to a new world order in which the problems of nations could be solved by resort to international consensus and cooperation. The only vehicle in place for marshaling that kind of teamwork, imperfect as it is, is the United Nations. To dwell on its infirmities and look exclusively to unilateral solutions is to throw out the baby with the bath water.[26]

In drawing some of that bath water, the grand parameters of the Cold War marginalized the Military Staff Committee. Now it could play a central role, even if the standing army idea is shelved for the time being. The committee is made up of the chiefs of staff of the five permanent members of the Security Council. It should also include the administrative heads of any nations voluntarily committing troops to U.N. efforts under Boutros-Ghali's recent proposal, and representatives of analogous committees from regional organizations like the OAU, ECOWAS, and the OAS. The function of the Military Staff Committee would be to construct and maintain an ongoing system of military cooperation, subsuming (like NATO) joint training programs and exercises, logistical support planning, and contingency planning for different situations and under different rules of engagement. War games, in effect, would give way to peace games. Future Somalias might be simulated in Arizona or Turkey, or the eventuality of Zaire's anarchy rehearsed in Brazil. Although national leaders would retain ultimate control over their own soldiers, by way of these "road tests," coordinated command-and-control mechanisms and the integrated participation of regional organizations would already be in place if and when the time for intervention arises. Such a system would both reduce the threat of U.S. domination of peacekeeping operations and increase the advantages accruing to those operations from unique American strengths.

Tight, institutionalized command-and-control will also attract high-caliber professional armies like, for example, Germany's. After the Germans' stint in Somalia—its first overseas deployment since World War II—its officers were put off U.N. peacekeeping because of UNOSOM II's lack of troop coordination.[27]

Finally, a guarantee of efficient coordination would make tenable the delegation of tactical, strictly military decisions from the Security Council to commanders in the field.[28] Such deference to the field commander has, at times, worked well in Bosnia. Certainly it is preferable to the intrusive hand the Security Council held over military operations in Somalia by virtue of Resolution 837, which authorized the pursuit and prosecution of Aidid. Security Council resolutions are awkwardly durable: they are binding on all members, not revocable by veto, and not subject to judicial review. This stickiness makes it difficult to reverse the momentum of an ill-advised resolution. In effectively making the hunt for Aidid policy rather than tactic, Resolution 837 tyrannized military strategy in Somalia for six months that culminated in disaster. Further, it replaced humanitarian relief and social reform with individual persecution as the focus of the peacekeeping mission.

In light of these considerations, a statutory prohibition on U.S. forces serving under any non-U.S. command, which Senator Dole has also proposed, is too rigid. The president will always have the power to withdraw troops where further engagement makes no sense, and the War Powers Act checks presidential indiscretion. Conceivably there will be circumstances in which the United States could make subsidiary military contributions with relatively few personnel. In those situations, there might be too few U.S. soldiers at risk to justify insistence on strategic command.

Presidential Decision Directive 25, issued in May 1994, offers adequate guidelines. It makes any commitment of U.S. troops subject to several conditions, including the advancement of American interests, the availability of personnel and funds, the support of Congress and the presence of clear objectives, the indispensability of U.S. participation, and acceptable command-and-control arrangements.[29] The other stated condition of the new policy—a clear projection of the end of U.S. participation—appears unrealistic. Again, assuming American troops are indispensable, the beneficiary population will tend to develop a dependence on them from which it must be weaned. It is impossible to set a timetable for this process in advance, as the Somalia experience has clearly shown. At the same time, control of the operation and a bold approach that keeps temporizing to a minimum will better enable the Pentagon to limit involvement and formulate an exit strategy once troops are on the ground.[30]

Basically, the Somalia experience put the lie to the post–Cold War proposition that reduced U.S. requirements for absolute force and the expectation of more cooperative military efforts also relaxes the need for fully independent command-and-control and intelligence capabilities. M.I.T. defense gurus Morrison, Tsipis, and Wiesner wrote in

February 1994 in *Scientific American*: "In the world we hope to enter, there is no reason for the U.S. to act so determinedly alone."[31] In light of Somalia, it seems rash to proffer this notion without qualification. October 3 came down, by default, to American capabilities. It is American strategic gospel that usable military power depends not on one scalar sum of firepower but on delivery through a multiplicity of vectors. Though obviously not forgotten, this dictate has been muted somewhat by the overwhelming force doctrine. It showed on October 3. Even if the U.N. Military Staff Committee is revitalized, the United Nations's ingrained phobia of intelligence operations will remain. And the new freestanding mechanism for harmonizing different armies will need cautious test runs, often with U.S. oversight. Clearly the need for flexible and comprehensive command-and-control and intelligence facilities, highly competent from White House briefing room down to Third World battlefield, is greater than ever. These are the sorts of capabilities that could be neatly lifted for detachment and put on loan to a U.N. peacekeeping operation, to which the United States could offer tactical support without insisting on overall command. Severable, freestanding tactical capabilities therefore are necessary and will flourish only if the U.S. military is maintained on the assumption that it will have to act without help. This approach favors small contingents, not huge ones like Operation Restore Hope's mobilization.

## FOURTH LESSON: LET SOLDIERS BE SOLDIERS

The small-force concept would automatically promote greater sensitivity than the Pentagon exercised in Somalia to the psychological limitations of ordinary noncommissioned soldiers. They do not typically consider themselves, as combat soldiers, to be suited to humanitarian efforts. Most enlisted personnel did not want to be in Somalia. Requiring U.S. troops to function as they were trained to function stands a better chance of keeping them alert—and therefore alive—than depositing them in a compound to serve as a passive deterrent. The barracks bombing in Lebanon in 1983, killing 242 U.S. Marines, is only the most obvious example. And if at all possible, the duration of their deployment as peacekeepers should be short. Keeping the peace simply is not a durable motivation to the line soldier. (As Delong and Tuckey note in *Mogadishu! Heroism and Tragedy* [7 and 83], GIs in Somalia—inspired by the then-popular movie of the same name—called every day

"Groundhog Day" because of the monotony of their mission.)

During the Clinton administration, the relationship between the military and its civilian leadership has reached a low point. The ebb was symbolized by President Clinton's initial refusal, on the advice of media advisor David Gergen, to make public appearances with the survivors of the October 3 firefight.[32] Most of the larger messages of the Gulf War and post-Vietnam military engagements have been muddled, but the one smaller message that is clear is that the U.S. volunteer military is a highly professional force that takes orders. It is an operational success. Arguably General Powell had enjoyed undue influence on the politics of the Somalia intervention—that is, in its being cast as the crowning vindication of the overwhelming force doctrine. If so, however, it is because civilian leadership neglected its role as the maker of defense policy. The military's function is to provide professional soldiering and render professional advice to the president and the Pentagon and not to lobby civilian leadership for a particular strategic approach the way a special interest group might. But when the executive branch has set forth no coherent policy, logically the military will feel obliged to fill the void.[33] General Powell, and General Shalikashvilli after him, have felt so obliged and as a result drew staff and field officers away from the line soldier. While they comforted hesitant newcomers in the Defense Department and the White House, they neglected thousands of soldiers sitting on their hands in a hot, remote desert, uncertain about why they were there.

Treating soldiers like soldiers would have helped. To use one of Thomas C. Schelling's old dichotomies, the American approach should be primarily one of "compellence" rather than deterrence.[34] Mishaps in Somalia suggest that in their general conception, overseas interventions are best structured as aggressive correctives of some misbehavior, not as mere shows of strength designed to deter by threat. Such a conception, by its formulation, calls for a firmly active, directed approach, finely tailored to a specific, limited goal. That approach, in turn, conforms to engagements designed to be limited in time rather than open-ended occupations, which are politically untenable to this Congress and foreseeable ones. On the psychological level, it embraces the reality that the men and women Washington sends overseas are professional soldiers trained to use force rather than diplomats used to waiting and cajoling. It's a simple point, but one worth noting, as it indexes a mindset quite different from that which dominated the Cold War.

## FIFTH LESSON: PREFER ACTIVE SECURITY TO PASSIVE FORCE

Energetic security enforcement is more effective in the static case than the passive stance suggested by the overwhelming force doctrine. Despite a thirty thousand–troop presence, the decisive battle for Mogadishu, such as it was, involved four hundred special-operations soldiers and an army quick-reaction force. (The October 3 operation qualifies in form as a focused and decisive strike, even though faulty intelligence doomed the mission.)

The mission also might have fared better with artillery and heavy armored support. In context, however, that sort of ordnance might well have infuriated Somalis used to UNOSOM II's inertia. The larger point, then, is that the United States should have established at the beginning of Operation Restore Hope that security would be territorial in scope rather than simply confined to areas occupied or convoys escorted by American soldiers, and its enforcement methods active rather than passive. UNOSOM II then could have reiterated the strategy, continued its execution, and in the process conditioned the antsy Somalis to genuine policing. Although there might have been some chance that Somalis would have viewed such an approach as intrusive, they could hardly have seen it as more egregiously occupying than a division-and-a-half that was, in the event, encamped inside their capital city. That kind of presence is neither necessary nor appropriate in operational environments like Somalia's. Eliot A. Cohen wrote astutely in *The New Republic,* "America's opponents ten years hence will surely have found other, less comfortable ways of securing success than by imitating Saddam Hussein. Indeed, as General Mohamed Farah Aidid has demonstrated in Somalia, they already have."[35]

Somalia should be the epitaph for the overwhelming force doctrine in all but out-and-out war. In particular, it should not apply to operations contemplating only urban guerrilla warfare with a dispersed enemy who is difficult to identify, as opposed to pitched battles with regular army units. On account of Vietnam, attrition was discarded as an overall military strategy, but the overwhelming force doctrine is not by itself a comprehensive alternative. If one objective of military action is political stabilization or nation building, force must be complemented with some form of pacification. Vietnam also demonstrated that ruthless schemes of dissident eradication like the Phoenix program don't work, either. One hopeful approach would appear to be to provide territorial security all the way down to the local level as a precondition for U.N.-aided political programs starting in the community and culminating in national reconciliation. In January 1993, Oakley himself observed that the singular lesson he took with him from Afghanistan was that "we must understand local development. Not much hooks Mogadishu to Somalia, just as not much hooks Kabul to the rest of Afghanistan."[36] That principle should have meant protecting traditional local political leaders from intimidation by the likes of Aidid.

In short, the prescription here is to trade off personnel for heavier weaponry and a greater degree of military activity. And that activity should include coercive disarmament and territorial security. As long as the indigenous population is forewarned and the cooperation of local authorities secured, the selective deployment of a relatively small, dynamic force could well be less provocative than a massive deployment like Restore Hope or UNOSOM II. Indeed, this is where warlord co-optation might have come in. In Somalia, the United States would have done well to negotiate with Aidid and Ali Mahdi in advance for the cooperation of their militias, perhaps as policemen subject to oversight, and distributed fliers before the marine landing explaining to Somalis that their presence would entail disarmament. Instead, Washington wasted the warlords' perishable receptivity by having troops storm Mogadishu's beach as they did Omaha and Utah in 1944. With misconception and procrastination, the idea of rejuvenating a Somali police force died on the vine and was not effectively revived for eighteen months.

The American initiative was at once grandiose and wishy-washy. There is some evidence that Washington is learning. In the wake of the February 5, 1994, bombing in Sarajevo, an American-driven NATO resolved to order air strikes against Serbian artillery emplacements unless the Serbs submitted those positions to U.N. supervision. When the stubborn and combative Serbs capitulated, the ultimatum proved sobering enough to compel compliance but also sufficiently modest to leave dormant the Serb penchant for military grandstanding.

The subsidiary point here is that there is still a place for controlled brinkmanship. In fact, it may be the operational standard for the kind of small-force peacekeeping urged here. Query, again, whether a military ultimatum to Aidid might have been a more effective means of compellence than a bounty hunt. In the postmortem of October 3, U.S. intelligence agencies admitted in retrospect that hunting for one military man intent on hiding on his own turf was folly. As camouflaged as Aidid's irregulars were, surely they made more identifiable and acquirable targets than the general alone. Gradually neutralizing them through capture and disarmament—with a promise of more military pressure, absent Aidid's capitulation—probably would have brought the general around with fewer political and human losses. Although the dynamic might sound suspiciously Vietnamesque, Somalia's relatively small and sparse population, clan divisions, and lack of a large outside arms wholesaler made the prospect of Aidid's replenishing his corps, unlike Ho Chi Minh's in 1967, very dim indeed. Greater military pressure, brought to bear earlier, might have given the warlords a stronger incentive to reconcile, particularly if linked to more energetic political brokering. Again, these are considerations that a more searching approach to tactical intelligence might have percolated up to the planning level.

Still, not all plans, even the best-laid ones, will have such agreeable results as the air strike gambit in Bosnia. Projecting the worst case should retain the time-honored place that it has among national security spoilers. As a practical matter, this rule-of-thumb will usually mean guarding against uncheckable escalation by controlling risks. Even here, NATO's action in Bosnia in early 1994 was a recent example. The United States and western Europe were wise in electing not to punish the Serbs with aerial bombardment without warning, and instead to issue a challenge. Their gravest concern was Russia, whose leading opposition politician stated that he would consider an air attack on the Serbs an attack on Russia, forcing Boris Yeltsin into the same stance, at least officially. Had NATO bombed immediately, domestic politics might have forced Yeltsin to move in the Serbs' defense. As it happened, the Western powers relinquished the initiative to the Serbs, and in doing so gave Yeltsin the political leeway to blame the Serbs for missing an opportunity and refrain from actively supporting them.

NATO's flexible firmness paid the added dividend of inducing Russia both to convince the Serbs to pull back and to unilaterally send eight hundred peacekeeping troops of its own. Although there was an element of ominous counteraggression to Yeltsin's move, ultimately it set a higher tone for regional involvement and resolution—precisely what the United Nations and the United States should encourage.

## SIXTH LESSON: KEEP VIETNAM IN PERSPECTIVE

Don't forget Vietnam, but don't be a slave to its memory either. The caveat is easy to say, hard to fulfill. Clearly the painful heritage of sixty thousand dead Americans in Vietnam inspired the doctrine of overwhelming force, honed to a fine edge with the succession of Grenada in 1983, Panama in 1989, and the Gulf War in 1991. More broadly, it reflects the rediscovery of American commanders' extraordinary parsimoniousness with the lives of their soldiers—particularly in World War II but nominally in Vietnam itself, where a 1-to-10 kill ratio favored the Americans. What the doctrine fails to embrace fully, however, is that the strategic philosophy that allowed American generals such impressive human conservation was one of flanking and maneuver, as opposed to head-to-head set-piece engagement. General Douglas MacArthur, World War II's biggest tightwad in terms of his own men, always advocated agility, diversion, and the element of surprise over attritional slugging matches. Applying such tactics requires relatively few soldiers in perpetual motion, not a sedentary assemblage standing like a Maginot line to face the enemy. At the same time, they call for the best and the most equipment. This too is consonant with American military tradition, in which combat technique has depended on the full use of industrial facilities. "We are holding the line with ammunition, and not with the lives of our troops," wrote Harry Truman in his diary during the Korean war.[37] For the president to retain the military flexibility the Constitution allows him as commander-in-chief, against Congress's secular disinclination to sacrifice American lives, that should remain the American philosophy.

Indeed, it should remain the American philosophy simply because it is both humane and self-protective. The efficacy of an approach stressing small, mobile units and high technology, however, depends critically on aggressive rules of engagement. The Vietnam War, it is true, also sensitized the U.S. military to both the moral impropriety and the public-relations disaster of civilian deaths from military operations "while trying to pound a tiny backward nation into submission on an issue whose merits are hotly disputed," wrote Robert McNamara.[38] But he was referring to the peasants killed with bombs and napalm dropped from the air. It is almost inconceivable that peacekeeping operations will ever call for such tactics. Civilian deaths will instead occur from an errant burst from the M-16 of the occasional jumpy soldier. American soldiers must be permitted to fire preemptively—that is, before they are fired upon. Provided they are appropriately trained, unjustified casualties would be kept to a minimum.

## SEVENTH LESSON: PLAN FOR DECENT INTERVALS

This is the Good Samaritan rule: though humanitarian intervention is an extraordinary remedy, once applied, its termination should be structured so as to allow the beneficiary population to be weaned of its dependence on foreign troops.[39] This means primarily two things. First, military commitments cannot be artificially limited. Although bold, quick strokes are intended to make the needs for foreign manpower manageably finite, inevitable discrepancies between planning and execution call for flexibility. Furthermore, in general, troop withdrawal should be accomplished in phases rather than in one massive, potentially traumatic redeployment. A graduated program to build overall self-sufficiency—bureaucratic entities, enforcement institutions like police forces, welfare agencies—should complement phased withdrawal in order to minimize any shock to the indigenous system.

Second, the secretary-general's office and the governments participating in the peacekeeping operation should ensure that development programs and U.N.-sponsored political management facilities are in place to maintain peace and generate self-sufficiency. Having invested the time, expense, and humanity to pacify a hell-hole, the United States and the United Nations derogate their own sacrifices if they fail to protect their gains. Such an objective, of course, must be fulfilled within affordable limits. Here, in contrast with the strictly military context, the United States might profitably insist on U.N. coordination and oversight. At present, USAID is providing virtually no supervision for CARE's monetization of food markets in Somalia with USAID food contributions. It cannot afford to do so—with Washington's current inclination toward frugality and insularity, the State Department is streamlining USAID's operations and may even eliminate it as a discrete bureaucratic entity. On the other hand, by the preamble to its charter, the primary brief of the United Nations is "to employ international machinery for the promotion of the economic and social advancement of all peoples." This, indeed, is putatively the principal mission of the secretary-general's office. The

United States contributes almost 32 percent of the budget of the United Nations.[40] That the United Nations should help administer U.S. development programs, then, is consistent with legal and financial reality. More than that, by lowering American administrative costs, exploiting the United Nations as an aid vector would free up more dollars for direct Third World benefit.

## THE FUTURE

Harmonized, these lessons call for: preventive diplomacy, flexibility in U.S. intervention policy, limited humanitarian intervention in the event of failure, a bolder approach to peacekeeping and a streamlined command structure, a clearer allocation of competence between the Security Council and ground commanders, and follow-up development. This guideline, though comprehensive, is hardly a revelation. It seems only a matter of common sense. In the future, it is worth recalling that common sense never really took hold in Somalia. If these lessons are taken to heart, Somalia's memory will serve as inspiration rather than lament.

Despite the forsaken opportunities, it is probably still not too late for Somalia. Washington and U.N. brass are to blame for losing sight of the political track of a "two-track" policy in favor of the military evisceration of Aidid. But solving Somalia's problems is not merely a matter of adjusting priorities. It also requires a harder look at the Somalis' unique brand of politics.

The chief problem is that Somalis' memories of anarchy are all too fond. Before Siad Barre took over in 1969, Somalia was in essence a pastoralist anarchy, in which clans and subclans co-existed in territorial equilibrium. When the balance was disrupted, one clan would side with an oppressed one until the aggressive clan was brought back into line, whether by crude battle or simply by camel raids. It was grazing land and livestock, not larger political power, that mattered.

Superpower backing gave Siad Barre the military means of shifting the balance permanently in favor of his clan. Now each clan wants what Siad Barre's had—essentially, absolute power—and would reach that end by the customary Somali method of shifting alliances. Thus, Aidid courted the United States; then, when he got the cold shoulder, turned to Islamic fundamentalists. With over one hundred thousand automatic weapons around and clans reluctant to disperse power, however, scrambling for political equilibrium gets a tad more brutal than rustling did in the old days.

Given these realities of Somali culture, it seems plain that broad, coercive disarmament was the appropriate first step to a political solution, and securing territorial stability for each Somali faction the second. But the American and U.N. commands, maladroitly defining their mission on the fly, undertook these tasks only tentatively and sporadically. Finally they gave up and let Somalis carry guns as long as they were registered.

By March 1994, the most feared enforcers were heading for home, and the United Nations faced a crisis of leadership and confidence; it was too late for UNOSOM II to start over. When the Security Council passed Resolution 865 on September 22, 1993, it nominally locked in the goal of nation building by authorizing a U.N. presence through 1995. In fact, though, at this point resurrection of the politic is essentially up to the Somalis themselves. The only useful product of the U.N.-sponsored Addis Ababa peace conference of March 1993 was the faction leaders' embryonic concept of a "transitional national council" with regional representation. A year later it hadn't translated into tangible progress because the Aidid bounty hunt precluded any attempts to create the right initial conditions. Once Aidid wore out the United Nations and turned into a virtual statesman, he became the sole occupant of a power vacuum in the capital of Somalia. The most realistic hope is that the United Nations, regional groups, or friendly interlopers like former U.S. president Jimmy Carter can prevail upon Aidid to try to disarm the civilian population himself.

The imam of Hirab, traditional Muslim leader of Aidid's clan, has also urged peace between Aidid and intraclan arch-rival Ali Mahdi Mohamed, and the clan elders are behind him. Although it is unlikely that his influence could extend outside his own clan, he could significantly check Aidid's bellicosity. Certainly a sound knowledge of local customs and culture and the consequent grooming of leaders like the imam should be elements of any U.S. or U.N. plan of political regeneration.

If the guns could somehow be confined to factional militia—which, by the way, was the linchpin of the American plan in March 1993—it is possible that, as in the nomadic Somalia of yore, skirmishing could become containable and equilibrium attainable. From that point, where each faction would enjoy a firm territorial power base, faction leaders might become sufficiently comfortable to engender some form of power-sharing body as a feasible vehicle for national governance.

It bears remembering that such a body might not square with Western democratic principles. Somalia watchers at the United Nations and elsewhere should be neither surprised nor alarmed if it does not. What's good for Switzerland is not necessarily good for Somalia. This is especially true for African cultures, like Somalia's, in which group entitlements are valued more than individual rights. "Free and fair" elections tend to bring civil degeneracy to African nations and pave the way for coups and dictatorships; Kenya, Angola, Nigeria, and Burundi are only the most recent examples. In Somalia, collective clan acclamation, lodged locally through traditional channels of elders, is likely to work better. Certainly it has kept the peace in Hoddur, for example, where Mohamed Nur Shoduk, the eighty-year-old elder, has quietly governed for fifty-five years through Siad Barre, the Ogaden war, and Aidid.

But prospects remain bleak. After four postponements of Somali peace talks over the neutrality of the venue, they were scheduled for May 30, 1994, in Nairobi, but neither Aidid nor Ali Mahdi showed up. Although Boutros-Ghali recommended a six-month extension of UNOSOM II, the United States, threatening a veto, cowed the Security Council into granting only a four-month reprieve. In November 1994, the Security Council decided to withdraw all U.N. troops by March 31, 1995. Meanwhile, aid agencies were asking for $70.3 million in emergency aid as Aidid's and Ali Mahdi's factions prepared to resume battle unimpeded.

## THINKING THE UNTHINKABLE

During the Cold War, Herman Kahn urged policy makers to "think about the unthinkable"—thermonuclear war—to ensure it would remain out of the question.[41] In the new world order, however, with U.N. peacekeeping facilities stretched far beyond capacity, the unthinkable has come to be the prospect of a failed state without recourse. It is a looming reality.

Washington and the United Nations are partially to blame for failing to redress Somalia's problems efficaciously. Yet disarmament and securing territorial stability were made difficult by the Somali factions' mobility and guile over a broad expanse of terrain. These factors arguably made large-scale military intervention inappropriate in the first place. I have suggested here what measures might have worked better in regenerating Somalia *given* intervention. Still, the very magnitude of the mistakes and the highly speculative nature of the alternatives offered lead ineluctably to the conviction that sometimes intervention is plain futile.

Rwanda is the latest test. The situation there is very different from Somalia's. Only two main tribes—the Hutu and the Tutsi—compete for hegemony in Rwanda, as opposed to the many clans that vie for control in Somalia. Two ethnically dominated armies, not several factional militia, are the agents of civil war in Rwanda. The precolonial framework in Rwanda was not anarchical but, to the contrary, feudal. Most importantly, whereas Somalia is sparsely populated, Rwanda's population is among the densest in the world.

From a humanitarian point of view, it is tempting to say that these distinctions make a large-scale military presence appropriate in Rwanda. A concentrated population is easier to control by overwhelming force; so are the regular and semiregular military corps that hold the weapons in Rwanda. And with only Hutus and Tutsis to worry about, the marginalization of less powerful factions that made an indigenous consensus so difficult to generate in Somalia is a far smaller threat in Rwanda.

But there are other less salutary differences. The majority Hutu appear to be engaged in a campaign of genuine ethnic eradication, which was one of the few banes that did not infect Somalia. Also, Somalia's large size makes it possible for each faction to establish a firm and discrete territorial power base, which might (some day) make faction leaders sufficiently at ease to arrive at some form of federal body. Such factional segregation is probably infeasible in Rwanda because of its minuteness. Under the interventionist argument, both distinctions would make direct and impartial policing an all-the-more-urgent prerequisite to political reconciliation.

Nonetheless, under the criteria set forth here, wholesale intervention in Rwanda remains dubious. Although once again the United Nations failed to assume an anticipatory and proactive role on the political front, and once again regional groups appear paralyzed, there are no bold, responsive military missions that a peacemaking/peacekeeping force could hope to accomplish. The conflict between the Hutu and the

Tutsi is starkly tribal, and the rebel Rwanda Patriotic Front's resistance to the government army relatively well organized and focused. Once on the ground, a large military force would have little to do besides enforce cease-fires and secure safe havens. Those tasks naturally do have an important immediate purpose—namely, saving lives. But the rub is that sooner or later, the United Nations's money and the contributing members' patience will run out, and the troops will have to leave. The chances that a U.N. political mission will be able to defuse the ancient tribal enmity during that period—that is, the prospects for a decent interval—are virtually nil. The solution to the Rwandan conflict, now as well as later, appears to rest squarely with the Rwandans themselves.

Provided the two opposing forces in Rwanda can at least reach truces to stop the slaughter on their own, the United Nations, the United States, and other member nations should be prepared to leave the pacification of Rwanda to its own people. (If that sounds cold, query whether the Somalis would be palpably worse off now had Operation Restore Hope never happened, remembering that the famine mortality rate had dropped most precipitously the month *before* the Americans arrived.) As an intermediary measure, the United Nations could make available the good offices of the secretary-general and their respective diplomatic corps, as well as a small military force to harbor refugees at the Rwandan borders.

The United States's misgivings, it is true, about where to deploy even a small (5,500-troop) force to Rwanda delayed an otherwise enthusiastic Security Council from immediately sending the soldiers.[42] This dilatoriness was roundly criticized by the international press as a combination of paranoia and exculpation stemming from the Somalia experience. In the *Independent,* Richard Dowden accused Washington of "trying to present its intervention in Somalia as some U.N. foul-up in which it unfortunately became entangled."[43] The explanations of American diplomats rather suggested that although failure in Somalia certainly informed their concerns, their intention was simply to use that experience constructively. Madeleine K. Albright, the U.S. ambassador to the United Nations, testified to Congress, "We want to be confident that when we do turn to the U.N., the U.N. will be able to do the job."[44] This reflected some appreciation for the fact that armed peacekeepers create a dependence that must be sustainable over the period of political resurrection—a fact that was neglected in the case of

Somalia. Indeed, Ambassador Albright characterized the Rwanda crisis as the first test of Presidential Decision Directive 25, which arose out of U.S. involvement in Somalia.[45]

By the same token, insofar as it operates inside the boundaries of a nation, the primary function of the United Nations or any other peacekeeping entity is to promote political stability consistent with indigenous culture, within certain broad limits imposed by human rights. If, in achieving that objective, the United Nations can effectively use blue berets or even armies, it should not be afraid to press member nations to provide them, or to encourage volunteers. The lesson of Somalia is not for member nations to eschew military intervention categorically but rather for them to examine carefully whether it makes sense under local conditions, which are particularly idiosyncratic in the Third World, and most acutely among the fifty-two countries of Africa. This imperative means acting sensibly and fairly and not necessarily instinctively. The world community's reflex is to send the cavalry to the rescue. But its endeavor must be to make sure the cavalry, as a scarce resource in heavy demand, can help enough to justify its withdrawal from the market.

# 10 The United States and the United Nations

The United Nations was conceived as the institutionalized exhortation to true internationalism: the resolution of global disputes by means of an international consensus harmonized by and embodied in a single agency. It has had its moments of apparent fulfillment, the most recent and dramatic being the Gulf War. But more often than not, it has functioned as little more than a front for the policies and viewpoints for the permanent members of the Security Council—in particular, the United States, its largest contributor. The degree of control the United States exerts over the Security Council became evident in May 1994, when it stalled an otherwise unanimously prointervention council from even voting on whether to send 5,500 troops into Rwanda merely by voicing its reservations. It did not have to exercise its veto formally, and at no time did Washington even contemplate sending American troops. U.S. officials said they feared "another Somalia."[1]

Unilateralism, then, is certainly not dead, but lately it has been ensconced in the trappings of multilateral U.N. action. Frankly, the Gulf War was an instance of unilateralism—the United States would have gone in regardless of the Security Council resolution. And President Bush probably would have launched Operation Restore Hope, in substantially the same form, even if the rest of the Security Council had blanched. But because the United Nations did tender resolutions, both engagements looked—and tried to look—like genuine triumphs of international consensus. In early 1994, John R. Bolton pointed out, "There is no multilateral system with a life of its own. There is only leadership by one or more like-minded nations that persuades the United Nations's other members to follow."[2] Although cosmetics have always mattered to the inspirational value of the United Nations, when things go wrong, cloaking unilateral initiatives in U.N. garb only ends up damaging the United Nations as an institution.

Nothing went wrong in the Gulf War. Plenty went wrong in Somalia. Indeed, UNOSOM II is an embodiment of U.N. flaws. Of the $1.6 billion earmarked to save Somalia, only about $72 million will be used for actual development assistance. Thanks to the precedent established by the sheer scale of Operation Restore Hope—a precedent very difficult to reverse—most of the money will go to the contributing governments to maintain a large troop presence there. The standard U.N. rates paid to members contributing armed forces are $1,063 monthly per soldier, with a $291 premium for those with special expertise. Each soldier also gets $1.28 per day to keep. In the United Nations's seven-month budget for November 1993 through May 1994, that translated to almost $200 million in compensation to member states for the nineteen thousand peacekeepers in Somalia. The costs of hardware depreciation, food rations, redeployment, aircraft leasing, spare parts, petroleum products, and infrastructure increased the bill by $225 million. The United Nations budgeted an additional $61.3 million for logistical support, as well as $6.3 million for death and disability payments.[3] The United Nations's disarmament, demobilization, and demining office was allotted only $7.6 million, for clearing mines.[4]

The payments are windfalls to poor countries like Bangladesh, which assigned almost one thousand troops to Somalia. But ideally, money should not be the primary motivation for participating in peacekeeping efforts. The more appropriate incentive would be a sense of duty combined with a practical desire to use soldiers for the function they have been trained to perform. As the American experience in Somalia has shown, however, national armies are not in fact trained for peacekeeping, generally do not much care for it, and are not very good at it.[5]

This reality is perhaps the best argument for the establishment of a specially trained standing U.N. army, though not one that has been forcefully put forth. Participants in the debate see expense as a major barrier to a standing army. If, however, the small-force concept were brought to bear, U.N. savings on downstream expenses would substantially offset initial investment and maintenance charges. Some would argue that a standing army would attract merely a new breed of mercenaries. But U.N. recruits, unlike the soldiers from national armies that now make up blue-beret corps, would be specifically trained for peacemaking and peacekeeping rather than the defense of the realm.[6] As suggested, they could also be conditioned in advance to work as a unit. Divergence among military styles made enforcement in Somalia far more difficult than it need have been. For example, the Americans were aggressive whereas the Egyptians were passive, so the Somalis skewed their aggression toward the Egyptians. On the other hand, the relative trigger-happiness of the Americans, both before and after October 3, initially led to exaggerated assessments of the Somalis' bellicosity and the military risk they imposed and ultimately became a self-fulfilling prophecy. Members of the Canadian Airborne Regiment, whet for battle rather than peacekeeping, ended up committing torture and murder.

Further, corruption contributed to ineffectual peacekeeping. Egyptians, with paltry salaries and their mere $1.28 daily U.N. stipend, would accept bribes from Somalis simply to feign resistance to raids and permit thievery. An integrated professional army, adequately funded and appropriately trained, would help solve all these problems. They may yet afflict the Haitian intervention, which was authorized by a Security Council resolution materially identical to the one that blessed Operation Restore Hope, likewise was to be led by the United States and drew only token initial support from four small and militarily inexperienced Caribbean nations.[7] And the fact is, after Somalia, most governments will be hard-pressed politically to order national armies to perform the ostensibly altruistic task of peacekeeping. Consider, for example, the difficulty the French encountered recruiting partners for their intervention in Rwanda.[8]

More refined and customized training would also address concerns about peacekeeping forces' neglect of human rights. Characterizing UNOSOM II's human rights practices as "disastrous," a January 1994

Amnesty International report stated: "The U.N. has so far failed to build essential measures for human rights promotion and protection consistently into its peacekeeping activities. It is time for the U.N. to develop a more coherent and comprehensive approach."[9]

Finally, a standing army would minimize the possibility of neocolonial action clothed as internationalism, of which the Americans were accused (baselessly) in Somalia,[10] and the French were accused (perhaps more defensibly) in Rwanda.[11] A force with a collegial mode of command, worked out before deployment, would tend to be less susceptible to unilateral manipulation.

Opponents of a standing U.N. army also raise a more substantial obstacle to its realization. Such an army, they say, would vest excessive power in the secretary-general and lead to supranationalism.[12] This fear can be assuaged only by clarifying to what extent sovereignty remains inviolate under international law, and when unilateral intervention can occur in place of U.N. action. If nations can be assured of nonintervention in their internal affairs under a consistent set of criteria, and of their legitimate power to act on their own to protect their interests or those of their friends, then a standing U.N. army would be less threatening and more palatable.

From the standpoint of U.N. legitimacy, too, it is surely better to call unilateral action what it is than to give it a U.N. rubber stamp and call it multilateral. UNOSOM II illustrates the point. In fall 1993, an Italian businessman named Giancarlo Marocchino was snatched by American Rangers, detained and questioned for five days, then deported to Italy. Admiral Howe reportedly suspected him of running guns to Aidid and considered him a public enemy. But clan elders and Ali Mahdi—Aidid's *enemy*—sent a letter to Howe saying they considered Marocchino a son, pointing out the fact that he was married to a Somali, and declaring that only Somalis had the right to deport him. Eventually Marocchino was allowed back into Somalia, but the damage had been done. Ali Mahdi was the one warlord who had welcomed the United Nations all along; now the U.N. special envoy had offended him. More generally, with the Americans having decisively alienated the Somalis, UNOSOM II missed a clear chance to look benevolent by comparison and rescue its tarnished reputation among the Somalis. In the end, though, unilateral American action in the guise of multilateral U.N. action only plunged the United Nations's esteem lower.[13]

Alluding to the October 3 disaster, *The Economist* observed: "The United States, acting on its own, has a fair chance of getting away with high-handed action. . . . The consequences are more damaging when America acts impulsively within the U.N.'s framework."[14] How, then, should the power to intervene be allocated between sovereign powers and the United Nations?

Morton Halperin has suggested that the United Nations extend a legal guarantee of a republican form of government, like that accorded states by the federal constitution, to nations, and that the United States confine military intervention explicitly to U.N. enforcements of that guarantee under chapter 7.[15] In other words, he proposes that the United States abandon unilateral intervention as an instrument of foreign policy. This is a radical proposal. In almost any civil war, the government won't consent to U.N. intervention, has interfered with no other country's dominion, and has not jeopardized international peace in any substantial way. In those circumstances, the U.N. Charter, even with Halperin's guarantee added, bars intervention.

Shirley Hazzard has pointed out, "The public interest has never been represented in U.N. Councils, except as dubiously interpreted by governments."[16] Neither unorganized populations nor their individual members have standing to initiate protests of mass mistreatment in the United Nations or the World Court; only sovereign states and the U.N. secretary-general himself have such standing. A sympathetic nation or the secretary-general may propose a repressed people's plight for redress, but there is no guarantee that it will produce actual relief. This failure could be due simply to a lack of authority, or it might result from the veto of some permanent member of the Security Council with its own agenda.

Yet to accord any subgovernmental group or individual the right to petition the General Assembly or the Security Council would portend a procedural nightmare. It makes better sense to acknowledge that the United Nations was created not to provide exclusive remedies for injustices visited by putatively sovereign powers, but rather to inspire their consensual alleviation by a community of nations. U.N. remedies needn't be exclusive.

Equity, then, favors a right of unilateral intervention. Lloyd Cutler actually proposed such a right in a conspicuously ignored 1985 article in *Foreign Affairs*.[17] The crux of Cutler's argument, like Halperin's, was that a repressed majority has a right to be liberated from an antidemocratic tyrant. Such a right seems an easy extension of human rights and the right of self-determination in the sense that liberation paves the way for the recognition of those rights.

The dicier issue is when another country may enforce that right militarily on the majority's behalf. There may be a few cases whose merit is intuitively obvious, but most post–World War II moves even remotely styled broadly as humanitarian rescues have been problematic: Vietnam, Grenada, Nicaragua, Panama, and now Somalia. Under what conditions could a right to unilateral intervention be contained?

The first condition is fairly obvious. The United Nations must have censured the activity of the target state. Otherwise the intervening state would be entitled to circumvent internationalist organizations that conventionally express the collective voice in the matter. Skirting the recognized authority of such groups would be rankly inconsistent with the sensitivity to global consensus that has become paramount in a shrinking post–Cold War world. A prospective intervener, as a member of the United Nations or other body, should first have to petition the Security Council for a resolution condemning the conduct of the target state and actually obtain such a ruling. Governments in civil conflict, of course, would also remain free to lobby against Security Council partisanship or involvement, as Yemen's government did in May 1994.

The second condition is almost as straightforward: a refusal to intervene by the United Nations (or the appropriate regional body). Again, multilateral remedies in general, and Security Council remedies in particular, should be preferred for the simple, compelling reason that consensus underpins international law. And again, fulfilling the condition would require a nation looking to make a move to propose a resolution calling for U.N. intervention to the Security Council and have it be rejected.

Third, to warrant unilateral intervention, a civil conflict should be of large enough magnitude to jeopardize regional security under chapter 7. In this vein, Cutler identified two useful, if somewhat attenuated, criteria: the existence of a prodemocratic insurgency and the complicity of a third state in the repressive action. The idea is that these circumstances reflect, respectively, an indigenous population's extreme dissatisfaction with the government, and the government's inability to enlist intramural support of sufficient strength to carry out its policies. Together, they spell the absence of a popular mandate in the target country that could produce refugees in such large numbers as to disrupt neighboring countries' economies and security through saturation and banditry. Somalia viv-à-vis Kenya or Ethiopia would qualify here, and Sudan is getting close, over one hundred thousand refugees each having poured into Ethiopia, Kenya, and Uganda.

A tandem of more direct criteria might include the exodus or attempted exodus of a large number of citizens and the repressive regime's operational dependence on a demonstrably criminal enterprise independent of the regime, like a drug cartel or a terrorist group. Consider, respectively, the flight of the Haitians and Manuel Noriega's "narco-military state" in Panama.[18] Neither condition in isolation seemed to justify intervention. Had both occurred in Panama, though, serious international objections to the United States's invasion might not have arisen.

Fourth, the unilateral action must not contravene international law. This means two things: either human rights or the right of self-determination must have been violated; further, the United Nations's refusal to authorize multilateral intervention must have rested on the judgment that the United Nations lacks the power to intervene, as opposed to its judgment that intervention is morally unwarranted. In practice, both elements will usually obtain when the United Nations has already censured a country's domestic policies. For instance, the General Assembly has overwhelmingly condemned Khartoum's conduct of the civil war in Sudan as a campaign of ethnic cleansing. But the Security Council is unlikely to authorize U.N. intervention because the government has not projected its military aggression over its borders and will not consent to any foreign troops inside them.

Under these four criteria, unilateral intervention would complement U.N. remedies rather than compete with them. In practice, such interventions would be considered acceptable only when the United Nations had condemned the conduct of the target country but determined that it had no power to act. Properly used, the remedy would be employed to defend the rights of repressed peoples with no coercive means of their own for doing so.

At the same time, the four conditions outlined here should ensure that any legal unilateral intervention will be in defense of general populations, as opposed to special interests. It's not a new idea. In 1988, Captain Benjamin Dean wrote in the *Military Law Review*:

> If self-determination as a coequal principle [to that of nonintervention] is to have any meaning in the law on the support of insurgents, it at least has to consider the legitimacy of a government in power, as viewed in the same way the people themselves perceive their government. The issue becomes whether the use of force has been applied against the political independence of a government that has its legal basis in the will of the governed. The issue also involves such factors as the state of the governed as a people, and the pervasiveness of state repression against fundamental freedoms.[19]

In his June 1992 report, "An Agenda for Peace," Secretary-General Boutros-Ghali himself noted, "The time for absolute sovereignty . . . has passed" and offered instead "a balance between the needs of good internal governance and the requirements of an ever more independent world."[20] Finally, a June 1992 General Assembly resolution made a government's request for and consent to humanitarian intervention merely preferable rather than mandatory, and qualified consent in any event as being popular rather than executive in principle.[21]

The unilateral right to intervene offered here calls for probing factual inquiries to determine the legality of particular interventions. It has overtones of "natural law" that may somewhat discomfit international lawyers long wedded to cautious positivism.[22] But if the choice is between black-letter rules that proscribe unilateral intervention absolutely and flexible but self-limiting rules that call for some consideration of facts and context, the latter seem preferable[23]—both from an internationalist standpoint and from the standpoint of potential beneficiaries of unilateral intervention.

The editors of London's *Independent* wrote of the United Nations in November 1993, "Harmonious chaos is an elegant description of the natural state of things, but it is not desirable for an organization guiding the world into a new century."[24] The world body then found itself engaged in fifteen new peacekeeping operations—more than double the number it had undertaken during its first forty years. Even excluding the Americans in Somalia, sixty thousand troops were under direct U.N. command. But the motivation of most of the governments supplying them was primarily financial; any commitment to peace through international consensus was vague and distant and tended to acquire focus only for the nations like the United States that could afford the luxury of idealism. Using unmotivated timeservers as peacekeepers could work during the Cold War, when defensive rules of engagement effected a passive deterrent. But Somalia has shown that a more aggressive approach is needed where combatants are no longer accountable to "made" dictators like Siad Barre. With that need comes the exigency of directed professional troops, driven by the principles of the institution that dispatches them. Strong consensus in the United Nations will draw such troops to the fore, but weak consensus probably won't. That is where unilateral intervention may prove useful.

Whether intervention is unilateral or U.N.-sanctioned, peace once made should be maintained over the long term. Although this responsibility is ultimately that of the indigenous government, failed and failing states need time—that is, decent intervals—in which to generate workable institutions. In *Foreign Policy*, Helman and Ratner suggested graduated levels of U.N. "conservatorship": governance assistance for failing states like, say, Zaire or Georgia; delegation of governmental authority to the United Nations for failed states like Somalia; and, if more oversight is required, international trusteeship.[25] Such a system would require substantial amendment of the U.N. Charter, which does not contemplate the first two forms of supervision and states that trusteeship does "not apply to territories which have become members of the United Nations."[26]

The appropriate amendments would, however, be consistent with the more qualified view of sovereignty espoused by Boutros-Ghali, among others, and suggested here. Helman and Ratner assert that properly drafted, the amendments would set forth selective criteria (perhaps resembling those for instituting voluntary and involuntary bankruptcy) for establishing and maintaining each of the three types of conservatorship; an administrative framework for oversight; an operational organ for managing conservatorship programs; and a financial plan. Through these structures, the United Nations could, as suggested, coordinate development projects as well as political reconstruction.

With its promise, the end of the Cold War has brought new problems. Superpower sponsorships have been lifted and no longer hold together intrinsically weak governments. Unless consensus dictates the abandonment of crippled states, which is improbable, world opinion will call for far more interventions than it has in the past. For the United States to guide the post–Cold War world, economically as well as politically, it must be an ethical standard-bearer as well as a main provider. This means helping to save even marginal states like Somalia. The quirks of sovereignty (however relaxed the working definition becomes) will often proscribe U.N. authorization of justifiable military intervention through the Security Council, whether or not there is a standing U.N. army at the ready. The United States should be prepared to step in. But once the spadework of pacification has been accomplished, only maintenance and development of the beneficiary country's self-sufficiency makes the game worth the candle. That, however, the United States cannot afford to provide. Although it can and should contribute development aid and perhaps provide residual military assistance, the operating costs of nation building should be borne by the world as a whole, through the corporate medium of the United Nations. Helman and Ratner's suggestions seem a good start.

By the same token, the United Nations's "corporate" resources are limited to what the contributions of the member nations can provide. Conservatorships cannot be blithely open ended and should be subject to periodic review under strict criteria. Although the $1.2 billion Congress appropriated in August 1994 was more than enough to cover the United States's $950 million peacekeeping arrearage to the United Nations, Congress refused to authorize the $300 million requested by the White House for the American share of operations in Somalia, the former Yugoslavia, and Kuwait.[27] The general approach should be to condition further peacekeeping and humanitarian aid on indigenous political progress, as the United States did in May 1994 by threatening to veto a six-month extension of the U.N. mission in Somalia absent palpable advances by July in reconstituting the government. (The Security Council settled on a four-month extension, subject to revocation.)

The centerpiece of U.S. and U.N. policy, then, should be to encourage troubled countries to help themselves to become reasonably self-sufficient, politically and economically. For the United States (or any other single country) to take on the wholesale burden of resurrecting or manufacturing a nation is generally inadvisable—that is among the lessons of Vietnam and one that Washington has tried, with great difficulty, to abide by in Somalia. Practically, the United States initially did stage a unilateral intervention, notwithstanding the U.N. banner. Officially, it withdrew relatively soon (after five months) and left the rebuilding of Somalia to the United Nations. Admittedly the task has not gone smoothly. But there is a silver lining in Somalia's cloudy example. The operative modality there was one nation spearheading military intervention, with the United Nations then assuming the long-term role of nation-rebuilder. It seems an approach that should apply as well to unilateral interventions undertaken in the breach between U.N. power and U.N. mandate in order to bring them into convergence. Whether the French are able to coordinate their intervention in Rwanda with the deployment of a U.N.-sanctioned force will apparently be the first test of this approach.[28]

More importantly, however, the gap between power and mandate should be narrowed institutionally and permanently, so as to minimize the need for intervention altogether. Mohamed Sahnoun offered the simplest prescription shortly after his reluctant departure as U.N. special envoy for Somalia. "The whole function of the United Nations is to develop an early-warning system and a process of intervention which must be constant," he said. "Wherever there's oppression or a violation of human rights, the secretary-general must take the initiative of sending wise men very quickly."[29] It is that capacity that the United Nations should develop and entrench above all others. The Anglo-French suggestion of a standing diplomatic corps of crack analysts and negotiators, to be dispatched during the early stages of gathering strife—a kind of diplomatic quick-reaction force—would make preventive diplomacy possible in its purest form.[30]

There would remain limitations inherent even in a retooled United Nations with a standing army, an institutionally shorter diplomatic response time, and broader conservatorship powers. Operation Restore Hope demonstrated that humanitarian intervention leads unavoidably to the task of political resurrection. And that task requires medium-term policing that no standing army could be expected to provide and a reconstruction of civil infrastructure that no conservatorship could accomplish on its own. Only sovereign nations are equipped to perform these functions. Optimally, the failed state itself would manufacture the sovereign power needed. In most cases, though, outside help from an established country would be the most expeditious solution, but that would entail a daunting commitment (military and diplomatic) that most nations would be loath to make. At the end of the day, then, it is likely that the country in need, having been helped to its knees, will have to struggle to its feet substantially on its own.[31]

The sticking point for U.N. or unilateral intervention remains the same: Whether it can work well enough at an acceptable cost. The tough question, of course, is what is "acceptable"? Military and political considerations are important and have occupied the lion's share of this book. Yet humanitarian intervention in general—and Somalia in particular—have acquired their poignancy through the moral pressure exerted by world opinion. Global outcry against the United Nations's neglect of Somalia, juxtaposed with its attentions to Bosnia-Herzogovina, prompted both the United States and the United Nations to take notice and act. More than two years later, the most delicate matter for decision makers is still to determine the precise relationship between what should be and what is possible in international relations.

# 11 Moral Compulsion in Foreign Policy

It goes almost without saying that even though the United States can plausibly assert a legal right to intervene unilaterally in certain cases, it should not do so in all of them. From a strategic, self-interested perspective, now that the Cold War has ended, the need to risk American lives and prestige to backstop free states against antidemocratic influences obviously has diminished. By the same token, from a military point of view, the United States can afford to be more adventurous. For example, the task of fulfilling the once-urgent geopolitical imperative of enveloping the Western Hemisphere as an exclusive sphere of influence is at once easier and less urgent.

Should, then, the United States take advantage of its current position by aggressively intervening on behalf of neglected or oppressed populations, against brutally antidemocratic regimes, when the opportunity presents itself? Or should it enjoy the luxury of waiting to see whether indigenous populations can generate their own viable opposition and overthrow those regimes? The quotidian but correct answer is: it depends.

Nations, like people, are subject to two basic impetuses: prudential interests and moral concerns. The United

States's prudential interests overseas include defense of the realm and its inhabitants, access to oil, secure lines of communication, and the stability of trading partners—what General John Shalikashvili, chairman of the Joint Chiefs of Staff, deemed "core interests" on *Nightline*.[1] In a democracy like the United States they are determined to some extent directly by the electorate, to some extent by political leaders in their exercise of discretionary (sometimes called "enlightened") representation. These are interests that must be served to preserve the United States's very sovereignty, its status as a nation. President Clinton tried to acclimate the American people to military intervention in Haiti by portraying such a measure as classically prudential. The interests he said Haiti's unrest implicated included drug interdiction, the preservation of democracy within the immediate sphere of influence, the protection of Americans living in Haiti and relatives of Haitian-Americans still there, and forestalling a panicky, massive, and disruptive influx of refugees.[2]

Whereas Western philosophical tradition makes individuals obliged to act on moral concerns affecting others, it does not burden nations with the same compulsion to act on behalf of other nations or their peoples. The reason is that by the definition of sovereignty, a government's paramount moral duty is to safeguard its own people. That duty, in turn, is tantamount to serving the nation's own prudential interests.

This, at least, was the Machiavellian dictate in the world of strict sovereignty that delivered the United Nations Charter.[3] But, with global depolarization and more relaxed notions of sovereignty now gaining currency, the world has become post-Machiavellian. Whereas publicly extolling and actually serving the sanctity of one's own nation's borders and people was once the exclusive imperative of maintaining benevolent power, now it is also essential for a world leader, if it is to retain that designation, to acknowledge and honor the needs of less fortunate nations as well. Internationally, the United States's moral concerns comprise securing human rights, maintaining the integrity of borders, and extending humanitarian aid.

The working relationship between the one set of concerns and the other seems quite simple: If the United States can address any of these moral concerns effectively without violating its duty to protect its own people—that is, its own prudential interests—it should do so. Thus, the United States is in an odd position. On the one hand, when doing right for others would impinge on the interests of its own citizenry, it is obliged to constrain itself. On the other hand, because international threats to those interests have diminished, the United States's moral obligation to help others has been heightened.

During the Cold War, the U.S. government apprehended a moral duty to its own populace and like-thinking foreigners to "contain" the designs of a sinister, expansionist regime. The Truman doctrine was an expression of that duty, and it was often distorted, sometimes tragically. The United States remains a compulsory guardian of the international interest, but what foreign involvements would serve it is far less clear than it was when the Soviet Union was such an easy foil. Nevertheless, one dictate of common sense can simplify the puzzle: The United States is under no moral compulsion to act unless it can really do some good. The weight of the evidence is that no magic quantum of money or resolve would have made the Somalis more compliant or Somalia's resurrection more manageable. Operation Restore Hope was both morally beyond the call of duty and imprudent. Doing right, then, involves hard, subtle decisions, not grandiose displays, and may well require looking wrong. To quote one more Hempstone gem from the eve of Restore Hope, "Statecraft is better made with the head than with the heart."[4] Meg Greenfield's is a sensible viewpoint:

> American security interests and, yes, humanitarian purposes are still very much alive and deserving respect, and it is possible to define them. But they tend to get lost in the razzle-dazzle of instantly proclaimed and instantly called-off foreign crises. We are not naturally suited to the old colonialist swagger through distant, turbulent parts of the world, imposing some sort of Pax Americana. And anyway, that sort of stuff went out decades ago. If the administration does not finally want to be overwhelmed in its foreign policy by a tide of hostile public opinion, it really needs to know how to make an honest, compelling case for those interventions it deems necessary and how to let go of the rest.[5]

The October 3 misfortune drove home the fact that the case for intervention must be well considered, well in advance. Testifying before the Senate Armed Services Committee in May 1994, Vietnam veteran Larry E. Joyce, having lost his son James in Mogadishu, matter-of-factly stated: "If we learn nothing else from this foreign policy debacle it should be this: Before we send American troops into combat, three questions must be asked. (1) Is the mission attainable? (2) Are American national interests at stake? (3) Are we willing to stay the course?"[6] In their basic outlines, these criteria make good sense.

Operation Restore Hope in Somalia, and arguably even the Gulf War, has suggested that legal intervention under U.N. auspices, although laudable, can be incendiary and ultimately counterproductive. (The popular and accurate perception is that both, though technically U.N.-sanctioned and multilateral, were at bottom American operations.) In Somalia, the allure of American sponsorship drove clan-based factions even farther apart and the United Nations's stock even lower. Bloodshed actually peaked after the Americans handed the operation over to a smaller U.N. force. Likewise, Saddam Hussein's resentment toward the Americans for the savage beating they gave him may have made him less inclined to cooperate with U.N. nuclear inspection teams, challenged him to prove his machismo by prodding the no-fly zone and renewing aggression toward Kuwait, and channeled his aggression back toward Iraq's indigenous Kurds.

The truistic lesson is simply that Washington must exercise particular caution when dealing with inscrutable local politics or megalomaniacs. As a rule of thumb it doesn't narrow the field. But cases like Bosnia's that implicate classically prudential interests as well as humanitarian concerns will likely remain the strongest candidates for intervention. Sudan is comparable to Bosnia in this regard. Africa's largest country, Sudan reflects both the geographical and the political transition of Islam from its stronghold in north Africa and the Middle East to the black subcontinent. Iran backs Sudan's fundamentalist government ideologically, financially, and militarily. For the United States, these features do give Sudan a strategic resonance that other Third World countries do not have. Moreover, the humanitarian problems there are every bit as compelling as those in Somalia were before Restore Hope and those in Bosnia are now.[7] If Somalia and Bosnia ever stabilize, the United Nations presumably will have to turn to Sudan. But the United Nations will find itself handcuffed by an all-too-identifiable central government in Sudan and Khartoum's inevitable refusal to consent to blue helmets within its borders. Even so, before going in, Washington would have to consider whether it would draw other countries (such as Iran itself) into the conflict, whether it could avoid protracted involvement, and whether intervention could really expedite a peaceful political solution.

With a disengaged Soviet veto in the Security Council, Washington alternately primps and lurks as the effective leader of the United Nations and its cynical alter-ego. From the latter position it is easier than ever for it to exalt expediency over principle in choosing to project its strength through or over the United Nations according to the global political climate.[8] But this administration and future ones will do well not to allow the new opportunities for multilateralism and peacekeeping occasioned by the Security Council's post–Cold War suggestibility to seduce them into an enveloping Dulles-like global moralism. The obvious example is again Somalia, where after an inaugural attempt to operate under a U.N. command structure, the United States found it necessary to prosecute its hunt for General Aidid with specially dispatched Rangers and Delta-force commandos. Washington would do best in the global community to avoid this sort of temporizing and obscurantism and simply come forward with frank explanations of the United States's actions, be they popular or condemned. Those explanations should be couched in terms of the moral calculus outlined here, and their rationality so demonstrated.

At the end of the day, moral caution is more likely than melodrama to lead to consensus and community—the linchpins of the internationalism the United Nations Charter envisages and U.S. policy professedly seeks to promote. Blustery, impulsive sanctimony in foreign policy, on the other hand, will tend to imply promises that cannot be fulfilled and result in a divisive Third World clamor for Western resources. These resources may well be needed by Western powers for defending their own clear interests—in the Middle East or south Asia, as well as Eastern Europe.[9] An American defense of South Korea, for example, could require four hundred thousand soldiers, take several months, and cost twenty thousand U.S. casualties.[10] Humility has an important place in both U.S. and U.N. policy. They haven't got a prayer of shaping an organic mechanism for handling world problems equitably and dynamically, unless they develop the capacity to admit that some problems are beyond the ken of redemption by intervention.

And to repeat, the moral duty of the United States to other peoples is strictly circumscribed by its obligation to its own. This consideration is manifested politically—Congress will balk at presidentially dictated military action once it costs a certain amount of money and a certain number of American lives—but it is in essence moral. General Shalikashvili told Ted Koppel, "We must not ask Americans to give their lives needlessly, but Americans have understood, perhaps better than most, that freedom isn't free."[11] Point taken. But on who else's freedom is the freedom of Americans contingent? It is often not a question that admits of short, easy answers: witness Vietnam. To further complicate the moral algebra of foreign policy, the American obligation clearly extends beyond preserving its own citizens' freedom, which is merely a prudential consideration. On the eve of U.S. withdrawal from Somalia, General Shalikashvili suggested that only American "core interests"—that is, those directly implicating its own long-term security—should drive its willingness to risk troops. Bosnia, he said, is one such interest, whereas Somalia is not. But given the status the United States currently enjoys (or at least endures), it is no exaggeration to say that remedying any political instability caters attenuatedly to its overall interests. If that is the realpolitik, how can Washington fairly discriminate among lesser interests?

The United States cannot financially or politically launch operations like Restore Hope on behalf of Sudan, Mozambique, Rwanda, and any of dozens of other Third World nations. Even without considering its U.N. dues, the United States has already spent about $2 billion on the Somalia intervention; and even the forty-three American lives lost in Somalia have pushed Congress to its breaking point. Indeed, in retrospect the Somalia effort seems morally arbitrary—more akin to awarding a sweepstakes winner than meeting a duty. This is an unprincipled and ultimately unconstructive way to conduct a foreign policy that is presumptively aimed at harmonizing an entire world and therefore aiding populations evenhandedly. It is arguable (though not obvious) that the United States owes Somalis and others a Cold War debt, but Operation Restore Hope was an inappropriate way to pay it back.

The more problematic extension of this logic is that the United States's and the United Nations's duty to provide humanitarian aid (military or civilian) is limited not only by what it can do for the intended recipient but also by whether it can subsequently provide a fair measure of comparable relief to other equally deserving or politically more important populations. "By too casually committing U.S. forces in situations that are not critical and where the commitment is thus halfhearted," wrote Paul D. Wolfowitz recently, "the administration runs the risk that it will not be able to commit forces later in truly vital situations, and that such a commitment would be presumed halfhearted in any case."[12] From a moral perspective, U.S. and U.N. humanitarian policy should focus on the durability and iterability of limited measures and not on isolated, absolute solutions. In short, to preserve their bona fides, they must pick their spots.

This means that the United States may often have a duty to help another nation, even if refraining from doing so would not adversely affect a "core interest." It depends on circumstances both at home and abroad. If, for example, the president decides that the plight of the south Sudanese calls for U.S. participation in a U.N. peacekeeping initiative, the troops are available without sacrificing national security, and other global moral concerns would not be compromised by participation, then an American contribution to the peacekeeping force might be considered compulsory. If, on the other hand, deploying troops to Sudan would mean none could be deployed to Bosnia for a foreseeable but not immediate emergency, assuming Bosnia represents a core (prudential) interest, the president would be duty-bound not to dispatch a U.S. contingent to Sudan. Of the stated American concerns about intervention in Rwanda, the most probative was whether the proposed commitment would leave the United Nations with the resources to help other trouble spots with potentially equivalent catastrophes.[13] That seems a major step toward developing a standard of fairness for allocating peacekeeping forces.

Operation Restore Hope was bad precedent. Ironically but fortunately, only its operational failure precludes a heightened demand for help the United States simply cannot supply and a new form of injustice. The intractability of Somalia's troubles, after the pliancy of Kuwait's, shows vividly that not all humanitarian interventions work. But neither do all interventions fail. The larger point is that neither Somalia nor any single intervention operation can usefully serve as a metaphor for a failure of foreign policy. Operation Restore Hope did fulfill its humanitarian purpose, though less militaristic means brought to bear earlier would have been far preferable. On the other hand, the operational shortfalls of Restore Hope do not translate automatically to situations elsewhere.

The lessons of this book dovetail delicately, but not, I think, unworkably. The United States must at once selectively choose its overseas beneficiaries and distribute its largess fairly among many nations in need. This mission calls for a more encompassing, forward-looking concept of "feasibility" under which no single crisis is considered in isolation from others that can be reasonably anticipated. The challenge is to avoid both the impetuousness of Operation Restore Hope and the paralysis that still afflicts ex-Yugoslavia. In other words, the United States and the United Nations must endeavor to move wisely enough and timely enough, but also often enough, to make a lasting difference.

John Keegan, when he wrote the words quoted in this book's epigraph, contemplated the continuation of the nuclear stalemate, a "post-heroic" world in which world powers had to settle for managing risks without vanquishing foes. A few years later, the Cold War suddenly ended, and the prospect of a new world order augured the renaissance of heroism. Controlling the risks of nuclear confrontation remains a diplomatic and military priority. Yet the crumbling of Third World governments suddenly on their own increasingly calls for humanitarian intervention and with it conventional conflicts with the traditional goal of securing territory (though not that of gaining dominion over it). If the Gulf War was the auspicious comeback of the United States after Vietnam, then Somalia was its sophomore slump. Keegan's next caveat still applies today: "There can . . . be nothing automatic about the exercise of power through force, whether naked or implicit, though long the power-holding and the power-hungry have sought such a secret. Force finds out those who lack the virtue to wield it."[14]

There is still a place for heroes. But in a new world order, if it is to crystallize and then endure, heroism is a matter of wisdom and probity as well as courage. In Graham Greene's 1955 Vietnam prophecy, *The Quiet American*, the cynical journalist despaired to the eponymous CIA faith-healer: "We shall do the same thing here. Encourage them and leave them with a little equipment and a toy industry."[15] It wasn't enough then, even when superpowers were willing to play vicious marionettes to keep the people away from communism. Surely it is not enough now, when we no longer have a reason to do anything but help.

# Notes

Unless otherwise indicated, all interviews were conducted in person by the author.

## INTRODUCTION

1. The cable is published in Smith Hempstone, "'Think Three Times Before You Embrace the Somalia Tarbaby,'" *U.S. News & World Report*, December 14, 1992, 30.
2. Hempstone, *Africa: Angry Young Giant* (New York: Praeger Publishers, 1961), 463.
3. Hempstone, *Katanga Report* (London: Faber & Faber, 1962).
4. Jeffrey Bartholet, "An American in Nairobi," *Newsweek* (international edition), December 2, 1991, 18.
5. Jonathan Stevenson, "Hope Restored in Somalia?" *Foreign Policy* 91 (Summer 1993): 138–49.
6. Ismat Kittani, interview held at UNOSOM II headquarters, Mogadishu, Somalia, December 30, 1992.
7. Hempstone, "'Think Three Times,'" 30.

## CHAPTER 1: DISSEMBLANCE AS ETHOS

1. Dr. Hussein Mursal, Medical Director for Somalia, Save the Children Fund, interview at SCF (U.K.) residence, Mogadishu, Somalia, December 4, 1992. See also Blaine

Harden, *Africa: Dispatches from a Fragile Continent* (New York: W. W. Norton, 1990), 139n; David Lamb, *The Africans* (New York: Random House, Vintage Books, 1987), 41; Scilla McLean and Stella Efua Graham, eds., 2d rev. ed., *Female Circumcision, Excision, and Infibulation: The Facts and Proposals for Change* (London: Minority Rights Group, 1985). Janice Boddy's "Afterword" in Virginia Lee Barnes and Janice Boddy, *Aman: The Story of a Somali Girl* (London: Bloomsbury, 1994) provides a particularly lucid and incisive overview of Somali culture and society.

2. Samuel M. Makinda, *Superpower Diplomacy in the Horn of Africa* (Kent, England: Croom Helm, 1987), 3, 110–34; Robert G. Patman, *The Soviet Union in the Horn of Africa: The Diplomacy of Intervention and Disengagement* (Cambridge: Cambridge University Press, 1990), 227–30.
3. I. M. Lewis, *A Pastoralist Democracy: A Study of Pastoralism and Politics among the Northern Somali of the Horn of Africa* (New York: Oxford University Press, 1961), 279, 294–96. This is the leading text on Somali clan culture.
4. Ibid., 119–26, 162–70.
5. See, for example, Lamb, *The Africans*, 11, 197.
6. Lewis, *Pastoralist Democracy*, 193–95. For a textured firsthand account of pre-Siad life in Somalia, see Barnes and Boddy, *Aman*.
7. Mohamed Jirdah Hussein, interview at Hotel Sahafi, Mogadishu, Somalia, December 14, 1992. On Siad Barre's degenerative affect on Somali culture generally, see *Somalia: A Nation in Turmoil* (London: Minority Rights Group, 1991), 17–22.
8. See Makinda, *Superpower Diplomacy*, 40–41, 215.
9. I. M. Lewis, "Somalia," *Africa South of the Sahara, 1994* (London: Europa Publications, 1993), 779–83.
10. Graham Roberts, CARE Logistics Coordinator, interview at CARE headquarters, Mogadishu, Somalia, August 5, 1992; CARE memorandum titled "Food Shipment-Related Security Incidents for the Period 17th/6/1992 [*sic*]–20th/6/1992," furnished to the author by CARE personnel.
11. For example, see John Prendergast, "The Forgotten Agenda in Somalia," *Review of African Political Economy* 59 (March 1994): 66–71. On conditions in Somalia before Operation Restore Hope, generally, see Edward R. F. Sheehan, "In the Heart of Somalia," *The New York Review of Books*, January 14, 1993, 38–43; United Nations, *World Economic Survey 1993* (New York: United Nations, 1993), 173–80.
12. "Gang Kills 70 and Rapes Women on Somali Refugee Ship," *Times* (London), June 27, 1992, 10.
13. Mohamed Sahnoun, interview at UNOSOM headquarters, Mogadishu, Somalia, August 25, 1992.
14. "Price of Charity," *Economist* (London), September 12, 1992, 42.

15. Carl Howorth, CARE Team Leader, interview at Mogadishu Port, Mogadishu, Somalia, August 5, 1992.
16. Africa Recovery Briefing Paper No. 7 (U.N. Department of Public Information), January 15, 1993, 12.
17. Jonathan Stevenson, "Food For Naught," *The New Republic*, September 21, 1993, 13–14.
18. Sahnoun interview, August 25, 1992.
19. Gregoire Tavernier, Deputy Head of Delegation—Somalia, International Committee of the Red Cross, interview at ICRC headquarters in Nairobi, Kenya, August 4, 1992.
20. "Population-Based Mortality Assessment—Baidoa and Afgoi, Somalia, 1992," *Morbidity and Mortality Weekly Report* (Centers for Disease Control) 41 (December 11, 1992): 916.
21. "Saving the People Who Should Not Be Starving," *Economist* (London), August 29, 1992, 35–36; "U.N. Begins Airlift to Save the Starving in Somalia," *New York Times*, August 16, 1992, A3.
22. On the Somalis' economic acumen and facility, see "A Daring Few Are Bullish on Somalia," *Washington Post*, March 22, 1993, A17. On the mercenary cynicism that took hold of the economy, see Jeffrey Bartholet, "The Road to Hell," *Newsweek* (international edition), September 21, 1992, 52–53.
23. Mohamed Abshir, Coordinator for Relief and International Relations, Somali Salvation Democratic Front, interview at Trattoria restaurant, Nairobi, Kenya, September 19, 1992.
24. "More Than We Can Chew," *Independent* (London), June 1, 1994, sec. 2, 1.
25. Osman Hassan Ali (Osman Ato), interview on board Piper Chieftain turboprop en route from K-50 airfield, Somalia, to Nairobi, Kenya, September 20, 1992.
26. The material discussing khat is based on Jonathan Stevenson, "Krazy Khat," *The New Republic*, November 23, 1992, 17–18, and on research undertaken and interviews conducted in preparing the article.

## CHAPTER 2: AMERICA'S PATRONAGE DURING THE COLD WAR

1. Lamb, *The Africans*, 204–7.
2. Zbigniew Brzezinski, *Power and Principle: Memoirs of the National Security Advisor, 1977–1981* (New York: Farrar, Straus, & Giroux, 1983), 446.
3. Makinda, *Superpower Diplomacy*, 111–12.
4. S. J. Hamrick, "The Myth of Somalia as Cold War Victim," *Foreign Service Journal*, February 1993, 32. See also Jeffrey Clark, "Debacle in Somalia," in special issue "America and the World, 1992–93," *Foreign Affairs* vol. 72, 110–12.

5. Makinda, *Superpower Diplomacy*, 112–18.
6. Lamb, *The Africans*, 205.
7. Patman, *Soviet Union in the Horn of Africa*, 208.
8. Lamb, *The Africans*, 204. See also ibid, 221–23; and Hamrick, "The Myth of Somalia," 32.
9. Hamrick, "The Myth of Somalia," 32.
10. Michael Maren, "The Food-Aid Racket," *Harper's*, August 1993, 11.
11. Cyrus Vance, "The United States and Africa: Building Positive Relations," *Department of State Bulletin* 76 (August 8, 1977): 169–70, quoted in Patman, *Soviet Union in the Horn of Africa*, 212.
12. Patman, *Soviet Union in the Horn of Africa*, 216.
13. Lamb, *The Africans*, 210.
14. Makinda, *Superpower Diplomacy*, 126–29.
15. Patman, *Soviet Union in the Horn of Africa*, 287.
16. Mohamoud M. Afrah, *Target: Villa Somalia*, 2d ed. (Karachi, Pakistan: Naseem, 1992), 41. This is the only firsthand written account of the fall of Siad Barre available. Although the book is disorganized, biased, and melodramatic, the basic historical points jibe with newspaper accounts and with firsthand oral reports of the events of Siad's demise.
17. Patman, *Soviet Union in the Horn of Africa*, 288.
18. Sanford J. Ungar, *Africa: The People and Politics of an Emerging Continent* (New York: Simon & Schuster, Touchstone, 1989), 376.
19. See, for example, Harden, *Africa Dispatches*, 47–54, especially 48.
20. Willy Huber, Regional Director for East Africa, SOS-Kinderdorf-International, interview at SOS village, Mogadishu, Somalia, January 12, 1994.
21. President George Bush, press conference, December 4, 1992.
22. Interview at Mogadishu International Airport, Mogadishu, Somalia, December 15, 1992.
23. See, for example, Robert Weil, "Somalia in Perspective: When the Saints Come Marching In," *Review of African Political Economy*, no. 57 (July 1993), 104.
24. Osman Ato interview, September 20, 1992; Mohamed Jirdah Hussein interview, December 14, 1992. See also "Amoco Oil's Exploring Machinery," *Chicago Tribune*, September 20, 1993, sec. 4, 1.
25. Osman Hassan Ali (Osman Ato), interview at residence, Mogadishu, Somalia, December 3, 1992.
26. "The Oil Factor in Somalia," *Los Angeles Times*, January 18, 1993, A1.
27. Robert Oakley, U.S. Special Representative for Somalia, interview at U.S. diplomatic residence, Mogadishu, Somalia, December 18, 1992.
28. Osman Ato interview, December 3, 1992.
29. Oakley interview, December 18, 1992.
30. Ibid.
31. Robert Oakley, press conference at U.S. diplomatic residence, Mogadishu, Somalia, December 17, 1992.

32. Osman Ato interview, December 3, 1992.
33. Robert Gosende, U.S. Special Representative for Somalia designate, interview at U.N. conference center, Addis Ababa, Ethiopia, March 15, 1993.

## CHAPTER 3: SIAD BARRE'S OUSTER: SOMALI RETRIBUTION RUN AMOK

1. The author was told the story by Willy Huber, Regional Director for East Africa, SOS-Kinderdorf-International, interview at SOS village, Mogadishu, Somalia, August 24, 1992.
2. Mohamed Farah Aidid, interview at Somali National Alliance headquarters, Bardera, Somalia, September 2, 1992.
3. Jeffrey Bartholet, "Land of the Dead," *Newsweek* (international edition), December 23, 1991, 23.
4. Aidid interview, September 2, 1992.
5. See Andrew Purvis, "Wanted: Warlord No. 1," *Time* (international edition), June 28, 1993, 28; and "An Elusive Clan Leader Thwarts a U.N. Mission," *New York Times,* October 7, 1993, A9; "Canada Puts Spotlight on Aideed's Refugee Family," *Guardian* (London), October 13, 1993, sec. 1, 11; "Aideed's Northern Exposure: Wife Faces Welfare, Immigration Fraud Investigation in Canada," *Washington Post,* October 29, 1993, A30.
6. Patman, *Soviet Union in the Horn of Africa*, 123, 126.
7. Mohammed Siad Barre, *My Country and My People, 1969–1974*, 2 vols. (Mogadishu, Somalia: Ministry for Information and National Guidence, 1974), 95; quoted in Patman, *Soviet Union in the Horn of Africa,* 128. See also I. M. Lewis, *A Modern History of Somalia* (London & New York: Longman Group Ltd., 1980), 205–25. Lewis has decades of personal experience with the Somalis and true affection and admiration for them. But he too concludes, "Certainly socialism was here a means rather than an end." Ibid., 225.
8. Patman, *Soviet Union in the Horn of Africa, 1994,* 301–2.
9. Ibid.
10. See ibid., 118, 221.
11. Afrah, *Target,* 5–10, 28–29.
12. Ibid., 34.
13. Ibid., 10–12.
14. Ibid., 59–70.
15. Ibid., Foreword, 42–43, and 59–70.
16. Ibid., 60.
17. Lewis, "Somalia," *Africa South of the Sahara, 1994*, 775–76.
18. Ibid., 776–77.
19. Aidid interview, September 2, 1992.

20. Osman Ato interview, December 3, 1992.
21. Abdulkadir Yahya Ali, interview at Ali Mahdi Mohamed's headquarters, north Mogadishu, Somalia, July 8, 1992.
22. Jeffrey Bartholet, "*This* Is the New World Order?" *Newsweek* (international edition), April 6, 1992, 21.
23. Stevenson, "Hope Restored?" 145; Ali Mahdi Mohamed, interview at his headquarters, north Mogadishu, Somalia, July 8, 1992; Mohamed Sahnoun, telephone interview from U.N. headquarters, New York, July 9, 1992; Aidid interview, September 2, 1992. On the Antonov incident, see "Death by Looting," *Economist* (London), July 18, 1992, 43; *Unicef Somalia Situation Report, July 1992.*
24. "Somalia: Death in Food Lines," *International Herald Tribune*, July 20, 1992, 1 [*New York Times* Service]. See also "U.N. Team Delays Somalia Visit as Red Cross Predicts Starvation," *New York Times*, July 12, 1992, A8.
25. "U.N. Pledges Somali Aid: 'Kids Are Dying Now,'" *International Herald Tribune*, July 30, 1992, 5.
26. Peter Hansen, Chief of U.N. Technical Team, interview at U.N. residence, Mogadishu, Somalia, August 7, 1992.
27. See, for example, "A Way Out of the Apocalypse," *Independent* (London), September 8, 1992, sec. 1, 9.
28. Africa Recovery Briefing Paper No. 7, January 15, 1993, 12. See also "In Somali Town, 'Only 65 Dead' Is Cause for Hope," *International Herald Tribune*, October 24–25, 1992, 5 [*New York Times* Service].
29. Carl Howorth, CARE Team Leader, interview at CARE headquarters, Mogadishu, Somalia, July 8, 1992.
30. Patrick Vial, Médecins Sans Frontières (MSF) Coordinator, interview at MSF compound, Mogadishu, Somalia, July 8, 1992. See, generally, Jeffrey Bartholet, "With the Workers: 'Very, Very Bad,'" *Newsweek* (international edition), September 28, 1992, 24.
31. Roberts interview, August 5, 1992.
32. Raymond Bonner, "First Buy Up the Youngsters' Guns," *International Herald Tribune*, December 3, 1992, 4 [*New York Times* Service]. For a more tempered view, apparently acquired over a few weeks, see Bonner, "The Dilemma of Disarmament," *Time* (international edition), December 28, 1992, 32–33.
33. Osman Ato, interview at Wilson Airport, Nairobi, Kenya, September 26, 1992.

## CHAPTER 4: UNOSOM I AND II: TWO SETS OF NOMENKLATURA

1. The analysis of Sahnoun's tenure is based on my article "Hope Restored in Somalia?" *Foreign Policy* no. 91 (Summer 1993), 138–54. See, generally, Mohamed Sahnoun, *Somalia: The Missed Opportunities* (Washington, D.C.: U.S. Institute for Peace, 1994).

2. "United Nations 100-Day Action Programme for Accelerated Humanitarian Assistance for Somalia," United Nations report, October 1992, 3.
3. See Jeffrey Bartholet, "The Poor Man's War," *Newsweek* (international edition), August 17, 1992, 19.
4. Sahnoun interview, August 25, 1992.
5. Stevenson, "Hope Restored?" 148.
6. Ibid. See also Tom Post, Anne Underwood, and Jeffrey Bartholet, "How Do You Spell Relief?" *Newsweek* (international edition), November 23, 1992, 18.
7. Osman Ato interview, December 3, 1992.
8. Stevenson, "Hope Restored?" 150–52.
9. Sahnoun interview, August 25, 1992.
10. Quoted in Sidney Blumenthal, "Why Are We In Somalia?" *The New Yorker*, October 25, 1993, 58.
11. Quoted in Blumenthal, "Why?" 57–58.
12. Jonathan Stevenson, "Seeking a Solution," *Foreign Service Journal,* February 1993, 33.
13. Blumenthal, "Why?" 57.
14. Ibid., 49–51. *Nomenklatura* is the term for the iron-fisted bureaucrats who once ran the Kremlin and the expression Sahnoun used for the middle managers of the United Nations.
15. Karen Breslau, "Can the United Nations Do the Job?" *Newsweek* (international edition), October 18, 1993, 15.

## CHAPTER 5: SNAFUS ON THE HOPE RESTORATION DETAIL

1. See the op-ed piece, Jonathan Stevenson, "Will Bungle Turn Into Betrayal?" *Evening Standard* (London), January 6, 1993, 16.
2. Nur Hussein, Project Officer for Water and Sanitation, UNICEF, interview at UNICEF headquarters, Mogadishu, Somalia, December 30, 1992.
3. "CIA Warns Bush on Somali Mission," *International Herald Tribune,* December 3, 1992, 6 [*New York Times* Service]. See also Fred Barnes, "Last Call," *The New Republic,* December 28, 1992, 11–13.
4. Colonel Fred Peck, USMC, UNITAF Spokesman, press briefing at Mogadishu International Airport, December 14, 1992.
5. Neil Sheehan, *A Bright Shining Lie* (London: Jonathan Cape Ltd., 1989), 713. "William Westmoreland thought that he possessed South Vietnam. What he owned was a lot of American islands where his soldiers stood."
6. Lieutenant General Robert Johnston, USMC, press briefing at Hotel Sahafi, Mogadishu, Somalia, December 12, 1992. See also Rod Nordland, Jeffrey Bartholet, and Jonathan Stevenson, "Hurry-Up Offense," *Newsweek* (international edition), January 4, 1993, 14–15.
7. General Joseph P. Hoar, USA, Commander-in-Chief, U.S. Central Command, press briefing at UNITAF headquarters, Mogadishu, Somalia, December 19, 1992.

8. Major Rudy Wormeester, USMC, interview at Mogadishu International Airport, Somalia, December 14, 1992.
9. Oakley interview, December 18, 1992.
10. See Jonathan Stevenson and Jane Whitmore, "When Is Quitting Time?" *Newsweek* (international edition), January 18, 1993, 31.
11. Colonel Fred Peck, press briefing at UNITAF headquarters, Mogadishu, Somalia, December 30, 1992.
12. Lewis, "Somalia," 776–77.
13. Dr. Hussein Mursal, Medical Director for Somalia, Save the Children Fund, interview at SCF (U.K.) residence, Mogadishu, Somalia, December 17, 1992.
14. Stevenson and Whitmore, "When Is Quitting Time?" 31.
15. Mursal interview, December 17, 1992.
16. "Background Notes" given to United States Marine Corps officers, shown to the author by a marine at Mogadishu International Airport, Somalia, December 16, 1992.
17. Corporal James Moore, USMC, interview at Mogadishu International Airport, December 16, 1992.
18. Sergeant Mark Oleck, USMC, interview at Mogadishu International Airport, December 12, 1992.
19. Quoted in "Marines' Ignorance Angers Somalis," *Independent* (London), January 11, 1993, sec. 1, p. 10.
20. Captain Tom Imburgia, USAF, interview with Jeffrey Bartholet, Nairobi Bureau Chief, *Newsweek,* in Mogadishu, Somalia, December 1992.
21. Interview at U.S. diplomatic residence, Mogadishu, Somalia, December 14, 1992.
22. Colonel Jean-Paul Perruche, French Army, 2d Regiment Etranger Parachutist, interview at French army headquarters, Mogadishu, Somalia, December 16, 1992.
23. Lieutenant Colonel Charles Borchini, USA, interview with Jeffrey Bartholet, Nairobi Bureau Chief, *Newsweek,* in Mogadishu, Somalia, December 1992.
24. Kittani interview, December 30, 1992.
25. Colonel Fred Peck, press briefing at Mogadishu International Airport, Somalia, December 16, 1992.
26. "Background Notes."
27. Lance Corporal Brad Vawter, USMC, interview with Jeffrey Bartholet, Nairobi Bureau Chief, *Newsweek,* in Mogadishu, Somalia, December 1992.
28. Interview at Mogadishu International Airport, Somalia, December 16, 1992.
29. Mark Stirling, UNICEF Representative for Somalia, interview at UNICEF headquarters, Mogadishu, Somalia, January 9, 1993.
30. Sheehan, *A Bright Shining Lie,* 160, 204.
31. Quoted in ibid., 537.

32. Quoted in "The Raid That Went Wrong," *Washington Post*, January 30, 1994, A27.
33. Brigadier General Imtiaz Shaheen, UNOSOM Force Commander, interview at UNOSOM headquarters, Mogadishu, Somalia, December 15, 1992.
34. Brigadier General Imtiaz Shaheen, UNOSOM Force Commander, interview at UNOSOM headquarters, Mogadishu, Somalia, August 6, 1992.
35. Quoted in Russell Watson, et al., "Troops to Somalia?" *Newsweek* (international edition), December 7, 1992, 26.
36. Corporal Darren Butto, USMC, interview at Mogadishu International Airport, Somalia, December 12, 1992.
37. Imburgia interview, December 1992.
38. Johnston press briefing, December 12, 1992.
39. On the roots of this rumor, see John R. Bolton, "Wrong Turn in Somalia," *Foreign Affairs* 73 (January/February 1994), 60–61.
40. Colonel Fred Peck, press briefing at UNITAF headquarters, Mogadishu, Somalia, January 15, 1993.
41. Corporal James Evans, and Private First Class John Berrest, USMC, interview at UNITAF headquarters, Mogadishu, Somalia, January 15, 1993.
42. Dennis Walto, Operations Director, International Medical Corps, interview at IMC compound, Mogadishu, Somalia, January 15, 1993.
43. Gemmo Lodesani, Deputy Director of Operations, World Food Program, interview at WFP headquarters, Mogadishu, Somalia, January 15, 1992.
44. Message Re: "30-Day Attitude Adjustment" from Major General Charles C. Wilhelm, USMC, posted in UNITAF headquarters, Mogadishu, Somalia, dated January 12, 1993.
45. Corporal William Hutchings, USMC, interview near Hotel Sahafi, Mogadishu, Somalia, January 15, 1993.
46. Lance Corporal R. E. Duarte, USMC, interview at UNITAF headquarters, Mogadishu, Somalia, January 15, 1993.
47. Evans/Berrest interview, January 15, 1993.
48. Colonel Fred Peck, press briefing at UNITAF headquarters, Mogadishu, Somalia, March 3, 1993.
49. "Canadian Guilty of Killing Somali," *Washington Post*, March 18, 1994, A26; "Torture by Army Peacekeepers in Somalia Shocks Canada," *New York Times*, November 27, 1994, 14.
50. Huber interview, January 12, 1994.
51. Quoted in Michael Elliott, "The Making of a Fiasco," *Newsweek* (international edition), October 18, 1993, 11.
52. "A Bitter Tale of Two Estranged Worlds in One Divided City," *Guardian* (London), November 27, 1993, 10 [*Washington Post* Service].
53. Dr. Hussein Mursal, Medical Director for Somalia, Save the Children Fund, interview at SCF (U.K.) residence, Mogadishu, Somalia, March 3, 1993.

54. Ibid.
55. Shaheen interview, December 17, 1992. See also Jeffrey Bartholet and Jonathan Stevenson, "When the Rules Aren't Clear," *Newsweek* (international edition), March 8, 1993, 32.
56. Shaheen interview, December 17, 1992.
57. Mohamed Ali Mohamed, Security Chief, SOS-Kinderdorf-International, interview in Mogadishu, Somalia, January 12, 1994.
58. Omar Ibrahim Salah, Project Director, SOS-Kinderdorf-International, interview at SOS village, Mogadishu, Somalia, January 12, 1994.
59. "Heavy Medals," *Washington Post,* April 3, 1994, C3.
60. Quoted in "After Today, Marines in Mogadishu Will Be 'Just the Few,'" *Washington Post,* March 24, 1994, A2.
61. "Marines Leave Somalia, Ending U.S. Mission," *International Herald Tribune,* March 26–27 1994, 4 [*Washington Post* Service].
62. "What Began as a Mission of Mercy Closes with Little Ceremony," *New York Times,* March 26, 1994, A1.
63. Ibid.
64. "Marines Leave Somalia, Ending U.S. Mission," *International Herald Tribune,* March 26–27, 1994, 1, 4 [*Washington Post* Service].

## CHAPTER 6: BUILDING THE PERFECT BEAST

1. Quoted in "Perspectives," *Newsweek* (international edition), October 18, 1993, 5.
2. "Welcome to the Lair of the Warlord," *Independent* (London), 15 October 1993, sec. 1, p. 1. For more on the Somalis' predisposition toward a leader like Aidid, see Barnes and Boddy, *Aman,* 302–3.
3. The author was told the story by Stephen Tomlin, Country Director for Somalia, International Medical Corps, interview at IMC compound, Mogadishu, Somalia, September 22, 1992.
4. Stephen Tomlin, interview at IMC compound, Mogadishu, Somalia, December 3, 1992.
5. Osman Ato, interview at residence, Mogadishu, Somalia, December 3, 1992.
6. Ibid.
7. Abdulkadir Isse Fara-adde, interview at IMC compound, Mogadishu, Somalia, December 4, 1992.
8. Colonel Peter Dotto, USMC, interview at O.A.U. conference center, Addis Ababa, Ethiopia, March 17, 1993.
9. Dr. Hussein Mursal, Medical Director for Somalia, Save the Children Fund, interview at SCF (U.K.) compound, Mogadishu, Somalia, March 3, 1993.
10. Osman Ato interview, December 3, 1992.
11. Tomlin interview, December 3, 1992.

12. Aidid interview, September 2, 1992.
13. Osman Ato, interview at residence, Mogadishu, Somalia, December 29, 1992.
14. Blumenthal, "Why?" 58.
15. Oakley interview, December 18, 1992.
16. Ibid.
17. Ibid.
18. Press statement, Somali National Alliance, Nairobi, Kenya, dated January 13, 1993. [Actual release date: January 14, 1993.]
19. On Aidid's machinations, see "Protesters in Mogadishu Assail U.N.," *Independent* (London), January 4, 1993, sec. 1, p. 9; "U.N. Struggles for a Role in Somalia," *Financial Times* (London), January 4, 1993, 6; "Warlords Drive Wedge Between U.S. and U.N.," *Financial Times* (London), January 6, 1993, 7; "Playing the U.S. Against the U.N.," *Economist* (London), January 9, 1993, 42; Andrew Purvis, "In the Cross Fire," *Time* (international edition), March 8, 1993, 37.
20. Lieutenant Colonel Andre Leroy, Belgian Army, interview at O.A.U conference center, Addis Ababa, Ethiopia, March 17, 1993.
21. Brigadier General James Cox, Canadian Army, Chief of Staff, UNOSOM II, interview at UNOSOM II headquarters, Mogadishu, Somalia, March 3, 1993.
22. Ibid.
23. Lewis, "Somalia," 778.
24. Aidid interview, September 2, 1992.
25. Osman Ato interview, December 3, 1992.
26. Jonathan Stevenson, "Still No Peace in Somalia," *Newsweek* (international edition), March 29, 1993, 31.
27. Stevenson, "Hope Restored?" 141–42.
28. Dotto interview, March 17, 1993; quoted in Stevenson, "Still No Peace," 31.
29. Gosende interview, March 15, 1993.
30. Rhodri Wynn-Pope, CARE Team Leader, interview at CARE headquarters, Mogadishu, Somalia, March 3, 1994.
31. Ismat Kittani, U.N. Special Envoy for Somalia, press conference at UNOSOM II headquarters, March 4, 1993.
32. "Warlord at Large," *Economist* (London), 12 June 1993, 52.
33. Mohamed Abshir Musa, Chairman, Somali Salvation Democratic Front, interview at O.A.U. Conference Center, Addis Ababa, Ethiopia, March 16, 1993.
34. Colonel Peter Dotto, USMC, interview at O.A.U. conference center, Addis Ababa, Ethiopia, March 20, 1993.
35. Agence France Presse (AFP) report, dateline Mogadishu, *The Nation* (Nairobi, Kenya), June 6, 1993, 6.
36. On the warlords generally and Morgan in particular, see "A New Shadow,"

*Economist* (London), October 17, 1992, 53–54; "Who's Who," *Economist* (London), January 23, 1993, 49.

37. Quoted in Elliott, "The Making of a Fiasco," 11.
38. See, for example, "Gun Law Thwarts Dreams of Civil Rule in Mogadishu," *Times* (London), 7 June 1993, 11.
39. United Nations Charter, chap. 14, arts. 92, 94(2).
40. Ibid., chap. 11, art. 73(c).
41. "U.S. Threatens to Quit Somalia as War Continues," Reuters, dateline Addis Ababa, 13 March 1993; "Aid Donors Tell Somalis to Show Greater Commitment to Peace," Agence France Presse (AFP), dateline Addis Ababa, 12 March 1993.
42. For a similar analysis, see Waltraud Queiser Morales, "U.S. Intervention and the New World Order: Lessons from the Cold War and Post–Cold War Cases," *Third World Quarterly* 15 (March 1994): 89.
43. Kittani press conference, March 4, 1993.
44. Admiral Jonathan T. Howe, USN (ret.), U.N. Special Envoy for Somalia, press conference at O.A.U. conference center, Addis Ababa, Ethiopia, March 19, 1993.
45. The meeting was reported to the author by Willy Huber, interview at SOS-Kinderdorf-International, Regional Office East Africa, Nairobi, Kenya, January 6, 1994, on the basis of Huber's conversation with Egal.
46. Elliott, "The Making of a Fiasco," 11, 40; "Aidid Goes Home After 6 Months," Reuters, dateline Mogadishu, May 20, 1994.
47. "Welcome to the Lair of the Warlord," *Independent* (London), October 15, 1993, sec. 1, p. 1.

## CHAPTER 7: NONCHALANCE REDUX

1. Sheehan, *A Bright Shining Lie*, 131, 168–73.
2. Huber interview, January 12, 1994.
3. David H. Hackworth, "A Christmas Story," *Newsweek*, January 4, 1993, 38.
4. P. J. O'Rourke, "All Guns, No Butter: Inside Somalia, A Starving Nation Armed to the Teeth," *Rolling Stone*, April 1, 1993, 40.
5. Osman Ato interview, December 3, 1992.
6. Robert Oakley, U.S. Special Representative for Somalia, press conference (Farewell Statement) at U.S. diplomatic residence, Mogadishu, Somalia, March 3, 1993.
7. U.N. Security Council, Resolution 794, December 3, 1992.
8. Quoted in Stanley Meisler, "From Guard to Enforcer: U.N. Peacekeepers in Somalia," *Foreign Service Journal*, February 1993, 24.
9. Melinda Liu, "The Father of All Warlords," *Newsweek*, February 22, 1993, 37.
10. "In Ruins of Somalia, A Brave New Voice," *International Herald Tribune*, February 19, 1993, 7 [*Washington Post* Service].

11. Walter Isaacson, "Sometimes, Right Makes Might," *Time* (international edition), December 21, 1992, 64.
12. Robert Oakley, U.S. Special Representative for Somalia, interview at U.S. diplomatic compound, Mogadishu, Somalia, January 9, 1993.
13. Oakley press conference, March 3, 1993.
14. Blumenthal, "Why?" 59.
15. Quoted in "U.S. Supported Hunt for Aidid: Now Calls U.N. Policy Skewed," *New York Times*, October 18, 1993, A1, A6.
16. "The Retreat," *Economist* (London), October 16, 1993, 66.
17. Quoted in "U.S. Supported Hunt For Aidid," A1, A6.
18. Ibid.
19. "Western Newsmen Die in Mob Attack," *Times* (London), July 13, 1993, 1. See also Donatella Lorch, "Four Friends," *The New York Times Magazine*, August 22, 1993, 48.
20. "The Raid That Went Wrong," A26.
21. "How the Warlord Outwitted Clinton's Spooks," *Washington Post*, April 3, 1994, C3.
22. "Clinton Purges Foreign Advisors," *Independent* (London), November 10, 1993, sec. 1, p. 8.
23. "The Raid That Went Wrong," A1.
24. "How the Warlord Outwitted Clinton's Spooks," C3.
25. "U.S. Supported Hunt for Aidid," A1, A6.
26. Ibid.
27. Quoted in ibid.
28. "How the Warlord Outwitted Clinton's Spooks," C3.
29. "Mogadishu Guerillas Expose Failure of 'High–Tech Toy' Tactics," *Times* (London), July 15, 1993, 12; Douglas Waller, "When the Bad Guy Has No Phone to Tap," *Newsweek* (international edition), October 18, 1993, 11.
30. "The Raid That Went Wrong," A1, A26–27.
31. Ibid.
32. Ibid. See also "Night of a Thousand Casualties," *Washington Post*, January 31, 1993, A1, A10-11. For a detailed and heartfelt account of the battle, see Kent DeLong and Steven Tuckey, *Mogadishu! Heroism and Tragedy* (Westport, Conn.: Praeger, 1994).
33. "How the Warlord Outwitted Clinton's Spooks," C3.
34. "Clinton Purges Foreign Advisors," sec. 1, p. 8.
35. "What Began as a Mission of Mercy Closes with Little Ceremony," *New York Times*, March 26, 1994, A1, A2; "The End of the Chapter," *Economist* (London), April 2, 1994, 56.
36. Mursal interview, December 4, 1992.
37. Quoted in Blumenthal, "Why?" 60.

38. Quoted in "In, or Out, or What?" *Economist* (London), October 9, 1993, 60.
39. Ibid.
40. "The Retreat," 65–66; Joshua Hammer and Douglas Waller, "At Least Someone Was Doing Something Right," *Newsweek* (international edition), October 25, 1993, 13; "How the Warlord Outwitted Clinton's Spooks," C3.
41. Blumenthal, "Why?" 48–51.
42. Ibid., 51.

## CHAPTER 8: HIGH-CONCEPT FOREIGN POLICY

1. Willam Shawcross, *Sideshow* (London: Andre Deutsch, 1979), 135, 144.
2. See George P. Shultz, *Turmoil and Triumph: My Years as Secretary of State* (New York: Charles Scribner's Sons, 1993), 683–86.
3. David McCullough, *Truman* (New York: Simon & Schuster, Touchstone, 1992), 454.
4. Sheehan, *A Bright Shining Lie*, 706–7.
5. Barnes, "Last Call," 12.
6. Quoted in Blumenthal, "Why?" 53.
7. Robert Stone, *A Flag for Sunrise* (New York: Knopf, 1981), 439.
8. Quoted in Blumenthal, "Why?" 53.
9. President George Bush, press conference, December 4, 1992.
10. Bolton, "Wrong Turn," 58–59.
11. Interview at military airfield, Mogadishu, Somalia, September 23, 1992.
12. Quoted in Michael Elliott, "The Making of a Fiasco," *Newsweek* (international edition), October 18, 1993, 9.
13. Colonel Michael Hagee, USMC, Commanding Officer, 11th Marine Expeditionary Unit, interview at military airfield, Mogadishu, Somalia, September 23, 1992.
14. Interview at U.S. diplomatic compound, Mogadishu, Somalia, December 14, 1992.
15. Elliott, "The Making of a Fiasco," 8.
16. Ibid.
17. Sheehan, *A Bright Shining Lie,* 285.
18. See Edward N. Luttwak, "Wrong Place, Wrong Time," *New York Times,* July 22, 1993, A13; Sheehan, *A Bright Shining Lie,* 558. General Powell himself did not see matters this way. In an article published just as Operation Restore Hope was launched, he wrote, "When force is used deftly—in smooth coordination of diplomatic and economic policy—bullets may never have to fly," and cited Somalia as a "successful" example of this axiom. Colin L. Powell, "U.S. Forces: Challenges Ahead," *Foreign Affairs* 71 (Winter 1992–93): 39.
19. See Blumenthal, "Why?" 57–60; Sheehan, *A Bright Shining Lie,* 364.
20. Bolton, "Wrong Turn," 59–50.

21. Quoted in ibid., 62.
22. Bolton, "Wrong Turn," 62–64.
23. Interview at U.S. diplomatic compound, Mogadishu, Somalia, December 14, 1992.
24. "U.S. Supported Hunt For Aidid," A1, A6.
25. Elliott, "The Making of a Fiasco," 10; "Somalia Hearing Examines Rejected Request for Armor," *Washington Post*, May 13, 1994, A40.
26. Ibid.
27. "U.S. Officials Were Divided on Somali Raid," *New York Times*, May 13, 1994, A8; "Somalia Hearing Examines Rejected Request for Armor," A40. See also DeLong and Tuckey, *Mogadishu!* 63, 99.
28. "As U.S. Exits, Somali Clan Chief Stands Strong," *New York Times*, March 2, 1994, A3.
29. "Weapons of War, Words of Peace Blur Somalia's Future," *Washington Post*, January 27, 1994, A18.
30. Quoted in Elliott, "The Making of a Fiasco," 8.
31. "Weapons of War, Words of Peace," A18. See also "President Resists Somalia Pull-Out Now," *New York Times*, October 14, 1993, A6.
32. See "Clinton Doubling U.S. Force in Somalia, Vowing Troops Will Come Home in 6 Months," *New York Times*, October 8, 1993, A1, A9; "'Like Rambo,' Eritrean Chief Calls the U.S.," *New York Times*, October 10, 1993, A8.
33. Hempstone, "'Think Three Times,'" 30.
34. M. A. Khan, Administrative Manager, CARE, interview at CARE compound, Mogadishu, Somalia, January 11, 1994.
35. "Somalis See Pact as a Last Chance," *New York Times*, March 27, 1994, A7; "Talks on Somalia Said to Collapse," *New York Times*, March 24, 1994, A9.
36. Sheehan, *A Bright Shining Lie*, 624.
37. "Somalis Begin to Build a Police Force as a First Step Out of Anarchy," *Washington Post*, March 25, 1994, A26.
38. "Gunmen Kill Two Italian Journalists in Somali Capital," *Washington Post*, March 21, 1994, A2.
39. Khan interview, January 11, 1994.
40. Letter to the author from Clay Burkhalter, Project Administrator, SOS-Kinderdorf-International, Somalia, February 22, 1994.
41. "U.N. Battles Looters in Somalia's Capital after U.S. Pulls Out," *New York Times*, March 28, 1994, A7.
42. Letter to the author from Clay Burkhalter, Project Administrator, SOS-Kinderdorf-International, Somalia, April 17, 1994.
43. Quoted in "U.S. Weighs Withdrawal from Somalia," *New York Times*, July 22, 1994, A7.
44. "Seven Peacekeepers Killed in Somali Ambush," *New York Times*, August 23, 1994, A4; "Somalis Kill Three Indian Doctors at U.N. Hospital, *New York Times*, September 1, 1994, A4.

45. See, for example, Graham Hancock, *The Lords of Poverty* (New York: The Atlantic Monthly Press, 1989), 43.
46. "As U.S. Exits," A3.
47. "Weapons of War, Words of Peace," A18.
48. Ibid.

## CHAPTER 9: LESSONS LEARNED

1. Robert O'Connor, *Buffalo Soldiers* (London: HarperCollins, Flamingo, 1993), 50.
2. Robert B. Oakley, "Somalia: Lessons of a Rescue," *International Herald Tribune,* March 22, 1994, 6 [*Washington Post* Service].
3. Quoted in "What Began as a Mission of Mercy Closes with Little Ceremony," A2.
4. See, for example, "Aidid Offers Talks As U.N. Rocket Injures Civilians," *Times* (London), June 15, 1993, 12.
5. Quoted in "How the Warlord Outwitted Clinton's Spooks," C3.
6. United Nations Charter, chap. 8, art. 52.
7. "Eight-Nation African Force Is Peacekeeping Model in War-Torn Liberia," *Washington Post,* April 2, 1994, A6; "War-Battered," *Economist* (London), September 3, 1994, 44–45.
8. "Night of a Thousand Casualties," *Washington Post,* January 31, 1993, A11; "Manhunt," *Economist* (London), September 18, 1993, 46.
9. "The Raid That Went Wrong," A26.
10. Quoted in Charles Lane, "The Master of the Game," *The New Republic,* March 7, 1994, 28.
11. Oakley interview, December 18, 1992; Oakley press conference, December 17, 1992.
12. Charles William Maynes, "Containing Ethnic Conflict," *Foreign Policy* 90 (Spring 1993), 14.
13. "Somali Clansmen Hold MPs Hostage for 24 Hours," *Independent* (London), February 11, 1994, sec. 1, p. 11.
14. Maynes, "Containing Ethnic Conflict," 11.
15. See, for example, "Dole Attacks America's Role in the U.N.," *Independent* (London), January 25, 1994, sec. 1, p. 9.
16. See, for example, Sheehan, *A Bright Shining Lie,* 418–19.
17. See, for example, "Boy's Death in Somalia Tests Uneasy U.S. Role," *New York Times,* February 20, 1993, A1, A4.
18. "Night of a Thousand Casualties," *Washington Post,* January 31, 1993, A11.
19. Tom Post, et al., "Fire Fight from Hell," *Newsweek* (international edition), October 18, 1993, 14. A more recent account suggests that the exchange did not involve a direct threat. See DeLong and Tuckey, *Mogadishu!* 64–65.

20. "Night of a Thousand Casualties," A11.
21. Testimony of James H. Smith before the U.S. Senate Armed Services Committee, May 12, 1994, witness's submission, 2–3.
22. "Dividing the Blame in Somalia," *International Herald Tribune,* May 21–22, 1994, 8 [*New York Times* Service].
23. Quoted in "What Began as a Mission of Mercy Closes with Little Ceremony," A2.
24. This use for the Military Staff Committee was proposed in Edward C. Luck, "This Isn't the Way to Have the United Nations Keep the Peace," *International Herald Tribune,* April 19, 1994, 8. See, generally, Luck, "Making Peace," *Foreign Policy* 89 (Winter 1992–93), 152–55.
25. For a pithy and impassioned assessment, see Shirley Hazzard, "System Failure," *The New Republic,* September 21, 1992, 16–17. See, generally, Michael S. Serrill, "Under Fire," *Time* (international edition), January 18, 1993, 11–15.
26. Brian Urquhart, "If the United Nations Is for Real, Give It a Police Force," *International Herald Tribune,* May 23, 1994, 6 [*New York Times* Service]. See also Urquhart, "For a U.N. Volunteer Military Force," *The New York Review of Books,* June 10, 1993, 3–4.
27. "Somalia Mission Fuels German Debate," *Washington Post,* February 25, 1994, A23, A27.
28. On the need for the U.N. to give field commander strategic flexibility, see, for example, "Lost in a World of Troubles," *Independent* (London), January 31, 1994, sec. 1, p. 14.
29. "The Peacekeeping Front: Clinton Is Pulling Back," *International Herald Tribune,* May 7–8, 1994, 3 [*New York Times* Service].
30. For more on the difficulty of balancing the need to withdraw against local dependency, see Chester A. Crocker, "How to Restore Public Confidence in the Necessary Art of Peacekeeping," *International Herald Tribune,* May 10, 1994, 6 [*Washington Post* Service].
31. Philip Morrison, Kosta Tsipis, and Jerome Wiesner, "The Future of American Defense," *Scientific American,* February 1994, 25.
32. "How the Warlord Outwitted Clinton's Spooks," C3.
33. For similar substantive observations but a harsher perspective, see Richard H. Kohn, "America's Upstarts in Uniform Should Go Quietly Back to Base," *International Herald Tribune,* April 11, 1994, 6 [*New York Times* Service].
34. Thomas C. Schelling, *Arms and Influence* (New Haven: Yale University Press, 1962; reprint, Westport, Conn.: Greenwood Press, 1976), 69–91, especially 72.
35. Eliot A. Cohen, "Down the Hatch," *The New Republic,* March 7, 1994, 16.
36. Oakley interview, January 9, 1993.
37. Quoted in McCullough, *Truman,* 898.

38. Quoted in Sheehan, *A Bright Shining Lie*, 685.
39. See Bolton, "Wrong Turn," 66. "The real lesson of the American experience in attempting to relieve the famine in Somalia is that any administration must play out the long-range consequences even of humanitarian decisions because of the complex political and military consequences inevitably entailed."
40. "The Peacekeeping Front," 3.
41. Herman Kahn, *Thinking about the Unthinkable* (New York: Horizon Press, 1962).
42. "Rwanda Stand Reflects New U.S. Caution," *International Herald Tribune*, May 19, 1994, 4 [*New York Times* Service].
43. "Don't Blame the U.N. for an American Mess," *Independent* (London), May 18, 1994, sec. 1, p. 16.
44. "Rwanda Stand Reflects New U.S. Caution," *International Herald Tribune*, May 19, 1994, 4 [*New York Times* Service].
45. Ibid.

## CHAPTER 10: THE UNITED STATES AND THE UNITED NATIONS

1. "America Hampers Dispatch of Extra UN Troops for Rwanda," *Independent* (London), May 18, 1994, sec. 1, p. 12.
2. Bolton, "Wrong Turn," 66.
3. "Few U.N. Dollars Get to Mogadishu's Streets," *Washington Post*, March 24, 1994, A1, A25. See also Michael Maren, "Spoiled," *The New Republic*, December 12, 1994, 13–14. For more glaring examples of U.N. inefficency, see "Waste in Somalia Typifies Failings of U.N. Management," *Washington Post*, January 3, 1995, A4. For a scathing broadside attack on U.N. inefficiency in general, see Hancock, *The Lords of Poverty.*
4. "Drifting," *Economist* (London), April 16, 1994, 77–78.
5. See Samuel M. Makinda, *Seeking Peace from Chaos: Humanitarian Intervention in Somalia*, International Peace Academy, Occasional Paper Series (London: Lynne Rienner Publishers, 1994).
6. On the political and operational awkwardness of compromises short of a standing U.N. army, see, for example, Stanley Meisler, "From Guard to Enforcer: U.N. Peacekeepers in Somalia," *Foreign Service Journal*, February 1993, 21–24.
7. U.N. Security Council, Resolution 940, July 31, 1994; "U.N. Authorizes Invasion of Haiti to Be Led by U.S.," *New York Times*, August 1, 1994, A1, A7; "U.S. Backed a Possible Invasion of Haiti," *New York Times*, August 31, 1994, A8.
8. See "French Press On with Rwanda Mission," *Independent* (London), June 21, 1994, sec. 1, p. 11.

9. Quoted in "U.N. 'Fails to Meet Standards on Rights,'" *Independent* (London), January 26, 1994, sec. 1, p. 10.
10. See, for example, "Operation Restore Hoax," *Environmental Action* 25 (Spring 1993): 6; Christopher Whalen, "In Somalia, the Saudi Connection: Is American Intervening in the Horn of Africa to Protect Persian Gulf Oil?" *Washington Post*, October 17, 1993, C1.
11. See, for example, Alex Shoumatoff, "Gallic Mischief," *The New Yorker*, July 18, 1994, 4–5.
12. Lee Hamilton, et al., "A U.N. Volunteer Military Force—Four Views," *The New York Review of Books*, June 24, 1993, 58–60.
13. The account was rendered to the author by Willy Huber, Regional Director for East Africa, SOS-Kinderdorf-International, interview at SOS village, Mogadishu, Somalia, January 12, 1994. On Italy's conciliatory position vis-à-vis Aidid in July 1993, see Lewis, "Somalia," 778.
14. "Assertive Multilateralism," *Economist* (London), September 25, 1993, 20.
15. Morton Halperin, "Guaranteeing Democracy," *Foreign Policy* 91 (Summer 1993), 105.
16. Hazzard, "System Failure," 16.
17. Lloyd Cutler, "The Right to Intervene," *Foreign Affairs* 64 (Fall 1985): 96.
18. See R. M. Koster and Guillermo Sanchez, *In the Time of the Tyrants* (New York: W. W. Norton, 1990), 367–68.
19. Benjamin Dean, "Self-Determination and U.S. Support of Insurgents: A Policy Analysis Model," *Military Law Review* 122 (Fall 1988): 183. See also Michael Levitin, "The Law of Force and the Force of Law: Grenada, the Falklands, and Humanitarian Intervention," *Harvard International Law Journal* 27 (Spring 1986): 651.
20. Boutros Boutros-Ghali, *An Agenda for Peace: Preventive Diplomacy, Peace-making, and Peace-keeping*, U.N. Doc. A/47/277, June 7, 1992. See also Boutros-Ghali, "Empowering the United Nations," *Foreign Affairs* 71 (Winter 1992/93): 89, an adaptation of *An Agenda for Peace*.
21. Cited in Gerald B. Helman and Steven R. Ratner, "Saving Failed States," *Foreign Policy* 89 (Winter 1992–93), 11.
22. For example, Charles Maechling Jr., "Washington's Illegal Invasion," *Foreign Policy* 79 (Summer 1990), 129–31.
23. See Anthony D'Amato, "The Invasion of Panama Was a Lawful Response to Tyranny," *American Journal of International Law* 84 (April 1990): 521.
24. "Chaotic Harmony or Just Chaos?" *Independent* (London), November 1, 1993, sec. 1, p. 14.
25. Helman and Ratner, "Saving Failed States," 11.
26. United Nations Charter, chap. 12, art. 78.
27. "U.S. to Pay Off Its U.N. Debt for Peacekeeping Operations," *New York Times*, August 20, 1994, A2.

28. See "French to Launch Rwanda Rescue," *Independent* (London), June 21, 1994, sec. 1, p. 1.
29. Quoted in Tom Post, Anne Underwood, and Jeffrey Bartholet, "How Do You Spell Relief?" *Newsweek* (international edition), November 23, 1992, 18. See also Stevenson, "Hope Restored?" 154.
30. See "The Limits of the Possible," *Independent* (London), November 1, 1993, sec. 1, p. 14.
31. This line of thinking is nicely developed in Michael Mandebaum, "The Reluctance to Intervene," *Foreign Policy*, no. 95 (Summer 1994), 3–18.

## CHAPTER 11: MORAL COMPULSION IN FOREIGN POLICY

1. "A Conversation with General John Shalikashvili," Ted Koppel, ABC, *Nightline*, March 15, 1994. General Shalikashvili's conception of core interests encompasses far more than military security, reflecting the revised post–Cold War view. See, for example, Joseph H. Romm, *Defining National Security: The Nonmilitary Aspects* (New York: Council on Foreign Relations Press, 1993).
2. "Clinton Tells Why Haiti Is So Vital," *International Herald Tribune*, May 21–22, 1994, 5 [*New York Times* Service].
3. Niccolo Machiavelli, *The Prince*, trans. George Bull (New York: Penguin Books, 1981), 71–73, 90–95.
4. Hempstone, "'Think Three Times,'" 30.
5. Meg Greenfield, "Intervention Fatigue," *Newsweek* (international edition), October 25, 1993, 16. See also Walter Isaacson, "Sometimes, Right Makes Might," *Time* (international edition), December 21, 1992, 64.
6. Testimony of Larry E. Joyce before the U.S. Senate Armed Services Committee, May 12, 1994, witness's submission, 6.
7. See Jonathan Stevenson, "Desert Storm," *The New Republic*, December 28, 1992, 17.
8. Brian Urquhart, "If the United Nations Is for Real, Give It a Police Force," *International Herald Tribune*, May 23, 1994, 6 [*New York Times* Service].
9. See Paul D. Wolfowitz, "Clinton's First Year," *Foreign Affairs* 73 (January/February 1994): 38-40.
10. "Pundits Ponder the Arithmetic of Death of Another War," *Independent* (London), June 11, 1994, 9.
11. "A Conversation with General John Shalikashvili," March 15, 1994.
12. Wolfowitz, "Clinton's First Year," 35.
13. "Don't Leap into Rwanda," *International Herald Tribune*, May 19, 1994, 6 [*New York Times* Service].
14. John Keegan, *The Mask of Command* (London: Jonathan Cape, 1987), 312.
15. Graham Greene, *The Quiet American* (London: William Heinemann, 1955; reprint ed., London: The Reprint Society, 1957), 103.

# Selected Bibliography

Afrah, Mohamoud A. *Target: Villa Somalia.* 2d ed. Karachi, Pakistan: Naseem, 1992.

*Africa South of the Sahara, 1994.* London: Europa Publications, 1993.

Barnes, Virginia Lee, and Janice Boddy. *Aman: The Story of a Somali Girl.* London: Bloomsbury, 1994.

Brzezinski, Zbigniew. *Power and Principle: Memoirs of the National Security Advisor, 1977–1981.* New York: Farrar, Straus, & Giroux, 1983.

DeLong, Kent, and Steven Tuckey. *Mogadishu! Heroism and Tragedy.* Westport Conn.: Praeger, 1994.

Greene, Graham. *The Quiet American.* London: William Heinemann, 1955; reprint ed., London: The Reprint Society, 1957.

Hancock, Graham. *The Lords of Poverty.* New York: The Atlantic Monthly Press, 1989.

Harden, Blaine. *Africa: Dispatches from a Fragile Continent.* New York: W. W. Norton, 1990.

Hempstone, Smith. *Africa: Angry Young Giant.* New York: Praeger, 1961.

———. *Katanga Report.* London: Faber & Faber, 1962.

Kahn, Herman. *Thinking about the Unthinkable.* New York: Horizon Press, 1962.

Keegan, John. *The Mask of Command.* London: Jonathan Cape, 1987.

Koster, R. M., and Guillermo Sanchez. *In the Time of the Tyrants.* New York: W. W. Norton, 1990.

Lamb, David. *The Africans.* New York: Random House, Vintage Books, 1987.

Lewis, I. M. *A Modern History of Somalia.* London & New York: Longman Group, 1980.

——. *A Pastoralist Democracy: A Study of Pastoralism and Politics among the Northern Somali of the Horn of Africa.* London & New York: Oxford University Press, 1961.

McCullough, David. *Truman.* New York: Simon & Schuster, Touchstone, 1992.

McLean, Scilla, and Stella Efua Graham, eds. *Female Circumcision, Excision, and Infibulation: The Facts and Proposals for Change.* 2d rev. ed. London: Minority Rights Group, 1985.

Makinda, Samuel M. *Seeking Peace from Chaos: Humanitarian Intervention in Somalia.* International Peace Academy, Occasional Paper Series. London: Lynne Rienner Publishers, 1994.

———. *Superpower Diplomacy in the Horn of Africa.* Kent, England: Croom Helm, 1987.

Patman, Robert G. *The Soviet Union in the Horn of Africa: The Diplomacy of Intervention and Disengagement.* Cambridge: Cambridge University Press, 1990.

Sahnoun, Mohamed. *Somalia: The Missed Opportunities.* Washington, D.C.: U.S. Institute for Peace, 1994.

Schelling, Thomas C. *Arms and Influence.* New Haven: Yale University Press, 1962; reprint ed., Westport, Conn.: Greenwood Press, 1976.

Shawcross, William. *Sideshow.* London: Andre Deutsch, 1979.

Sheehan, Neil. *A Bright Shining Lie.* London: Jonathan Cape, 1989.

Shultz, George P. *Turmoil and Triumph: My Years as Secretary of State.* New York: Charles Scribner's Sons, 1993.

Stone, Robert. *A Flag for Sunrise.* New York: Alfred A. Knopf, 1981.

Ungar, Sanford J. *Africa: The People and Politics of an Emerging Continent.* New York: Simon & Schuster, Touchstone, 1989.

United Nations. *World Economic Survey 1993.* New York: United Nations, 1993.

———. *Yearbook of the United Nations 1992.* Dordrecht, The Netherlands: Martinus Nijhoff Publishers, 1993.

# Index

# About the Author

Jonathan Stevenson graduated from the University of Chicago in 1978 and from Boston University School of Law in 1982. For the ten years following, he practiced law in New York and Connecticut. In 1992 he turned from law to journalism and moved to Nairobi, covering sub-Saharan Africa (mainly Somalia) for *Newsweek, The Economist,* and the (London) *Sunday Times.* Mr. Stevenson has also written on Somalia for *Foreign Policy,* the *Foreign Service Journal,* and *The New Republic.* He now lives in Belfast, Northern Ireland, where he is at work on his second book.

The Naval Institute Press is the book-publishing arm of the U.S. Naval Institute, a private, nonprofit society for sea service professionals and others who share an interest in naval and maritime affairs. Established in 1873 at the U.S. Naval Academy in Annapolis, Maryland, where its offices remain, today the Naval Institute has more than 100,000 members worldwide.

Members of the Naval Institute receive the influential monthly magazine *Proceedings* and discounts on fine nautical prints and on ship and aircraft photos. They also have access to the transcripts of the Institute's Oral History Program and get discounted admission to any of the Institute-sponsored seminars offered around the country.

The Naval Institute also publishes *Naval History* magazine. This colorful bimonthly is filled with entertaining and thought-provoking articles, first-person reminiscences, and dramatic art and photography. Members receive a discount on *Naval History* subscriptions.

The Naval Institute's book-publishing program, begun in 1898 with basic guides to naval practices, has broadened its scope in recent years to include books of more general interest. Now the Naval Institute Press publishes more than seventy titles each year, ranging from how-to books on boating and navigation to battle histories, biographies, ship and aircraft guides, and novels. Institute members receive discounts on the Press's nearly 400 books in print.

For a free catalog describing Naval Institute Press books currently available, and for further information about subscribing to *Naval History* magazine or about joining the U.S. Naval Institute, please write to:


Membership & Communications Department
U.S. Naval Institute
118 Maryland Avenue
Annapolis, Maryland 21402-5035

Or call, toll-free, (800) 233-USNI.